Living with Others

Living with Others
A Survival Guide

David Ruby

Jefferson, North Carolina

ISBN (print) **978-1-4766-9276-0**
ISBN (ebook) **978-1-4766-5593-2**

LIBRARY OF CONGRESS CATALOGING DATA ARE AVAILABLE

Library of Congress Control Number 2025018271

© 2025 David Ruby. All rights Reserved

No part of this book may be reproduced or transmitted in any form or by any means, electronic or mechanical, including photocopying or recording, or by any information storage and retrieval system, without permission in writing from the publisher.

Front cover image: created using Shutterstock AI Generator.

Printed in the United States of America

Toplight is an imprint of McFarland & Company, Inc., Publishers

Box 611, Jefferson, North Carolina 28640
www.toplightbooks.com

Table of Contents

Acknowledgments   viii
Preface   1
Introduction   3
Disclaimer   4
The Key Players and Their Roles   5

Part A—Growing Up

1. Childhood to Adulthood   8
2. The College Years   10

Part B—Finding Somewhere to Live

3. Your Choices as a First-Time Roomsharer   21
4. Wising Up Before Committing to a Roomshare   30
5. How to Avoid an Agency Ripping You Off   35
6. How Do You Know If This Is the Right Roomshare for You?   38
7. Your First Professional Roomshare   44
8. The Veteran Roomshare   46

Part C—Getting Roomsmart

9. Getting Lawsmart   50
10. Getting Rentsmart   55
11. Getting Costsmart   63
12. Staying Roomsmart When Idiots Can't Pay Their Costs   67

Table of Contents

Part D—Finding Roommates

13. Attending a Roomshare Interview — 72
14. By the Way, Discrimination Is Legal in Roomshares — 77
15. How Old Is Too Old to Be Living with a Roommate? — 82
16. Establishing a Group Dynamic That Works — 90
17. What to Do When a Roommate Leaves — 102
18. Interviewing People for Your Roomshare — 104

Part E—Rules of Roomshare Living

19. Cooking — 111
20. Working from Home — 116
21. Having Friends Over — 120
22. Living with Pets — 122
23. Decorating a Roomshare — 124
24. Weekends — 127
25. Big Occasions — 130
26. The Roomshare Taboos — 135

Part F—Rules of Hygiene

27. The Communal Areas — 148
28. Bathroom — 151
29. Individual Behavior — 153
30. Washing Your Dishes — 157
31. Drying Your Clothes — 160

Part G—Romance Kills the Roomshare

32. Dating in a Roomshare — 165
33. Living as a Couple in a Roomshare — 168
34. A Single Person Living with a Couple — 171
35. Living with a Partner — 175
36. Living with Your Ex — 178

Table of Contents

Part H—The End of the Roomshare

37. Accidentally Living Alone	182
38. When the Landlord Asks You All to Leave	185
39. You're Technically Homeless	187
40. Moving In with Family	190
41. What's Next?—Buying Your Own Home?	193

Part I—Actually Living with Idiots

42. This Is Literally Idiot Central	203
43. How to Get Out of Living with Idiots	205

Part J—Actually Living in Paradise (As Close as You Can, Anyway)

44. What It Takes to Live in Paradise (Metaphorically)	210
Final Thoughts	213
Appendix: Checklists	217
Index	219

Acknowledgments

This book is dedicated first to my wife. Without her by my side this book would have never seen the light of day. Thank you for supporting me, for reading every version of the manuscript (and there were multiple), and for providing invaluable advice day in and day out. And most importantly, for surviving sharing a home with me.

And the second dedication is to anyone out there who has ever shared a home, is currently sharing one, or is about to share one. It's a journey riddled with bumps, trials and tribulations. My hope is that this book will smooth the adventure and make things just a little bit easier for you. If I can survive living with others, anyone can. At least that's what my wife says.

Preface

Living with Others has been almost two decades in the making. Two decades of overpriced rooms, terrible roommates, and dodgy landlords. I've seen it all so no one else has to. This book will enable all current and upcoming roomsharers to ease the pain of living in a shared home and make their sharing experience brilliant.

After reading this book, every reader will have the knowledge and skills to find their own affordable perfect roomshare.

People always say "write what you know," which is exactly what I did. But not only that, I sought out experts in their field and quizzed them at length. I interviewed dozens of professors and psychologists to get a well-rounded view of the roomsharing industry and tied everything up in the present book. The real USP of this book is the research and expert knowledge that complements my hands-on experience-based advice.

I felt compelled to write this book to help others get through what is now a standard life experience of having to share with others. I firmly believe that any roomsharing experience can be joyful rather than terrible, and I hope every reader can absorb this knowledge to live a better life.

Introduction

"Life is a journey that must be travelled no matter how bad the roads and accommodations."
—Oliver Goldsmith

From birth to now, I've been living with "other people." That's close to 40 years. Based on Malcolm Gladwell's assertion that you need 10,000 hours to become an expert on a subject, I have clocked 350,400 (and counting) hours of experience. If there were a PhD in living with other people, I'd ace it in no time. In fact, there probably *is* a bachelor's degree (online only) from the University of As Long as You Pay Us Tuition We'll Give You a Piece of Paper Claiming You Have This Degree. That makes me more than qualified to comment on the topic.

So, how do I still get it wrong? Is Malcolm Gladwell wrong?!

Despite almost 40 years (and counting) of shared living experience, I still get surprised. The number of times I've come home and questioned my own sanity when seeing what some of my roommates had been up to…

The thing is, everyone is different, no matter how long you've been living with people. And that's the beauty (and horror) of the human experience. Every individual is unpredictable. You could have six psychology degrees and still screw up understanding someone. *No one* can predict what it will be like to live with people *until* you live with them. No matter how often you google "dishes roommate etiquette" (867,000 results at the time of writing), the answer will be unique for every living situation. Life is hard enough as it is, so if this book can make one part of living with other people better for you, then it will have done its job.

That's why I've taken matters into my own hands. With advice from psychologists, academics, and CEOs, I've compiled the best possible guide for navigating roommates to make shared living a little easier. Everyone lives with others at some point. And I mean *everyone*, from the cramped student roomshare with six people sharing one (usually dirty) bathroom to the recently divorced billionaire (with staff, neighbors, and ex-spouses to contend with) on an estate with several (obviously spotless) bathrooms for every guest.

No one lives completely alone unless they're living on Mars. And even then, are they *really* alone? Now, this is *not* a guide to living alone or sharing a home with just your partner. This book is specifically tailored to anyone living with roommates. Whether it's just one other person (with no romantic connection) or 20 strangers in a communal warehouse with an allotment everyone must attend to once a month on a rotating calendar. The same broad advice for living in a shared space applies whether with one person or 20.

This book is for you to read at your leisure—you don't even have to read from beginning to end! The chapters are numbered by life stages, so you can head straight to the stage that most applies to you. My goal is to help you learn *how* to live with other people. Living with difficult roommates has a big impact on your well-being, and this is a practical guide to dealing with it when (not *if*) it happens to you (if it hasn't already). More importantly, it will show you how to *avoid* living with them in the first place.

Disclaimer

Nothing in this book should be considered legal, psychological, or financial advice. This is a collection of tips and advice from experts worldwide collated with decades of collective experience from me, curated to help you live better in a shared living space. So, please don't file a class-action lawsuit (or any kind of lawsuit, actually) if your own roomshare doesn't work out.[1] I can't afford the fees!

---

1. Lawsuits sound so threatening when lawyers call them "class-action." Either way, I'm happy for you to email me if you have a query, and I'll do my best to help without the need for lawyers! Who knows ... your story might even influence the next edition of this book (assuming this first one goes well).

The Key Players and Their Roles

Several terms throughout this book refer to the types of people you'll encounter on your roomsharing journey, so it's best to clarify before you start reading.

Agent: For simplicity, I'll use "agent" as an overall term. In that sense the "agent" is whoever you deal with to secure access to your property while living there. It is also the person you get in touch with for any issue related to your roomshare.

Idiot: The difficult roommate. The type of person who does everything you hate and makes your roomshare a nightmare.

Management company: Management companies are usually reliable as they need to maintain a good reputation if they're to stay in business. Unless the "management company" is actually the child of the property owner (this has happened to me), then it's a nightmare. If that's the case, avoid the property at all costs. The good news is that, in the U.S., more than half of owners use a property management company and this trend is rising.[1] Not having a management company isn't a red flag, but it does mean you're at the mercy of a property owner who may respond slowly (if at all) to your messages about a broken shower…

Property owner: Exactly as written, this is the person who owns the property. They either directly rent their property to a tenant or use a management company. I recommend renting a property that uses a management company. Property owners are often "mom-and-pop landlords" (in the U.S., 41 percent of property owners fall into that category) and most have no idea what they're doing.[2] It can be painful to deal with them if they have no experience

---

1. Buildium. 2016. "Survey Finds Majority of Rental Property Owners Use a Property Manager, with Rates Expected to Rise in 2016." Business Wire. May 24, 2016. https://www.businesswire.com/news/home/20160524005289/en/Survey-Finds-Majority-of-Rental-Property-Owners-Use-a-Property-Manager-With-Rates-Expected-to-Rise-in-2016.
2. Reed, Catherine. 2023. "35 Insightful Landlord Statistics—2023." Flex | Pay Rent on Your Own Schedule. January 9, 2023. https://getflex.com/blog/landlord-statistics.

and are particularly stingy with their cash. At least a property owner who uses a management company leaves the maintenance of your home to the professionals. Management companies (in theory) know what they're doing and abide by local rules and regulations. Well, the good ones do anyway...

Randoms: People you didn't know before moving into a roomshare.

Real estate agent: I call the real estate agent[3] "the first point of contact in the rip-off chain." They'll say anything to get you to take the property. You'll hear claims of "great value," "brilliant location" and "back-to-back viewings." However, you'll need to learn to spot which are spurious and which are real.

Depending on where you live, if demand outstrips supply, you'll be in a difficult negotiating position. The real estate agent will always claim the property is in high demand even if it's been on the market for a while. They'll also do anything to sell the property, from hiding the rattling boiler booting to life after you go to bed, to scrubbing the surface-level grime hiding a fungus problem behind the toilet.

Real estate agents claim ludicrous selling points to get you to sign on the dotted line (yep, this happened to me). They cannot be trusted. They are self-interested and only want to make a deal, and after you, they'll move on to the next client to hit their sales target. Now, I'm not the only one who doesn't trust them: 89 percent of surveyed Americans said the same.[4] Even bankers ranked higher in trust! And this survey was gathered *after* the banking-induced financial meltdown of 2008.

Roommate: Someone you co-habit with, whether in an apartment, a house, a boat, or whatever dwelling you end up living in. Or as the Urban Dictionary defines it, a roommate is "what you get when you can't pay all of the rent to stay by yourself."[5]

Roomshare: The property you'll be sharing with others. It will have at least two bedrooms with no set maximum and a communal bathroom and living space. It could literally be anything from a two-bedroom caravan in rural Ohio to a multi-bedroom mansion in California.[6]

---

3. If a real estate agent is also a member of the National Association of REALTORS® they're also known as a REALTOR®. All REALTORS® are real estate agents, but not all real estate agents are REALTORS®.

4. Purplebricks. 2018. "An Era of Eroding Trust: National Study Reveals Occupations Americans Find the Most—or Least—Trustworthy." Business Wire. September 18, 2018. https://www.businesswire.com/news/home/20180918005181/en/An-Era-of-Eroding-Trust-National-Study-Reveals-Occupations-Americans-Find-the-Most-%E2%80%93-or-Least-%E2%80%93-Trustworthy.

5. Sunshine14. 2009. "Roommate." Urban Dictionary. 2009. https://www.urbandictionary.com/define.php?term=roommate.

6. Remember Hype House? To their credit if you're young and can arrange to live in a huge mansion for the same price as a small apartment why wouldn't you? Lorenz, Taylor. 2020. "Hype House and the Los Angeles TikTok Mansion Gold Rush." *The New York Times*. January 3, 2020. https://www.nytimes.com/2020/01/03/style/hype-house-los-angeles-tik-tok.html.

Part A

Growing Up

"There's no place like home."
—Dorothy, *The Wizard of Oz* (1939)

Looking Back to Your Pre-Adulting Days with Envy…

Growing up, no one realizes how lucky they are not to think about bills, rent, mortgages, and jobs. You wake up with a roof over your head. You go for breakfast, and there's food on the table. Same for lunch and dinner. Day after day, everything is served up. There are always exceptions, but as a kid with a normal childhood, you're usually expected to turn up and eat what you're given, wash when you're told to, go to school, and sleep where your bed is.

When you become an adult, you realize how ungrateful you were growing up.[1] In childhood, everything is taken care of. In adulthood, you are yourself responsible for earning money to sustain your livelihood, including where you live and what you eat. It's hard work that no one else will do for you, and it is not "fun" in the traditional sense. In other words, life as an adult is hard (which is partly why I wrote this book). I can't help with food, jobs, or romantic relationships, but I can help you live better in a roomshare.

Everybody experiences living with people they barely know. Living with randoms is inevitable in today's financial climate of overpriced rental homes and unaffordable mortgages. The book is important to me because I have experienced years of living with idiots. Where and how you live will affect you financially and emotionally.

Pick wrong: your life will be miserable.

Pick right: you'll live out your happiest days.

---

1. I'm also fully aware this could have just been me and that other people might actually have been more self-aware growing up.

1

Childhood to Adulthood

Whether you're born an orphan or a Mormon, you're born into a home in one way or another. This is your first experience of living with other people. Granted, these are the people you depend on to live, but you're still sharing a living space with them. It just so happens you didn't have a choice in your home's location, value, or decor. You were literally born into it.

Some people have loving sets of parents, others only have one, and a few have grandparents, other relatives, or foster parents raising them. Whatever your situation is growing up, it is out of your control. And it will be until you decide to legally get out of there.

Every childhood is different. You can be born into an Oregon vegan hippie commune while someone else is born into a Texan meat-and-potatoes-every-day-and-church-on-Sunday ranch. Whatever you are born into is the luck of the draw. It's where you *decide* to live that matters.

How and what you decide to do is influenced by "grit" and forms the basis of the *New York Times* bestselling book *Grit: The Power of Passion and Perseverance* by pioneering psychologist Angela Duckworth.[1] The "grit" which leads to achievement is a blend of persistence, passion and sheer hard work and ambition.

Your drive and personality determine how well you do at school, at work, and in life. It's up to you to decide whether to go to that house party and drink until you vomit or stay in and study. In my teenage years, I hosted the parties.

You can stay in school beyond the legal requirement, get a job, or start a business. I'll never forget being 12 years old and getting a "D" on my school report. *Oh*, I thought, *D for David...*

Academically, nothing changed for me until my trip to Italy as a wide-eyed 14-year-old. Hanging by the Trevi fountain, I met some

---

1. Duckworth, Angela. 2016. *Grit: The Power of Passion and Perseverance*. New York: Scribner.

18-year-olds selling bracelets to Rome's too-polite-to-say-no tourists. All they wanted to do was make enough selling these cheap bracelets to buy weed and smoke on the beach all day. *My God*, I thought. *If I screw up at school, is that my future?*

No thanks, people! I did not want to goof off in the street, living day-to-day. As soon as I got home that summer, I turned my life around. I studied hard, stopped partying, and went from being the worst performer at my school to graduating top of my class. If you have opportunities, make the most of them. There are so many people out there who don't even realize how lucky they are to have them in the first place. Suppose you don't, create your own. Opportunities, no matter how you obtain them, open doors for you (literally). And when they're open, you have more choices; when you have more choices, you'll have a better chance of living somewhere you'll be happy with.

2

The College Years

Movies and sitcoms portray the unending tussle between parents and their kids debating whether to attend college. It's a debate that has raged as long as colleges have been around. It will continue to rage for as long as they exist. Deciding on going to college is a personal choice. If you're more of an entrepreneur with a head for business who thinks college is a waste of time, you're probably right. There are plenty of books and websites to read to help you decide whether to go.[1] This book isn't one of them. Only you, the person going, knows what's best for *you*.

Going to college was a necessity for me. I didn't realize how much I needed those four years to figure out my future. It's cheesy, but I found myself during college and always feel grateful I had the chance to go.

So, if you're like over half of the country's high school population, eagerly waiting to start college and emerge four years later with massive loans that will take literally decades of your life to pay off, read along.[2] This will be the first time you decide where to live. There's a lot to think about. And let's face it, no matter what people say or how much it costs, going to college is *awesome*.

The Debate: Living in College Accommodation or Going Private

According to a National Real Estate Investor study, 22 percent of U.S. college students live in on-campus dorms.[3] This is partly due to the

---

1. Rampton, John. 2015. "6 Pros and Cons for Entrepreneurs to Get, or Skip, a College Degree." Entrepreneur. February 10, 2015. https://www.entrepreneur.com/leadership/6-pros-and-cons-for-entrepreneurs-to-get-or-skip-a/242768.
2. Marcus, Jon. 2022. "U.S. Sees 'Alarming' Decline in Number of High School Graduates Going to College as Many Ask: Is It Worth It?" NBC News. August 10, 2022. https://www.nbcnews.com/news/us-news/americans-are-increasingly-dubious-going-college-rcna40935#.
3. Anthony, James. 2020. "40 Essential Student Housing Statistics You Must Learn: 2020 Data & Demographics." FinancesOnline. March 9, 2020. https://financesonline.com/student-housing-statistics.

fact that of the country's 175 largest universities, only 21.5 percent provide on-campus dorms for undergraduates.[4] The numbers change for first years as almost half of first-year students at private non-profit colleges live on campus, and over a third of first-year students studying at public four-year colleges stay in dorms.[5]

You usually always have a choice to live on-campus, off-campus, or with your parents. It's just that neither of those last two options is as fun as living in dorms with your peers. Once you get to your second, third and fourth years, going private and living off-campus becomes a question of personal taste. If it's your first year, it's a no-brainer: secure a place in dorms (assuming there's availability as there might not be room for everyone). You'll want to mingle with other first years. Especially in SOAR (Student Orientation, Advising, and Registration Week), also known as Fresher's Week in the UK and Ireland, when you'll probably meet the people you'll hang out with for the rest of the year. You're likely to also meet older students who can guide (or misguide) you.

Now, college housing is expensive. Unless your family are multimillionaires and money is no object (although with inflation and the cost-of-living crisis, being a millionaire doesn't even seem enough these days), paying for dorms is a healthy chunk of change.

Of course, the kind of housing offered depends on your college. There will be a selection of options from the unattainably expensive to the "affordable" options. Remember, there will never be such a thing as "everyone is the same" and "everyone lives in the same kind of apartment." Oh no.

- Rich kids will have nicer places
- Poor kids will have the crappier places

This is just a fact of life since humans formed a conception of status and wealth in the Bronze Age. Accept it and move on.

One final thing… If you're a "mature student," i.e., maybe you never went to college and are finally taking the plunge, or perhaps this is your second degree in your late twenties, thirties, or eighties, don't be a weirdo and live in college accommodation with the first years. It's just wrong. While mature students are a big part of university life in the U.S. (over a third of students are 25+), and countless college blogs boast of the benefits of on-campus living for those same mature students, these should be

---

4. Mohamed, Reem. 2023. "Student Housing Statistics: A Case Study." Casita. 2023. https://www.casita.com/blog/student-housing-statistics-a-case-study.
5. Kelchen, Robert. 2018. "A Look at College Students' Living Arrangements." Robert Kelchen. May 29, 2018. https://robertkelchen.com/2018/05/28/a-look-at-college-students-living-arrangements.

ignored.[6] Colleges are just trying to get more money from everyone attending. And that includes convincing mature students to keep their dollars within the college and live in college housing. If you fall for that trap, every first year will talk about you as the "older person." Sure, they'll be polite to your face, but don't kid yourself unless you're a celebrity like Martin Sheen (who did go to college in his twilight years). Even then, everyone would only hope for an autograph or you covering a round of drinks at the bar.

Get your own place and leave the teenagers to be teenagers…

Living in Dorms

#1: Living away from home for the first time is exciting

You're going to college. You have an allocated room. Again, that's just down to luck and the college itself. In the U.S., during your freshman year (which, in my eyes, is outdated and should be really called "freshperson year" or "first year"), you usually share a room with someone else.

I went to Trinity College in Dublin, Ireland, where I had my own room with an en suite bathroom. Plenty of Americans were there; ironically, travelling and paying tuition in Ireland was cheaper than attending college back home. Whatever your situation is, whether you are sharing a room, a dorm, or a corridor, the same rules apply as you're still living with other people. Either way, the one thing you must remember is that it's incredibly exciting. This is your first time away from living with whomever you were raised with. It's also your chance to reinvent yourself. I met people who adopted nicknames, changed their fashion style, and became free enough to express their true sexuality. You can try any new activity, such as acting, painting, or writing. Anything you want to do, college is there to provide it. It's all down to your own grit and what you make of it.

#2: You'll meet friends, frenemies and people you just can't stand

A big lesson I learned when living with randoms who, overnight, were no longer strangers at all was that some will become your best friends, and some will always be jerks.

As Benjamin Franklin said, "Nothing can be certain, except death

---

6. Uresti, Shannon. 2022. "I Know First-Hand That Adult Learners Need a Variety of Supports to Succeed." Times Higher Education. December 6, 2022. https://www.timeshighereducation.com/campus/i-know-firsthand-adult-learners-need-variety-supports-succeed.

and taxes."[7] I'd rewrite that to say, "Nothing can be certain except the existence of douches." Some people will inevitably be carbon copies of the characters from *Mean Girls*, and some will be great wherever you go and wherever you live.[8]

Don't expect to be everyone's best friend. All you can do is be polite and kind and see where the friendships develop. Don't let this worry you. You won't like everyone, and not everyone will like you. This will likely be your first dose of realizing it's *just how the world operates*. You'll need to find "your people" and develop your own community of friends, supporters and advocates. One of the toughest parts of being an independent adult is sifting through everyone you know and removing the energy drainers from your life. This has taken me years to learn (and I'm still learning), and it's only something you truly realize is needed once you're an adult.

#3: Keep your room clean at all costs

If you're lucky to have your own room, keep it clean. There's nothing worse than coming back to a musty and messy room. It's supposed to be your sanctuary. And if you "get lucky" on a night out, there's nothing more embarrassing than having someone over and them seeing your dirty underwear on the floor or skid marks in the toilet.

Advice #3 might sound dumb; if it does, you're one of the rare people who keeps their room clean. While I was in college, most rooms were disgusting, with overflowing bins and bathrooms covered in hair and stains. If this sounds like a nightmare, I wish I had lived with you in college.

There is also a difference between *thinking* your room is clean and your room *being* clean. Dedicating five to ten minutes daily to cleaning your room can ensure it stays hygienic and tidy.

#4: Outside your room, always have footwear

In the communal areas, you must hope for the best and prepare for the worst. One of the most important rules to remember when living communally is never, ever go barefoot anywhere once you leave your room (I'd even argue to keep your footwear in your bedroom). If you have a communal bathroom, bring shower shoes. Wear slippers with a hard sole when entering your kitchen and living room. I recommend Crocs with socks as they're sturdy, comfy, and easy to slip on. Not only will this avoid dirty feet, but it will save you when you accidentally step on the broken glass

---

7. Wikipedia. 2024. *Death and Taxes (Idiom)*. March 27, 2024. https://en.wikipedia.org/wiki/Death_and_taxes_(idiom).
8. Waters, Mark, dir. 2004. *Mean Girls*. Paramount Pictures.

your drunk roommate forgot to clean up after coming home in the middle of the night....[9]

Your roommates will trek mud and dirt from outside, drop food, drinks, and a myriad of other foul solids and liquids. The communal floors you walk on will be covered in invisible (and visible, often very much so) hazards to the naked eye. Don't risk anything. Wear protective footwear. I'll sleep better at night knowing that you are.

The reason for dirty apartments is that the human brain is naturally wired to embark on "the path of least resistance." As the University of London's Dr. Nobuhiro Hagura explains, "Our brain tricks us into believing the low-hanging fruit really is the ripest."[10] And what does that mean, practically, in real life?

If someone picks up the slack and starts cleaning regularly, others will leave them to it and hope they continue. And, unless they love cleaning or don't mind being a sucker, then it's usually grim for the person conscientious about hygiene.

This is the first "reality check" when you realize people have different priorities and washing the living room floor isn't always top of *their* priority list. Until this point in your life, I will assume the house you grew up in (or apartment, trailer, castle) was clean and tidy, and you always had clean dishes to use when eating.

Unless you somehow land into a college dorm where your roommates are neat freaks who keep everything where it should be and empty the trash regularly, your dorm *will* be messy.

In my first college apartment, rats didn't overrun the place because our Accommodation Office imposed regular inspections. Students were fined if standards were found less than satisfactory. Back then, we thought it was draconian and unnecessary and a way to get more money out of us when we were inevitably charged "cleaning fees" for them to clear up our dorm to a standard they found acceptable. Looking back, I feel lucky that I didn't contract hepatitis just making tea.

One roommate, Ben (real name, not even bothering to change it), would leave his teabag in the sink. And we're not talking about leaving it there while he drank his tea to then wash his cup and throw the teabag away. Oh no, he'd leave the bag in the sink—for days—even though the trash can was under the sink. Yep. The trash can was literally right there. I asked him why on multiple occasions, but he never got the hint. He always shrugged until one day, he said: "I just can't be bothered to put

---

9. And yes if this sounds like I know what I'm talking about, it's because I do...
10. UCL, NICT (Japan) and Western University (Canada). 2017. "Humans Are Hard-Wired to Follow the Path of Least Resistance." UCL News. February 21, 2017. https://www.ucl.ac.uk/news/2017/feb/humans-are-hard-wired-follow-path-least-resistance.

it in the trash." I never knew how to answer that without sounding like the cleaning sheriff. Sometimes, he attempted to put it in the trash. When I say "attempted," I mean he'd boil the water, put his teabag in the cup, and walk over to the couch to watch *Coronation Street* (a British soap like *General Hospital* set in the countryside with worse acting). Then he'd realize his teabag was still in his cup and aim the bag at the trash can from the comfort of the couch. Was he on the basketball team with perfect aim? Nope. Did he miss every time? Yep. So, did he ever get up and deal with it? Ha!

In the name of keeping the peace, I didn't argue. Quite simply, there's no point in arguing when you're living with an idiot.

Living with others that first year also gave me the first sense of "roommate envy." Not every apartment was substandard. I'd find others immaculate and nicely decorated. There'd be flowers in the corner, throws on the couches, and pillows on the seats. It'd feel like a home—It just wasn't *my* home.

But that's like everything ... there are always exceptions. The well-kept apartments were few and far between. So, for any first-year student living in dorms and sharing communal areas, strap in for a year of unclean kitchens, bathrooms, and fridges. And if your experience is better than that, count your lucky stars.

My advice: pay for a cleaner. And, if no one wants to chip in (they usually won't), pay for it yourself. It's not worth arguing over who last cleaned the oven. It may be painful for your student budget, but you can't put a price on cleanliness.

#5: Hide your staples so your college roommates don't steal them

Don't expect others to buy their own when you purchase staples like butter, bread, and salt. No, no, no. They'll just use yours and never tell you. You'll regularly find someone has used your milk, and you won't have enough left to make a cup of tea. There's even a Buzzfeed listicle outlining which foods are okay to steal from your roommates.[11] These include milk, leftover pizza, chips, candy, cheese, spices, alcohol, eggs, cakes, and ice cream. And they're just the popular ones.

My advice: keep non-refrigerated staples in your room. You can't keep a secret fridge in your room (well, you could actually buy a mini-fridge), so only buy small amounts of refrigerated items at a time (juices, milk, etc.). If you buy a lot of milk and keep it in the communal fridge, someone will use it, especially if they're feeling brazen (i.e., hungover and too lazy to

---

11. Stopera, Matt. 2017. "19 Foods You Can Always Steal from Your Roommate." BuzzFeed. November 7, 2017. https://www.buzzfeed.com/mjs538/we-have-all-been-there-before.

go to the grocery store). Even if you don't notice anyone stealing, you can guarantee they will be. It's what happens in communal living as a student.

Also, don't tell anyone you're keeping your own staples in your room. Never, ever explain. They might think you're a selfish douche, and when living with others, you sometimes must be, or you'll end up subsidizing everyone else living there. Paying for your roommates' milk and bread isn't fair. When you know it's unfair, it's best to do something about it secretly rather than being ostracized as the "strange one" in your friendship group.

Living in Private Housing

Congratulations. You've survived your first year on campus, made friends for life, coped with teabags in the sink, and realized your best friend had been stealing bread from you every week (yep, this happened to me). And yet, you're still friends. I mean, come on. You won't lose a lifelong friendship over a piece of toast, right?

Now, it's time for the next phase… Do you move out of college dorms and move in with your new friends? Well, it can be a lot cheaper. Also, it can be much more fun because you *choose* to live with people you *like* rather than be lumped with strangers. Also, you can finally host those crazy house parties without fear of being shut down by college security. All in all, the advantages outweigh the disadvantages.

I advise living with friends off-campus after your first year (if possible). If you do it right, it will be cheaper and fun. But you will want to live on campus in your final year. The stress of exams and essay deadlines means you'll want to live as close to lectures and libraries as possible.

So, you've got the right group of friends. You've got the perfect house. What should you expect next?

#6: Don't expect your security deposit back

You must mentally prepare to lose your security deposit. Unless you live in a beautiful place you've kept immaculate from start to finish (these are the dream roommates who are the 1 percent of people you want to live with), agents will do everything to keep your security deposit.

In the U.S., security deposit laws are different in every state, so getting hard facts about the return of security deposits to students is difficult. However, if the UK is any indication, 14 percent of students say they struggle to get their deposit back at all.[12] After all, students are messy. Everyone

---

12. Bushi, Ruth. 2020. "National Student Accommodation Survey 2020—Results." Save the Student. February 18, 2020. https://www.savethestudent.org/accommodation/national-student-accommodation-survey-2020.html.

knows they break things and have parties. Agents will find any excuse to claim the costs of fixing whatever "damage" the students wrought on their homes. In fact, it's so hard to oppose agents' opinions that I've always considered the security deposit as another month's rent. On the rare occasions I had my deposit back, I saw it as an unexpected bonus.

#7: Sort out the bills to avoid any problems

In college, accommodation bills are included in the cost of rent, so you never have to worry. But once you're out in the "real world," bills get real, too. I was at college before the iPhone, which meant bill-splitting apps hadn't been invented yet. Different people were responsible for different bills, and some often forgot to pay. It was a total nightmare.

My advice: Each of you should download a bill-splitting app like Splitwise, and then one of you will pay all the bills, and the others will pay them back. If no one can pay for all the bills upfront, then each of you should send your share over first so the lead person can pay. The worst thing is being reminded to pay. If this happens, *you* become the roommate everyone talks about behind their back, and everyone will be talking about how they can't wait to stop living with you. Bills are like wrinkles; they're inevitable, and everybody hates them. So, pay your share, and pay it on time.

Part B

Finding Somewhere to Live

"The best part of living in constant terror is you always have a place to live."

—Dana Gould

Welcome to the School of Life

Hurrah! You've now graduated to the *School of Life*. You're ready to attack the real world, get a job, and be properly independent. There are big decisions ahead.

Every year in the U.S., over four million college graduates must decide on their next steps.[1] This is on top of the estimated 18 million Americans aged between 16 and 24 not in education.[2] If I had known everything I know now about roomsharing, I would have avoided going on to live in horrifically cramped roomshares paying over-the-market rate for the privilege.

Talking of paying over-the-market rate, I definitely panicked when I left college for London. I had no trust fund or family home I could live in for free while looking for work. I literally started from scratch with $2,000 in savings from a summer job.[3] I was (and still am) part of the majority who need a job to survive.

Don't panic: You will get a job

One thing to remember is that there is always a reason why it's a bad time to look for work. Whether it's Christmas and the hiring manager is

---

1. Hanson, Melanie. 2024. "College Graduation Statistics." Education Data Initiative. March 15, 2024. https://educationdata.org/number-of-college-graduates.
2. Review of *College Enrollment and Work Activity of Recent High School and College Graduates Summary*. Economic News Release. U.S. BUREAU OF LABOR STATISTICS. April 23, 2024. https://www.bls.gov/news.release/hsgec.nr0.htm.
3. This was back in 2007: $2,000 then is worth around $3,000 in 2024. Just goes to show how wild inflation is over the long term.

on vacation, or it's coming to the end of the tax year, and there's a hiring freeze. Add the cost-of-living crisis, high inflation, and spiraling interest rates; companies have plausible excuses not to hire. If you need a job, you're competing with millions attempting to get a foot on the career ladder. In parallel, there are also experienced ex-employees who are happy to take a pay cut and a job title demotion if it means they can eat. It's easy to get overwhelmed when thinking about how competitive the job market can be.

Don't panic. There's a role out there with your name on it. Everyone who wants a job and works hard for it will find one. It may not be your dream job, but it will be a job. Need some stats to back it up? According to the U.S. National Center for Education Statistics, 80 percent of those aged between 25 and 34 are employed full-time, rising to 88 percent for those with college degrees.[4]

I'm not saying you'll be able to live in a luxury duplex, save a ton of cash every month, and go on exotic vacations every weekend. But there's an 80 percent chance you'll be able to pay rent and eat. Now that it's been established that the majority of the U.S. population can be gainfully employed and afford a roof over their head, let's look at the choices you have about where to live.

---

4. National Center for Education Statistics. 2024. "COE—Employment and Unemployment Rates by Educational Attainment." 2023. Nces.ed.gov. May 2024. https://nces.ed.gov/programs/coe/indicator/cbc.

3

Your Choices as a First-Time Roomsharer

This is the second adult decision you need to make (the first one being whether to go to college): Do you live independently and pay rent or move back in with your family? If you have a family home in the area you want to work in, it's a tough call: live for free or live independently.

Who Should You Actually Live With?

#8: Trust your instinct on what's right for you to decide who to live with

There's no longer a stigma for an adult to be living with their parents, and it's been a rising trend for the last 20 years. In the U.S., 45 percent of adults aged between 18 and 29 live with their families, the highest ratio since the Second World War.[1] This is especially true in big cities like Los Angeles, New York, and London. As Professor Kath Scanlon from the London School of Economics explains, "If you are lucky enough to have parents with a home in London, it is just the absolute norm that you go away to university and then you move back in with your parents, for often several years to save up to rent your own place or to save for a housing deposit."[2]

Personally, I had no choice but to live independently and pay rent. My family home was far away from London, so if I wanted to start my career there, I had to find an affordable roomshare. I loved living independently and occasionally visiting family. Of course, you must do what's right for you, but personally, living this way taught me so much about life

---

1. Napolitano, Elizabeth. 2023. "More Young Adults Are Living at Home Across the U.S. Here's Why." CBS News. September 21, 2023. https://www.cbsnews.com/news/gen-z-millennials-living-at-home-harris-poll.
2. Scanlon, Kath. 2020. Phone interview. December 11, 2020.

and living—in a good way. Your family will always love you, and I'm sure they'll welcome you with open arms. However, deep down, they may want some space. Prof. Keith Tuffin of the University of Massey in New Zealand explains, "Depending on how you've managed your adolescence, your parents want you to leave as well. And it's not the end of the relationship. It's just another phase. Your parents are thinking, you've lived with them for twenty years, time you moved on."[3]

But let's face the facts. Returning to your family home is increasingly common. Just as half of young adults in the U.S. live with family, it's a similar story in the UK, Ireland, and France.[4] In fact, the average age for leaving the family home in the European Union is 26.2 years old.[5] And, in a country like Italy, it's completely normal to live with the family until you marry and start a family of your own. Forty percent of Italians in full-time employment aged between 18 and 34 live with their parents.[6] Financially, living at home while working makes sense. Matt Adamo, an estate agent specializing in luxury real estate in Los Angeles explains that "the cost of living has increased and the amount of income that people are getting is not in line with how much houses cost. People make two hundred grand, and they're living paycheck to paycheck."[7]

You're lucky if you like living at home and get on well with your family. Not everyone has the good fortune to live rent-free while climbing the career ladder and building a life. Personally, this level of comfort is great but risks making someone comfortable and less motivated to strive for more. If you're constantly thinking about a pay raise to afford a better apartment and save money, you will be more ambitious and hungrier for a promotion.

Living away from family teaches you crucial lessons about money. I had to live on what I earned and ensure I had enough to pay rent. I had an aversion to credit cards and overdrafts, and my spending never spiraled. I know a lot of people living at home in LA, New York, and London who had sky-high spending habits like they were the rich kids of Instagram—except they weren't rich. They just had lots of credit cards.

---

3. Tuffin, Keith. 2021. Phone interview. January 19, 2021.
4. Office of National Statistics. 2023. "More Adults Living with Their Parents." Office of National Statistics. May 10, 2023. https://www.ons.gov.uk/peoplepopulationandcommunity/populationandmigration/populationestimates/articles/moreadultslivingwiththeirparents/2023-05-10.
5. Rosswen. 2020. "Age of Young People Leaving Their Parental Household." Eurostat Statistics Explained. August 6, 2020. https://ec.europa.eu/eurostat/statistics-explained/index.php?oldid=494351.
6. Statista. 2024. "Share of young Italians aged between 18 and 34 years who live with their parents in Italy as of January 2018, by occupational status." Statista. July 31, 2024. https://www.statista.com/statistics/804700/share-of-young-italians-living-with-their-parents-in-italy-by-occupational-status.
7. Adamo, Matt. 2023. Phone interview. March 31, 2023.

3. Your Choices as a First-Time Roomsharer

#9: Beware of credit card debt no matter where you live

Clocking up credit card debt while being reassured by the banks that there's nothing to worry about is a common tragedy. Once the cards are maxed, all there is to show for it is an overpriced wardrobe you barely wear and a multi-year repayment plan, trapping ordinary folk in years of debt and an inability to save a deposit for a mortgage. They're then stuck at home because they can't afford to move out. And this isn't just anecdotal. This is real. According to Bankrate, 35 percent of Americans carry debt from month to month, with the average American household on the hook for $96,371.[8]

Kudos to earning your own money and paying your way, which gives you a flair of confidence that nothing else can provide. You're your own safety net. Not only that, when you're a financially independent adult, you can do whatever you like.

#10: Living independently is better in the long run

You can go out until the early hours without your parents commenting about it the next day. Want to go out drinking until five in the morning and sleep until four in the afternoon? No one will judge you—except your liver. Your liver will hate you for it.[9] And that's what you do when you're 23. You can go out all night because you're an adult and earning money—to hell with everyone else. No judging parents, no questions.

At 35, life is different. There's nothing more thrilling than going to bed at ten and then waking up feeling lucky you didn't get up for a whiz in the middle of the night. Ultimately, if living with family is what's best for you, then go for it. It just wasn't for me and never will be. You may have circumstances where you have no choice but to live with family. Every person has unique reasons for the choices they make. Hopefully, these are right for them.

#11: Roomsharing with others has advantages living alone can't match

When living with family isn't for you, and you're paying your own way, you have an important choice: live alone or with roommates.

---

8. Gillespie, Lane. 2023. "Average American Debt Statistics." Bankrate. January 13, 2023. https://www.bankrate.com/personal-finance/debt/average-american-debt.

9. If you have an Apple Watch which tells you your "body battery" level, it will be easy to see the difference between going out drinking tequila until the small hours versus having a peppermint tea and going to bed at nine p.m.

According to the environmental psychologist Lee Chambers, the concept of living alone comes from humanity's "individualistic culture." This is a "culture where we have these kinds of life milestones that we should all expect to pass through."[10]

One of these expected milestones is living alone, but more so, this consists of living alone in a property you own (outright or through a mortgage). As Chambers explains, this "has become embedded, especially since the 1980s, that that is a way for you to show your life's progress, and also a way for you to own your own stamp of land on this earth that we live in. Naturally, that has bled through to society, for millennials, there's an expectation that that is the life stage one of you will pass through."[11]

I find the expectation of living alone compared to the judgment and stigma associated with shared living to be unfair. Living with others is often an economic choice done out of necessity at not being able to afford your own place. Roomsharing is fundamentally cheaper. No one should be judged negatively for wanting to spend less money. Nor should people be *expected* to take out unaffordable mortgages to live alone. As Chambers explains, the assumption that having a mortgage and living independently is better leaves "people feeling that if they're not achieving that, and they're not in a place to do so, that actually, they are the ones who are missing out on this idea of a place where you can call home."[12]

According to Chambers, "If we look across the world, there's a wide variety of different ways of living."[13] And there is no stage of one's life that isn't appropriate to live with other people. In Chambers' mind, it can be an appealing and formative experience as people who roomshare "become very adaptive and flexible."[14] They "learn about other people's cultures" and "understand how people can respond differently to the same thing."[15]

Whatever you choose is highly personal. There is no wrong answer, there is only the right choice for you. The number of people living alone has grown exponentially since the end of World War II. In the last 50 years in the U.S., it has doubled, while, in cities like Stockholm and London, many of its citizens live alone.[16]

I would hate to live by myself. You wake up, and there's no one to say good morning to. You work all day, get home, and there's no one to

---

10. Chambers, Lee. 2021. Phone interview. February 15, 2021.
11. Chambers, Lee. 2021. Phone interview. February 15, 2021.
12. Chambers, Lee. 2021. Phone interview. February 15, 2021.
13. Chambers, Lee. 2021. Phone interview. February 15, 2021.
14. Chambers, Lee. 2021. Phone interview. February 15, 2021.
15. Chambers, Lee. 2021. Phone interview. February 15, 2021.
16. Ortiz-Ospina, Esteban. 2024. "Loneliness and Social Connections." Our World in Data. March 2024. https://ourworldindata.org/living-alone.

listen to you rant about colleagues and bosses. It's ... lonely. Some may hate the idea of sharing a living space, and sometimes they're better off living alone. Psychologist Donna Dawson says, "If you've got a moderate degree of OCD, or something that actually means you can't live with anybody, you need to be on your own because you like everything just so."[17]

There is no doubt that sharing accommodation has its challenges ... which is why this book exists. The same can be said for living alone. Unless you're anti-social and hate talking to people, living alone increases the risk of social isolation. Going home alone when you have an extroverted and lively personality is, at best, boring and, at worst, lonely. Of course, there are introverts who may avoid large social occasions. Yet, introverts like company, too. Just not in the same way.

There is a massive difference between being alone and feeling lonely. You can find time to be alone if that's what you want. You can go for a walk, go away for the weekend or stay in your bedroom. But not feeling lonely is hard when living alone, especially when you're single. This is why having fun roommates can be such a rewarding experience. You may not have as much privacy as you want, but you'll have company. And, as the CEO of roomsharing service Diggz Rany Burstein explains, having roommates "helps people with their social skills. Because you're forced to get along, compromise, live with people that might be a little bit different from you in all kinds of aspects."[18]

When living with people is done right, there's nothing better.

#12: Mentally prepare to roomshare with strangers

Sharing with friends is the natural option for your first time living independently. Why would you want anything else? For instance, if your college friends are all moving to the same city, it makes sense to continue living with them. You already know what they're like, and living with them works for you. Initially, this would be the preferred route. It's more comfortable and you can get to know your neighborhood together.

Eventually, your friends' casual flings will develop into long-term relationships. Those friends may decide to find a place with their partner. Within a few years, your initially dependent circle of friends is almost non-existent. In the long term, some friends will have less time and more responsibilities. They can't party all night and go on last-minute vacations anymore.

---

17. Dawson, Donna. 2023. Phone interview. April 14, 2023.
18. Burstein, Rany. 2023. Phone interview. March 31, 2023.

Even if, decades after leaving school, you still have a circle of close single friends, deciding where and how you will all live together is complicated. Scanlon explains that coming together as friends in a single roomshare "requires that everybody wants to live in the same area, everyone has an income that can support it, and everybody wants to move at the same time."[19]

The chances of these factors aligning shrink as you age, as everyone's careers and relationships progress. As Scanlon puts forth, finding something that ticks all your preferences means you'll eventually have to leave your usual friendship group and "go out and find another group of people."[20] And this is when adulthood really kicks in. Living with randoms is inevitable once you no longer have a circle of friends available to live with. So, you need to mentally prepare for this…

#13: Living with randoms means you keep your current friendships safe

Living with randoms also means you don't risk your pre-existing friendships. Dr. Chris Martin from the University of New South Wales in Sydney explains that when he was roomsharing, "it was almost always with strangers." This means when "things didn't end on a great note, I haven't lost that friend."[21]

This is the risk when sharing with friends. You may live together and discover you're incompatible. Dr. Martin comments, "You may end up losing that person as a friend. Whereas there might be less to lose and more to gain if you're looking to share with strangers."[22]

One of the reasons why sharing with randoms can be easier is, as Lee Chambers explains, friends usually "build a friendship based around not cohabiting together." Still, once these friends start living together, it "becomes sometimes more difficult to challenge pre-existing friendships when it comes to a cleaning rota, or when it comes to things that are upsetting each other. It sometimes becomes more difficult to talk, and it doesn't really give us that acclimatization and that adjustment period that we always give to strangers."[23]

In other words, when moving in with people you don't know, expectations are lower, and you have time to adjust to each other's schedules, habits, and routines.

---

19. Scanlon, Kath. 2020. Phone interview. December 11, 2020.
20. *Ibid.*
21. Martin, Chris. 2021. Phone interview. February 4, 2021.
22. *Ibid.*
23. Chambers, Lee. 2021. Phone interview. February 15, 2021.

#14: New roommates can become lifelong friends

Prof. Tuffin's research concludes that if "sharing arrangements work brilliantly"[24] then "friendships can develop from that."[25] And this couldn't be more verifiable. As Professor Sue Heath from the University of Manchester explains, "New friendships evolve when you're moving in with strangers. One of the very strange things about shared housing when you look at it from a step back is that very accelerated intimacy that comes of necessity. Particularly when you move in with strangers. The day before, you've never met them; the next day, you're wandering around the house in some state of undress. There's a kind of acceleration of the processes of friendship."[26] The people you live with automatically become the circle you hang out with. So, it makes sense to see them as friends and not just roommates.

As psychologist Bella DePaulo, author of *How We Live Now: Redefining Home and Family in the 21st Century*, explains, people "aren't just looking for roommates, they are looking for people to share life experiences with, even if only temporarily."[27] While Dr. Sophia Maalsen of the University of Sydney explains that when "you're moving cities or somewhere new, your roomshare becomes your social network. And when all goes well, in the best of share houses, these are people that come to life."[28] When you live with roommates you like, you'll be hanging out, meeting their friends, friends of friends, and building your own social circle. You can build a new life through your roommates.

#15: Avoid living with someone else's family

I will tell you one thing, though—avoid moving in with someone else's family. I once lived with a partner and her family for six months while we were saving for a deposit to buy our own property… It was hell.

They were the loveliest people, but there was no privacy. I felt permanently judged. I couldn't watch the shows I loved because they had their own to watch. If I wanted to read a book in my bedroom by myself, I was judged because I wanted to read a book in my bedroom. Mealtimes were also difficult. We had little in common, so conversation was stilted. In my own family, a good bottle (or three) of wine papered over any cracks. My partner's family barely drank, which prevented any free-flowing loose

---

24. Tuffin, Keith. 2021. Phone interview. January 19, 2021.
25. Tuffin, Keith. 2021. Phone interview. January 19, 2021.
26. Heath, Sue. 2021. Phone interview. January 6, 2021.
27. DePaulo, Bella. 2020. Email interview. December 19, 2020.
28. Maalsen, Sophia. 2020. Phone interview. December 22, 2020.

conversation that would have come from alcohol. To describe our meals as awkward would be an understatement.

Obviously, there are likely to be examples where it works out well. When moving into someone else's family home, you're moving into an established household with years of routine, habits, and expectations. It's hard for an outsider to adapt.

In my own case, moving in with my partner's family raised red flags I willfully ignored because we were living there for free. After six months, we had saved a big enough deposit and bought our apartment. We broke up four months later.

Determine Where's Best for You

#16: *Your choice of home reflects your personality*

Your personality and preferences determine the home you'd prefer to live in. It's like the research that has proven that dog owners usually own dogs who look like them.[29] Every home reflects the people who live there.

- If you like peace and quiet, being out of town, near a forest, might suit you best.
- If you prefer easy access to shops, restaurants, and bars, somewhere in the city center will work.
- Someone who can't imagine living anywhere but a house will avoid high-rise apartment blocks point-blank.

When you already know what you prefer, finding your ideal roomshare is easier. Even if you know what you want, it's worth exploring different types of properties. You might have never dreamed of living in a warehouse, but after visiting one, you may realize it's brilliant. Visiting different types of homes can confirm what you like and don't like.

When deciding where to live, the beauty of sharing and renting is that you can test different types of homes and decide on your favorite. Want a garden but are worried your allergies will flare up? Do you prefer an open plan kitchen with an integrated living room or a completely separate living room? Have you ever considered living in a warehouse with ten other people? Renting gives you the freedom to experiment without being financially tied long-term.

The type of space you choose to live in will attract others of a similar disposition. This applies to your home, your neighborhood, your city, and your region.

---

29. Hamer, Ashley. 2024. "Why do dogs look like their owners?" Live Science. July 20, 2024. https://www.livescience.com/animals/dogs/why-do-dogs-look-like-their-owners.

3. Your Choices as a First-Time Roomsharer

#17: Where you live influences how you live

As the psychologist Sam Gosling, author of the book *Snoop: What Your Stuff Says About You*, explains: "Even if you're genetically low on, say, the trait of openness, if you live in New York or London, you're just going to be exposed to new ideas and ways of being."[30] Living in big cities like these and being around new people, cultures, and trends will make you more open, or at least as "high in openness as your genes will allow."[31]

Living by the beach means you'll have a lifestyle different from someone living on a farm. Gosling explains that with these "sort of physical differences in the space, you can just do different things if you live in a mountainous space, or the desert or the coast."[32] This, in turn, influences what you do outside of work in the evenings and weekends.

The activities and people also vary depending on where you live, too. In a seaside neighborhood, people are likely to eat and drink in casual beach bars, dress differently, and be used to the salty, humid air. The people you hang out with there will likely be surfers or have jobs related to being near the ocean. Everyone is likelier to drive wherever they go, as well. Compare this to someone living in an apartment block in a busy city where they nip over to upmarket bars and restaurants better suited to shirts and dress shoes. Accordingly, their friends are probably working office-based jobs and take public transportation.

#18: Don't worry if it's not your perfect home yet

You'll only discover your true likes and dislikes when you start to live and share your life with different people in different types of homes. Subsequently, your choices will evolve. One thing you can count on is that it will take years before you find your dream home. And you'll probably "kiss a lot of frogs" along the way, or if I were to rewrite that expression to better suit a roomsharing analogy, you'll "kiss a lot of keys." But don't worry about this. If you're not in it yet, you're only one imperfect home away from your dream one.

As you hop from roomshare to roomshare, the main thing to ensure is that the place is clean, affordable, and occupied by people you like. If those three key criteria are ticked, everything else (usually) falls into place.

---

30. Gosling, Sam. 2021. Phone interview. February 23, 2021.
31. Gosling, Sam. 2021. Phone interview. February 23, 2021.
32. Gosling, Sam. 2021. Phone interview. February 23, 2021.

4

Wising Up Before Committing to a Roomshare

When I was growing up, my mother always said I was smart at school and dumb on the street. I think the only reason I didn't get mugged every day is simply out of luck. The same thinking applies to roomshares: it pays to be smart with them.

You'll spend at least one-third of your life at home, and it's easy to fall into the trap of quickly agreeing to somewhere that, on the surface, has everything you're looking for, until you move in and realize that below the surface everything is wrong. Choosing a new home is one of the most important decisions in your adult life and must be approached with the diligence you adopt when looking for a new job. The most important question to ask before moving in is: Will this be a good fit?

Living with idiots is real, and they make being at home unbearable. Trust me, I've lived with too many and vowed never to again. And, if reading this book means you'll have avoided living with even one idiot, I will have done my job. I write this fully aware I sound like a concerned (and arguably patronizing) parent. Don't care. I only care that you don't have to go through what I did.

The Financial Basics

#19: Know the rules and regulations around renting

People who own property as buy-to-lets aren't charitable personalities. They get into this business to make money. I should know, I own two buy-to-let properties myself. Unless there's an exception to the rule, property owners do everything they can to avoid spending money. And then some.

With this in mind, rules and regulations have improved in a tenant's

4. Wising Up Before Committing to a Roomshare

favor. It's beyond the remit of this book to go into detail for every state, but each one has different laws regarding renters' rights. For instance, in California, security deposits for renters are limited to two months' rent if a property is unfurnished and three months if a property is furnished.[1] In Washington, D.C., and Alabama, the limit is one month. Best to check the latest rules where you live as they may change over time.[2] A website like Avail is a great starting point as it lists the rules per state:

https://www.avail.co/education/laws

What is often universal, regardless of location, is that agents can decide to charge fees for maintenance, background checks, and contract renewals. In fact, if an agent could, they would charge $10 for every email you send them to read and reply to.

When I first moved to London in the UK in 2007, there were fees for:

- Signing the tenancy contract (you read that right, just for my signature)
- Running a background check
- Renewing my tenancy (even when done over a single email, it cost $250)

Security deposits varied in price and length. Some agencies requested anything from one week to three months' rent. The UK government eventually scrapped these ridiculous and inexplicable fees (they were money-making exercises punishing the tenant), and introduced a five-week security deposit cap.

This brings me to one of my most important points for your roomsharing journey: always check the rules and regulations for the location you are renting in. With Google and ChatGPT available on your phone, there is no excuse. Most people I know never look them up. It's like when signing up to a service online and not reading the fine print. Hardly anyone does. To prove this point, one study ran a test and managed to get 99 percent of respondents to agree to completely ridiculous terms and conditions (like giving up naming rights to their first-born children) just to prove how few people bothered to read them.[3]

And why would you? Terms and conditions are long, in a tiny font, and the risk generated by ignoring them is usually low. Even employment

---

1. Realtor.com Network. 2024. "California Landlord-Tenant Law." Avail. 2024. https://www.avail.co/education/laws/california-landlord-tenant-law.
2. Realtor.com Network. 2024. "Landlord Tenant Laws by State for the U.S." Avail. 2024. https://www.avail.co/education/laws.
3. Sandle, Tim. 2020. "Report finds only 1 percent reads 'Terms & Conditions.'" Digital Journal. January 29, 2020. https://www.digitaljournal.com/business/report-finds-only-1-percent-reads-terms-conditions/article/566127.

contracts are neglected, with one study claiming 84 percent of people do not thoroughly read them.[4]

If people aren't even reading their employment contracts, why bother reading their leases? I'm stating the obvious (to check the rules where you live) because of a personal experience that happened to me when I was looking for a place to live in London. And at the time, it was legal....

After making an appointment to see a property, I realized on arrival that I had been sent to the office of the agency letting out the property, not the actual apartment. Fine, I figured an agent would take me to a viewing. When I sat down, the agent thanked me for coming, checked which property I wanted to see and said, "Great. So, visiting the property will cost you £50."

"What?" I choked.

"Yes, sir?"

"Sorry, what do you mean it costs £50."

"Not sure I understand the question. It's a standard admin fee to arrange for someone to come and accompany you to the apartment and view. It's non-refundable whether you take the room or not, by the way."

"You're kidding, right?"

They looked at me like I'd just told them I'd seen the real Elvis busking on a street corner that morning. I walked out of there and never looked back. I'll repeat for clarity: the fee was to *visit* the property. And it was non-refundable! If I didn't like the room (again, I'm repeating myself.... I wanted to *see* a roomshare), they would have kept the £50. Others were viewing the property, too, so even if I had decided I wanted to move in, there was no guarantee the room was mine. It was a complete scam. And it was a legal scam. My only regret is that I never alerted the local housing authority. But then, what could they have done? The agent wasn't forcing anyone to hand over money. They created a service people willingly paid for. It was capitalism at its most ruthless, and the government turned a blind eye (most politicians own their homes, so the problems of renters aren't even on their radar).

In a metropolis like London, so many wide-eyed ingenues arrive en masse with no sense or knowledge of what's normal or not normal. When you're told this is normal, how would you know otherwise? It's like being sold a concert hoodie for $200 even though you know it probably cost $10 to stitch. You still take out the credit card and pay because what other choice do you have if you want the hoodie and the memory of the concert to cherish forever?

---

4. Kashyap, Karthik. 2022. "Only 16% of Employees Read Their Employment Contracts Entirely Before Signing." Spiceworks. October 7, 2022. https://www.spiceworks.com/hr/recruitment-onboarding/articles/only-few-employees-read-their-employment-contracts-entirely.

4. Wising Up Before Committing to a Roomshare

I once visited a property, and the person showing me around said they were about to redo the bathroom. *Great*, I thought. *There'll be a nice new bathroom.* And then I realized. "Wait," I said, "there's only one bathroom in the property."

"Oh yeah," they replied. "There's a gym down the road where you can use the toilet and shower there while the renovations are ongoing."

"So, let me get this straight. For the entire time the renovations happen, we won't be able to use the toilet or the shower?"

"Yeah, that's what I said."

"For how long?"

"Two months, maybe four."

"And will you pay for the gym fees or reduce the rent equivalent to the cost of that membership while it's all happening?"

"No, of course not."

I was looked at as if I were an alien from Saturn migrating to Earth.

But the worst part? *Someone* rented that room knowing they'd have to shower at the local gym for months, and if they needed the bathroom in the middle of the night while the gym was closed, they'd have to… What? Use an empty bottle?

It's almost worse than being asked to pay £50 to visit a property. Yet I think what *is* worse is that people clearly *did* pay that fee, not knowing any better. In a big city, greedy, cynical agents will always be out for your cash.

According to a survey by Dwellsy, over 90 percent of renters experienced attempted rental fraud or suspicious activity online,[5] and "over 50% reported an actual loss in the past year, with the average loss being over $1,000,"[6] and these cases are just the ones people bother to report.[7]

#20: Visit the property before handing over money

You've seen pictures and videos, and the place looks great. You're desperate for somewhere to live, and the agent emails you that the only way to secure it is to send over the deposit to avoid it getting snapped up by someone else. No problem! Except it *is* a problem…

It sounds obvious, but if you're looking online for somewhere to stay and you're coming from a different state or country, *wait* to see it in person first. Even if the agent pressurizes you to secure it ASAP and you're

---

5. Socure. 2024. "Socure Case Study: Dwellsy Increased Fraud Capture by 464%." Socure. 2024. https://www.socure.com/resources/casestudies/dwellsy.

6. Socure. 2024. "Socure Case Study: Dwellsy Increased Fraud Capture by 464%." Socure. 2024. https://www.socure.com/resources/casestudies/dwellsy.

7. Socure. 2024. "Socure Case Study: Dwellsy Increased Fraud Capture by 464%." Socure. 2024. https://www.socure.com/resources/casestudies/dwellsy.

thinking it's the only nice place you've seen in weeks of online searching. Be wary of scams.

A friend from New Jersey tried to secure a place in Paris (France) and sent over the deposit after seeing it online. When we went to the address to pick up the keys, we found a primary school. Thinking she got the address wrong, she tried calling. No answer. She emailed multiple times. No answer. She texted multiple times. No answer. We were ghosted, and my friend was down $5000 with nothing to show. Legally, nothing could be done. The money had been sent over voluntarily to a bank account in Spain. The worst part was that the French police just shrugged and puffed on their cigarettes. They said my friend was an idiot for sending the money without seeing the place. Not that I disagree, but … could they not have been a little nicer about it?

#21: Use a professional agency

With an established agency, you can be assured that they must abide by the rules and regulations of running properties. You'll also avoid being duped into paying a deposit for a roomshare that doesn't exist in the first place.

In my first ever roomshare in Camden, London (when Amy Winehouse used to hang in the neighborhood), Gus (the owner) would turn up unannounced to "say hi," often on a Friday or Saturday evening. *How nice*, I thought. I never imagined London property owners to be so caring. My Pollyanna view of his visits was quickly shattered by my more experienced roommates. He didn't care about us. He was checking if we were having a party or smoking. The apartment was his baby, and we were the hazards risking permanent damage. I didn't know how illegal this was (and still is). Years later, I learned that England's tenancy laws require agents to give tenants 24 hours' notice before entering a lived-in property.[8] And even then, the tenant needs to agree first. Most states in the U.S. have similar laws.[9]

Before signing a lease, search the agency's name, ratings, and reviews online. In ten seconds of research, you'll know more than if you forced an agent to take a lie-detector test—because you know they'd pass it with flying colors.

---

8. Shelter England. 2023. "Repairs and inspections: access to your rented home." Shelter England. September 27, 2023. https://england.shelter.org.uk/housing_advice/repairs/repairs_and_inspections_access_to_your_rented_home.

9. Stewart, Marcia. 2024. "Entry by the Landlord to Rental Property." Nolo. 2024. https://www.nolo.com/legal-encyclopedia/free-books/renters-rights-book/chapter8-2.html.

5

How to Avoid an Agency Ripping You Off

Be Financially Wary

#22: Protect yourself financially before committing

Before moving in, inventory the property and assess any existing damage. Catalogue everything from scuff marks to the dust behind the TV (take a ton of photos and videos). Your inventory should include a clear description of any contents you provide, as well as fixtures and fittings and, ideally, the condition of the property itself. Needless to say, descriptions should be based on the condition of the items at the time—not what they will be if repairs or replacements are in the pipeline.

Examples:

- Appliances—ensure they're all working as they should be (dishwasher, fridge, freezer, washing machine, tumble dryer)
- Ceilings—check for marks and cracks
- Fittings—bathroom suites and kitchen accessories such as taps and sinks
- Flooring—condition of all floor surfaces including carpets, laminate and wood
- Furniture—every item you provide should be included with a description of its condition, even small items like cutlery, glasses and crockery
- Garden and outdoors—any furniture, plant pots, condition of the grass, sheds and garages
- Paint and wallpaper—intact or peeling, chipped or flaking
- Permanent fixtures—ceiling and wall lights and the state of radiators
- Storage—both built-in or standalone wardrobes, cupboards, chests of drawers
- Walls and doors—check for scuff marks, scratches and cracks

- Windows—note the state of windows and blinds or curtains provided

When you leave, anything and everything could be an excuse to take money off your security deposit. Before signing a contract send everything you've catalogued to the agency and have them acknowledge the damage in writing. If you don't, you risk making yourself liable for repairs for pre-existing damage from before you moved in. Agents are like the wolf in Red Riding Hood. They'll smile, convince you everything is fine, and then gobble your money.

The same level of precaution applies when you send over your security deposit. Always send it to a verified account owned by the agent. A sneaky roommate who's leaving the roomshare might try to convince you to pay them your security deposit, claiming you'll just get the same amount back from the agency anyway when you leave. Never do that. Ever. Because the following happened to me.

A roommate was moving out and told me that since we were paying the same agency and I'd get his deposit back from the agency, it was normal for me to pay him his share to make everything go quicker as that's what he had done with the previous departing tenant when he had moved in. At the time it made perfect sense to me, so I handed over the money.... I never saw him or the money again. I'm convinced my deposit paid for his flight back to Australia.

If the agency requests that you pay a departing tenant your share of the deposit, refuse and move on because this is not an agency running its affairs by the book. Once your money is gone, it won't grow legs and run back to you no matter how much you cry. So, how do you avoid living in a roomshare with a rip-off agent?

#23: Spot all the red flags telling you the roomshare is going to be trouble

Red Flag #1: An agency is slow to respond

An agency should be quick with enquiries. Especially as tenants usually only get in touch when there are problems. Although this isn't the biggest red flag, if they're slow during the move-in process, don't act surprised when your boiler breaks and they reply a week later asking for more details about the problem while you've been suffering cold showers.

Red Flag #2: An agency refusing to give you a phone number is a big red flag

How are you supposed to get in touch in an emergency without a phone number? Looking after property isn't a nine-to-five job. When you get home at ten p.m. and there's a leak in the ceiling (and yes, this happened to me), you can't just email the agent and wait for a response when they get into the office the next day. You need to be able to call your agent at any time, day or night, in case of an emergency. That is just part and parcel of being in the property business.

Red Flag #3: The agency not having a physical office is the biggest red flag

Having a physical location you can go to for a complaint is absolutely necessary. The only exception to this would be if you're renting from a private owner who owns only one or two properties. In this situation, it would be a waste of money for them to have an office. But if an agent who has a dozen properties on their books tells you they're "fully digital" with no physical office, this screams "managed by idiots" at best and "managed by scammers" at worst. When an agency manages multiple properties, they need staff in the same office to function cohesively. This also means you always have a fallback if you can't reach them by phone.

Red Flag #4: Use your instinct to catch other red flags

Is the agent late to the viewing? Are they shady about the inventory? The deposit? The contract? Are they hitting on you? Your roomshare is your safe space. You'll be the one living there, so make sure the agent you're dealing with isn't going to make your life harder than it needs to be. One of the best defense mechanisms we have as humans is our survival instinct. If it feels wrong, it probably is. All you have to say to an agent is, "Thank you, but no thank you." Agents don't care. They will move on to the next idiot willing to part with their cash.

6

How Do You Know If This Is the Right Roomshare for You?

According to Google, home is:
- The place one lives permanently
- A family or social unit occupying a permanent residence
- Where something flourishes or originates from

When looking for a roomshare, you're not just looking for a bed to sleep on (sometimes you are; there are always exceptions). You're hoping for somewhere to spend quality time and relax, where you'd be happy to entertain friends, family and loved ones. In essence, you're searching for a home.

How do you know it's the right home? I call it instinct, intuition, or a sixth sense. It's personal, depending on tastes, budgets, and circumstances. Below are recommended universal non-negotiables to help your search and ensure you know what you're willing to accept (or not).

#24: Live with the smallest number of roommates your budget can afford

U.S. federal law has predefined National Occupancy Standards (NOS), which means that every household, at a minimum, needs one bedroom for every cohabiting couple and one bedroom for every non-cohabitating household member aged 18 and over.[1] This means that technically, as an adult in the U.S., it is illegal for an agent to rent a single bedroom for two strangers to share. Unless you're a couple, the agent must, by law, provide one bedroom for every single adult. Legally, there's no limit to the number of roommates you have as long as everyone has a bedroom. Saying this, the roomshares I've lived in where I was sharing with four or five other people have never been nice. In a roomshare of this size, it's hard to get to know

---

1. Law Insider. n.d. "National Occupancy Standards Definition." Law Insider. n.d. https://www.lawinsider.com/dictionary/national-occupancy-standards.

everyone. You all have different schedules, and inevitably, one or two will claim they're never in the apartment and never use the kitchen, so they think it's unfair they should contribute to communal tasks.

If you can, live with just one person. This is if your budget can stretch. Some people love living in a hippie-style commune with ten others. This is great, too. Everyone is different. I can't deal with too many people in the same living space as it's too noisy; someone is always moving in or out, and the bathroom is always busy. The fewer people you live with, the more amenities are available. The bathroom is cleaner. You'll have a better chance of watching that show you like on TV. There's even a better chance of having some quiet time when others are out.

After a few roomshare experiences, you'll know your limit on the number of people you can live with. In a big city like New York, 54.4 percent of apartments have only two or three bedrooms.[2] Apartments with four or more bedrooms account for less than 8 percent of the housing stock.[3] So, if you live in the Big Apple, the chances of having only one roommate are high anyway.

#25: *Live somewhere compatible with your own tidiness levels*

Pop quiz: How tidy are you on a scale of one to ten? With ten being the cleanest, be honest with yourself. If you're reading this at home, look around your bedroom. Are you closer to one or to ten? If you're a ten out of ten, you're either lying to yourself or you're a neat freak.[4]

The point is knowing your own levels of tidiness and what you can tolerate. When you're visiting a roomshare, you see it at its best (and if not, these are alarm bells). Sam Gosling explains, "The person who is the potential new incomer can get a lot of information by looking at the space. People have different standards for what is tidy and clean."[5] So, if one person is "incredibly tidy," living with "someone who's not can be a big source of discord."[6]

How a roomshare is presented to you when visiting will tell you a lot more than you realize about the people living there. Do they leave their clothes out? How clean is the bathroom? How is the food cupboard organized? All these details reveal what it'll be like living together to help you decide if it's right for you.

---

2. Timmons, Matt. 2024. "New York City Renters Statistics and Trends." Value Penguin. January 10, 2024. https://www.valuepenguin.com/new-york-city-renters-statistics#quick-facts.
3. Timmons, Matt. 2024. "New York City Renters Statistics and Trends." Value Penguin. January 10, 2024. https://www.valuepenguin.com/new-york-city-renters-statistics#quick-facts.
4. I love living with neat freaks, by the way. I think they're the best roommates.
5. Gosling, Sam. 2021. Phone interview. February 23, 2021.
6. Gosling, Sam. 2021. Phone interview. February 23, 2021.

It goes without saying that you'll want to live with people who have similar standards of tidiness and cleanliness. When you visit an apartment and the cushions aren't fluffed, dirty dishes are piled high, clothes are strewn everywhere, and there's a faint stench making you squirm, you know it's a pass. But, if it makes you as happy as the ending of a Reese Witherspoon movie, you've found a perfect match!

#26: Have a dishwasher

Only half of U.S. households have a dishwasher, making it sound a little ridiculous that one of my non-negotiables would be having one.[7] Despite the stats, believe me, every roomshare needs a dishwasher. For every roomshare I've lived in without one, arguments about dishes continuously erupted. No exceptions. It is wild when you think about it, as you would hope people naturally do their dishes once they finished eating.

They don't.

Even when there are two of you, you'll annoy each other over the dishes. One of you will have a way of washing the dishes the other doesn't like. You might leave them soaking overnight, let them air-dry, or insist on washing them immediately. Your roommate might prefer to relax and watch TV after dinner and wait until the morning to do them. Having a dishwasher removes any friction regarding who needs to do the dishes and how to do them. Sure, there might be disagreements over who bought the last dishwasher tablets and who last emptied the machine, but compared to the emotion and annoyance caused by handwashing dishes, they pale in comparison.

#27: Live close to the neighborhoods you love with a work commute that works for you

Ensure you're within walking distance (if your budget allows) to where you'd like to be (for example, where you want to eat, drink, and go out). Being close to your preferred social hangouts is crucial to your mental well-being. You could have found a great home, but you'll be miserable if it's in a neighborhood you hate. Of course you may not know what kind of neighborhood you like yet.

Unlike buying a home, when you rent, you're not committed to staying in one place longer than you wish to be. You can try new things, and if they don't work out, you can move. Roomshares are like samples at the ice

---

7. Bashir, Umair. 2024. "Household appliances ownership in the U.S." Statista. August 13, 2024. https://www.statista.com/forecasts/997158/household-appliances-ownership-in-the-us.

cream store. You can try before you buy. And if, like me, you like to read on your commute, then having an hour-long journey is great for finishing all the books you've been meaning to read for years. A movie-buff friend of mine based in San Francisco loves his 90-minute commute each way as he'll watch one or two movies a day. He'll even watch the ones on Amazon Prime that no one's ever heard of. But, if you're the kind of person who likes to walk to work, make sure you factor this in before even visiting the place. You might be working at the same office for years, so finding somewhere to live where you can walk to work is critical for your professional success (to get there on time every day) and, by extension, your happiness.

#28: Working from home needs to be comfortable

The pandemic showed us that working from home is possible, and studies have proven that hybrid working environments lead to higher productivity and job satisfaction. When you visit a potential roomshare, visualize yourself working there. Is there a separate space for working? Do your roommates work from home, too? It's doubtful that you can all work from the living room at the same time. Can you work and make phone calls from your bedroom without disruption?

Chapter 20 goes into a lot more depth on the topic of working from home. As a first step though, make sure when you view a property that you can envision yourself working from home in some capacity (assuming you want to) which will be key to you being able to live there long-term.

#29: Observe if the decor is compatible with your tastes

Pay attention to how the apartment is decorated. Are the walls white-washed? Are there plants on every available surface? Is it cluttered with furniture from the 1970s?

When you go on a first date, you notice what someone wears and how they hold their knife and fork when eating (oh, that's just me? OK). It's the same when you see a roomshare for the first time. How a roomshare is decorated will say a lot about the dynamics of the home. A tidy, well-decorated, and freshly painted place will tell you the people there care about their home. If the walls look like they haven't been painted in years, there's a mess on the kitchen table, and laundry is everywhere, this will tell you the people living there don't care.

Of course, this all depends on what you're looking for. Do you prefer a cheap place to crash, shower, and sometimes eat? Even if this is the case, you'll want to live with people who care about their home life. Again, I sound like a concerned parent who likes to repeat a joke about being a concerned parent. And, yes, I'm happy to be that parental figure if it means you won't live in a dump which will emotionally scar you for the rest of your life (dramatic much? Me?).

#30: A roomshare needs a living room

If you're young and budget-conscious, living on a first-job salary, you're probably thinking, I'd rather have a bigger room in a home with no living room than a smaller room with access to a living room. After all, it's only a place to sleep and shower, and you barely spend any time there… Right?

Patrik Schumacher, who runs Zaha Hadid Architects, publicly said that "private hotel room-sized" apartments with no living room are perfect for younger generations.[8] Well, let me tell you now: Patrik Schumacher is wrong, and fundamentally so. There's no debating this.

In a city like New York, residents are protected by section §27-2075 of the Housing Maintenance Code, which states that "every person in an apartment or a one- or two-family home must have a livable area of no less than 80 square feet."[9] In London, a study published in *The Guardian* revealed that over 90 percent of advertised roomshares had no shared living room.[10]

I have lived with and without a living room, so trust me, not having a shared living room is worse than living with idiots. Without a living room, you have nowhere to:

- Eat (except maybe in a tiny kitchen)
- Put your feet up and relax
- Read a book or watch TV
- Hang out with friends and roommates

Sure, you can do all these things in your bedroom. What, are you 12 years old and having a sleepover? A self-respecting adult isn't going to eat all their meals in their bedroom every day. Nor will they invite someone over to "hang in their bedroom" unless it's code for "we've been on a few dates

---

8. Oppenheim, Maya. 2018. "Millenials don't need living rooms, says top architect." *The Independent*. April 26, 2018. https://www.independent.co.uk/news/uk/home-news/patrik-schumacher-millenials-living-rooms-adam-smith-institute-studios-a8324201.html.

9. Glascott, Maggie. 2018. "Roommate Law: How Many People Can Legally Live Together?" StreetEasy. June 18, 2018. https://streeteasy.com/blog/legal-number-people-nyc-apartment.

10. Saner, Emine. 2019. "Nine out of 10 shared houses don't have a living room. Here's why we need them." *The Guardian*. September 30, 2019. https://www.theguardian.com/money/shortcuts/2019/sep/30/shared-houses-dont-have-living-room-landlords-communal-space-into-bedrooms-tenants-socialise.

6. How Do You Know If This Is the Right Roomshare for You?

now, and it's time we get it on." A living room is a fundamental human right—end of. Any prospective agent telling you otherwise, trying to convince you a living room isn't necessary as your bedroom is big, is lying. The only reason your room *is* big is because it probably *was* the living room. I will bet you anything that not a single agent in the world lives in a home without a living room. And if they do, it certainly isn't by choice. Choosing to live without a living room for budgetary reasons is not worth the cost to your mental health. Especially after the pandemic, everyone needs somewhere they can chill.

If an agent is being misleading, an advert for a roomshare will gloss over the fact that there's no shared living space. I would personally double-check that there is one before committing to a viewing. Some scrupulous agents interpret having a table in the kitchen as the same as having a living room. The living room can be an extension of a large open-plan kitchen as many homes are designed that way. As long as it feels separate enough to relax, eat, and watch TV, it's fine.

A living room isn't a luxury. It's a necessity.

7

Your First Professional Roomshare

This is the most fun and exciting step in your adult life. You're about to start living independently. You might have a dream job lined up (or you're looking for it) and need a place to stay with other professional renters because one-bedroom apartments are extortionate. You conduct a bunch of viewings and find what looks like the perfect roomshare. Everyone is a similar age, has a fun-sounding job, and is up for going out. Great!

You'll live with interesting people, make new friends, and have dinner parties. It's a whole new world, and you have money to burn, wine to drink, and shots to take. Waking up on a Tuesday with a throbbing hangover is the definition of fun. If you want to make new friends, your roommates are your first port of call. They might have a circle of friends already, so make sure they're aware you're open to hanging out and getting to know them. Particularly when you're living with new people for the first time, becoming friends will make living with them much smoother.

Be prepared to make all sorts of mistakes. Simple things such as stashing your shoes neatly, labelling your food, and ironing that suit won't seem important at first. With your first professional roomshare, cut yourself some slack. The one mistake you can't make is being late paying your share of the bills. The easiest way to become enemy #1 is being chased for your half of the electricity bill. It goes without saying you should at least get these basics right. When it comes to communal bills, groceries, and toiletries, paying your fair share is expected. These small things go a long way to keeping the peace with your roommates.

You're young, inexperienced, and not expected to be aware of the standard etiquette. At least, this is what your roommates should be aware of. Talking of inexperience, it feels like a big lesson here, but don't let a more experienced roommate take advantage of the fact you're young and new. If they ask you to vacate the apartment just because they want a

7. Your First Professional Roomshare

dinner party with their friends, that's not fair, and they should at least be courteous enough to invite you.

Remember that when you start living together after meeting during the roomshare interview, you're in what Yale University professor Margaret Clark calls "ground zero," which is the "relationship initiation."[1] As Clark explains, having a friendship isn't a guarantee. Your roommates might not "want to become friends."[2] They "may just want a person who will split the rent and keep a place clean."[3] And if this is the case, that's okay.

As Donna Dawson explains, there shouldn't "be the assumption that you're gonna be best friends with all your roommates. A basic friendly relationship is expected, but beyond that, it's down to circumstance and how well your personalities blend together."[4] It should be discussed before you move in, and if your roommates aren't interested in becoming friends, you can decide whether this will work for you or find another roomshare with roommates who want to become friends.

---

1. Clark, Margaret. 2023. Phone interview. May 17, 2023.
2. Clark, Margaret. 2023. Phone interview. May 17, 2023.
3. Clark, Margaret. 2023. Phone interview. May 17, 2023.
4. Dawson, Donna. 2023. Phone interview. April 14, 2023.

8

The Veteran Roomshare

It's been years since you started roomsharing, and you've lived in quite a few. You know which neighborhood you want to live in, how many roommates you're looking to live with, and what your budget can stretch to. You're just looking for a peaceful roomshare to sleep, eat, and hang out in.

Once you've notched up a few roomshares and experienced living with friends, friends of friends, and randoms, you're likely to prefer living with strangers as they're easier to handle (they have fewer expectations of you). At this point, you'll probably want to spend more on your home comforts. You're likely to have an established routine, and no matter how long you'll be staying in this roomshare, you'll want to take time to make your home cozy. It will make a world of difference coming home and feeling comfortable. If you treat your roomshare like a hotel, you'll never be relaxed. The first step to being comfortable is to ensure that coming home is something you look forward to. Everyone has a different definition of "homely." For some, it's hanging up posters. For others, it's lots of cushions and blankets. Others prefer minimalism. Whatever works for you as long as you feel at home.

Veteran Etiquette

#31: Avoid mixing veterans with first-timers

If you're a first-time roomsharer reading this paragraph, this advice is not for you. The reality is, when sharing with someone who's been doing this for a while, you're their worst nightmare. First-timers are likelier to get things wrong because they don't know the expected etiquette. How would they? They've never done it before (and probably haven't read this book yet).[1] At the same time, it's not your job to teach them what to do or

---

1. If that's the case, buy it for them now and email me for a discount code 😉.

not do; you're not their parent. The best thing a veteran roomsharer can do is avoid living with a first-timer in the first place (or give them this book to read).[2]

The problem isn't that a first-timer will make mistakes. A first-timer will likely be younger and lead a completely different lifestyle than someone who has lived in roomshares for a while. Getting drunk on a Monday night and stumbling in with five strangers in tow to keep drinking is something a first-timer is likelier to do. This may not suit a veteran's lifestyle. Mundane things like taking out the trash and avoiding dirty dishes are learned behaviors one acquires over time. Your life will be made a lot easier by picking a roommate with the same level of experience. This is why, as a veteran roomsharer, avoiding younger roommates is better.

#32: Embrace living with one roommate

It's tempting to live with multiple people in a bigger place. The financial benefits are obvious: cheaper rent and lower bills. The problems are bigger, too. The kitchen is used more often, and you have fewer opportunities to cook when it suits you. The bathroom is used more. The television gets hogged. Overall, your home is busier, dirtier, and noisier. The fewer people you live with, the higher the quality of your roomshare.

This is why, as explained earlier, I encourage living with a small number of roommates. With one roommate, you may not be able to save as much money, but it will be worth every dollar. There'll be only one person to discuss chores with, and the chances of you having the roomshare to yourself once in a while are higher. Also, everything is easier when needing to communicate with only one other person. It does come with risks, of course. If you're not compatible, you're stuck living with them until you can figure out a solution (which is usually moving out). The rewards are worth the risks. You'll have a cleaner apartment, more space to enjoy, and more opportunities living in a peaceful environment.

#33: Living with one person is similar to living with a partner

When you're married or cohabiting full-time with a partner and no longer roomsharing with randoms, society views this as "success." Yet, this co-living is no different from sharing a home with someone who is not a romantic partner.

Living together means you:
- Share a bathroom

---

2. Please ☺.

- Cook (together or separately)
- Share rent
- Split bills
- Decorate together

Everything a couple does (minus the romance and kids) is the same as what two people roomsharing do. The key differences are that you're not in love and you have your own bedroom. And unless you have a strange (some would call it special) friendship you'll never shower together. In fact, this sounds exactly like marriage.[3]

---

3. *Kidding.* Sort of…

Part C

Getting Roomsmart

"Staying in bed all day is my way of saving money."
—Anonymous

Why Knowledge Will Enable Better Decisions

You've all heard it before: knowledge is power. It's true. Reading this book and learning to navigate roomshares will help you lead a better life. Back in Chapter 4, I briefly mentioned how my mother used to say I was smart at school and dumb on the street. When you're an adult living in a roomshare, whether you're smart or dumb at the office and on the street, you need to be roomsmart. When it comes to the law, rent, and dealing with idiots, being well-informed will give you a huge advantage.

9

Getting Lawsmart

This isn't a legal handbook by any stretch, but when money is being exchanged, it's important to have a basic overview of your legal rights regarding a roomshare. It's not exhaustive, but you should know some basics to prep you living there.

#34: Get everything in writing before moving in

Dr. Chris Martin advises that, before you start your roomshare, you must know "where you stand legally."[1] This is the most basic advice any lawyer will give you (I should know; I dated one). You may assume everything is fine, and in most cases, everything is. In situations when things go awry, you need to be ready. If you're living somewhere through a handshake, get a basic agreement in writing, signed by the people receiving your share of the rent. Martin explains that "the fact that it is in writing makes a difference" as "there'll be less likelihood of a problem arising."[2]

Sometimes, an informal arrangement is better than signing a 12-month contract. The flexibility of a handshake deal can be freeing. But as Martin elaborates, "If you're entering a roomshare, even if you don't want to insist on the full tenancy arrangement, you should at least ask for some of the basic details to be written down and for some sort of written record of your rent payments."[3] Only a written and signed agreement between all parties will clarify your rental situation. This is crucial in the event of a disagreement. At the bare minimum, you need to have written acknowledgment about the amount of deposit you've paid and what you're due back once you leave.

If you only take away one piece of advice from this chapter, it would be to ensure a paper trail of rents and deposits. Otherwise, everything becomes a case of "they said this" and "they said that," and everyone loses.

---

1. Martin, Chris. 2021. Phone interview. February 4, 2021.
2. Martin, Chris. 2021. Phone interview. February 4, 2021.
3. Martin, Chris. 2021. Phone interview. February 4, 2021.

9. Getting Lawsmart

#35: Read all documents in full before signing anything

In the past, I've made the mistake of assuming that a standard tenancy agreement is basically the same everywhere. I'd skim through, sign, and send back. In one apartment, the fridge broke, so I emailed the agent. Their reply? "As per the terms of the contract, we are not liable for any damage to the white goods in the property, including fridge, washing machine, and dishwasher." Brilliant. So, because I hadn't read the contract properly, I now had to shell out hundreds of dollars for a working fridge. Six months later, the washing machine broke. I didn't even bother letting the agent know.

And there are plenty of other scenarios that have happened to me or friends of mine:

- Getting a pet and being given 30 days to remove it or vacate the premises
- Putting up a shelf in the bedroom, then being told to take it down
- Accidentally forgetting to pay the rent (ex., you're on a long flight and the time zone difference got you muddled) and a day later accrue a 10 percent fine

Andrea Shapiro, Director of Program and Advocacy at the MET council in New York City, recommends New Yorkers should not believe "everything the landlord says" because "New York City landlords are infamous for lying."[4] To make things worse, New York's "leases are infamous for being wrong."[5] This is why Shapiro advises everyone, particularly New Yorkers, to pore over "the document you're all signing, looking at the apartment you're going into and asking lots of questions."[6]

Before you sign, read all agreements thoroughly to know what you're agreeing to. You're the one signing it, so you will only have yourself to blame. By reading the lease, you can check whether the agent includes basic tenancy rights such as hot water, heating, and privacy. If, after you've moved in, your roomshare falls short on any of those items (and it usually will at some point), you can quote the agreement.

I lived in a roomshare where the boiler broke down. The agent said they couldn't get hold of the owner to arrange for a plumber. Then, the agent was on vacation (allegedly). I kept following up, and the back-and-forth took weeks with excuse after excuse (e.g., sorry your email went into our spam folder, your last email was missed, etc.). When I looked up my rights (thank you, Google), I discovered it was UK law

---

4. Shapiro, Andrea. 2023. Phone interview. May 3, 2023.
5. Shapiro, Andrea. 2023. Phone interview. May 3, 2023.
6. Shapiro, Andrea. 2023. Phone interview. May 3, 2023.

for agents to provide their tenants with permanent access to hot water and heating. If a tenant is not receiving help from the agent, they can go to the local council. As soon as I flagged this, the agent miraculously arranged an appointment the same day, and it was fixed by the time I got home from work.

The thing about contracts is that they're deliberately onerous. As Richard H. Thaler and Cass R. Sustein write in *Nudge*, the "fine print contains that information the seller is required to tell you but does not want you to read."[7] Which is all the more reason to read everything. If you can re-watch ten seasons of *Friends* multiple times, you can read a contract putting a roof over your head.

#36: Always check your local tenancy rights

Wherever you live in the world, always (and I mean always) check your local tenancy rights. Now, I'm not suggesting you consult a lawyer every time you move. Not at all. One search on Google for "[INSERT STATE OF CHOICE] tenancy rights" will be enough to get hold of the highlights. To give you a flavor here's how they look when doing a quick search... (Obviously; I couldn't list every state in the U.S. from Alabama to Wyoming; they would dwarf this book!)[8]

Results When Searching for Tenancy Rights

CALIFORNIA

"The Tenant Protection Act of 2019 protects a majority of California's renters against unlawful rent increases and unfair evictions. Many cities also have stronger local rent control measures with lower caps on how much your landlord can increase your rent."[9]

FLORIDA

"Florida is one of the most landlord-friendly states in America. Landlords can evict tenants after giving them a 3-day notice for non-payment of rent, and they can terminate leases after giving tenants 15 days' notice."[10]

---

7. Thaler, R.H., and Sunstein, C.R. 2008. *Nudge: Improving Decisions about Health, Wealth, and Happiness*. London: Penguin, p. 141.

8. Thank goodness for Google so that I don't need to list the rights for every U.S. state from Alabama to Wyoming. If this book had been published in 1995 it would have been different...

9. Tenant Protections. 2024. "Tenant Protections." 2024. https://tenantprotections.org.

10. Gaddis, Agnes. 2024. "Top 20 Most and Least Landlord Friendly States of 2024." Real Wealth. July 9, 2024. https://realwealth.com/learn/landlord-friendly-states/.

Kansas

"Kansas is a moderately landlord-friendly state. There are no rent control laws, and tenants are unable to withhold rent unless it is for repairs."[11]

New York

"New York is considered a landlord-friendly state since rental prices are usually higher, compared to other states. It's also considered a tenant-friendly state because there's a high rate of rent control clauses."[12]

As you can see, tenants face different legal scenarios depending on where they decide to make their home, so you'll need to plan and research accordingly. Thanks to Google, you have the world's biggest digital law library on your phone. It's like a pocket legal counselor—free of charge. And everyone loves a freebie—even rich people.[13]

#37: If something feels wrong, do your research

Even though Gus was the owner and had keys, when he turned up unannounced at my apartment in Camden, it felt weird, and I couldn't explain why. No other roommate thought it was strange. If I had bothered to read our rights as tenants, I would have known Gus wasn't allowed to do this. Like the broken boiler situation, my gut told me it was wrong. Only years later did I realize it was not just wrong; it was illegal.

Humans are blessed with great instincts (most of the time). However, when choosing the right job or partner, our instincts can sometimes be off (case in point: 43 percent of first marriages end in divorce).[14] We are great at noticing when something is wrong. And, when we feel something is wrong, it probably is. The beauty of the world we live in is that nothing is a secret anymore. No tenant can hide behind a lack of knowledge. Information on tenancy rights is accessible to all. So, only the people that can't be bothered to use Google properly are at risk of getting screwed over. The internet has made it simpler to protect yourself. I'm making it sound like Google is the answer to everything. It is… To an extent. You know what I mean, right?[15]

---

11. Sanford, Jeanne. 2024. "Kansas Lease Agreements & Landlord-Tenant Law." Turbotenant. September 1, 2024. https://www.turbotenant.com/state/kansas.
12. Bitton, David. 2024. "New York Landlord Tenant Rental Laws & Rights for 2024." Doorloop. June 24, 2024. https://www.doorloop.com/laws/new-york-landlord-tenant-rights.
13. Particularly rich people.
14. Bieber, Christy. 2024. "Revealing divorce statistics in 2024." Forbes. May 30, 2024. https://www.forbes.com/advisor/legal/divorce/divorce-statistics.
15. You also need to be "Googlesmart" to make sure you can distinguish between the truth and misinformation. Which is another topic out of the scope of this book!

#38: Contracts are always negotiable

The laws have changed in recent years as various governments have realized that renters are on the rise and buying property is increasingly difficult. The younger generations are starting to believe they'll rent forever. In just four years (from 2018 to 2022), the proportion of millennials stating they'll be renting for the rest of their lives almost doubled from 13.3 percent to 24.7 percent.[16] And, if that belief becomes reality, having your say over where you live is more important than ever.

However, it all comes down to the contract between yourself and the agent. The thing is, you have the upper hand when it comes to moving in. You need to stand strong with your demands because there are so many properties out there you do not have to worry about losing the perfect one. There will be others. You just have to make sure you don't get screwed over while trying to get it. Securing a tenancy is like everything else in life. It requires two parties to sign on the dotted line, and that line can always be moved. Nothing is off-limits. Money is your limit, of course. Everything always comes down to money.[17]

---

16. Statista Research Department. 2023. "Share of millennial renters who expect to always rent in the United States from 2018 to 2022." Statista. 2023. https://www.statista.com/statistics/1222083/millennial-renters-expect-to-rent-forever-usa.

17. Another big lesson in life. Money solves everything. Except a broken heart. Even then…

10

Getting Rentsmart

"I want this place. Let's offer what they're asking."
—Roommate 1

"There is so much competition we need to offer over the asking price."
—Roommate 2

"Never pay the asking price. There is always room for negotiation."
—Roommate 3

The above quotes illustrate the three most common universal negotiating stances. Remember that prices are invented by the seller and validated by the buyer. In other words, the market value of a roomshare is whatever someone is willing to pay for it.

When I was a lead tenant and arranged all the visits for the other two bedrooms in my three-bedroom apartment, I always listed the price on the higher side. People offered less, but all I needed was one acceptable person to commit to the higher price, and I always found one. Every time it got me thinking: Could I have gotten more rent out of them for their room so that I could pay even less for my own?[1]

No matter what you're selling, if people are willing to pay full price, no questions asked, then you're always left wondering: How much was left on the table? Am I underselling? This is true for concert tickets, cars, and houses. This is why the travel industry computerized dynamic pricing in the 1980s. The cost of airfare varies depending on demand. Boston to Los Angeles is priced differently depending on whether you're flying on a Sunday evening or on a Wednesday at six in the morning. Everyone expects this.

---

1. The agent didn't care who paid the rent as long as they received the full amount every month, which came from me when the other tenants moved out and I took over as lead tenant. Demand for the rooms was so high that I eventually managed to get those in the other two bedrooms to pay me 110% of the apartment rent, which covered everyone (including myself), and I kept the surplus. No one had any idea I was doing this.

So, when it comes to renting, everything depends on the current state of the market. If people are queueing to view a home, you can be sure the agent will receive over-the-asking-price offers. The question then becomes: What are you willing to bid?

Unless you're desperate to live in that one oversubscribed roomshare, just let it go. You'll be happier knowing you're not a sucker paying too much for too little just because a lot of people happened to be viewing the same room the same weekend. The underlying issue is overcrowded cities with too few rental properties catering for too many people. Renters are facing unprecedented competition to secure a decent home they like. The optimal scenario, and it's rare, is if the agent looks beyond the price and considers your application holistically. Someone could offer way above the market rate, but if they're going to trash the place and complain all the time, the hassle for the agent isn't worth it. Your key assets are being a reliable tenant with great references. If an agent cares about the long-term maintenance of the property and not just a fast buck, you're in the front row to be selected.

Finding a roomshare can often feel like a beauty pageant. You need to look the part and have the skills to persuade a committee of strangers to pick you as the winner. This chapter is all about how to financially rig the pageant in your favor.

How to Approach Rent

#39: *The asking price is flexible (when approached correctly)*

Agents love to brag about a property getting "incredible offers," and the place you're interested in will "get snapped up in no time."[2] Always take these statements with a pinch of salt. Ask them how long it's been on the market. A week? A month? Longer? If so, sweet. You're in a strong position to negotiate. But *always* ask if the owner is open to negotiation. You'll be surprised at how many agents say there's no wriggle room (and it's true, there sometimes isn't) when, in fact, whoever is paying the mortgage on the home is just grateful someone is moving in.

Property owners will always prefer having a tenant paying slightly less than an empty asset generating no income. On top of this, offering less will make the agent think they have overpriced the property. In a situation where every property you like is getting snapped up before you can even view it, either suck it up and pay full rate or widen your net. It's like modern dating via apps. You either go on dates until you lose the will to live and settle for someone because you're desperate, or you get creative in finding a perfect match (assuming perfect matches exist).

---

2. I could write a whole book on agent clichés. Just saying.

#40: Build a business case to negotiate the asking price

A rent negotiation process is like building a business case. It doesn't have to be complex if you are precise with your numbers. If a room is advertised at $950 a month, instead of suggesting a rounded $850 or $900, offer $812 (or any other weirdly precise number like that), and include a link to an equivalent room at $800. You then explain that, compared to similar rooms in the area, the one the agent is offering is overpriced. You prefer their building, and this is your offer. And if the agent can't budge, you'll go with the $800 room.

You want to make an unusually precise offer because studies have proven that they have a higher chance of getting accepted than rounded ones.[3] It's a simple and effective psychological tactic that makes the recipients of the counteroffer subconsciously believe your business case is stronger. Which is the trick to a successful life, isn't it? Making people believe you know what you're doing...

#41: Stay confident you'll find the right roomshare

Even if you lowball an offer and miss out, plenty of other roomshares exist. Large cities have a particularly high turnover as people change jobs, start families and move away.

Be prepared to miss out on (what feels like) the perfect home. You will find yours eventually. If you overpay for a roomshare because you feel you must, you'll feel cheated and grow resentful. Before long, you'll be looking at your options, and the cycle starts again.

Whatever you do, don't sign anything if it doesn't feel right. It's like picking fruit at the grocery store. You sort through the bad ones and pick the best.

#42: How to split the rent before moving in

> "My room is smaller with a single bed. I should pay less."
> —Roommate 1

> "You have the en suite so you should pay more."
> —Roommate 2

> "I was told the rent was a take-it-or-leave-it situation."
> —Roommate 3

---

3. Mason, Malia F., Lee, Alice J., Wiley, Elizabeth A., Ames, Daniel R. 2013. "Precise Offers Are Potent Anchors: Conciliatory Counteroffers and Attributions of Knowledge in Negotiations." *Journal of Experimental Social Psychology.* January 1, 2013. https://business.columbia.edu/faculty/research/precise-offers-are-potent-anchors-conciliatory-counteroffers-and-attributions.

There are two types of contracts when it comes to splitting the rent:

- Contract #1: You sign a contract to rent a room and just pay for that
- Contract #2: The entire property's rent is split between all tenants

If you're in a Contract #1 situation, you can skip this section. The agent sets the rent for each room in what is usually a "take it or leave it" scenario, where they'll accept anyone on a first-come, first-serve basis. In Contract #2, the agent rents out the whole place (it's simpler for the agent), and the people moving in split the rent between themselves.... If every room in the roomshare is equal in size, amenities, and storage, you're lucky, and it's a no-brainer; everyone pays the same level of rent as everyone else as you're all sharing the communal spaces.

The reality is, not every room is created equal. Case in point: I once lived in a three-bedroom apartment where the overall rent was $2000. Every room was different:

- The first room had a queen-size bed with an en suite
- The second room had a double bed and shared the communal bathroom
- The third room had a single bed and shared the communal bathroom

In this clear-cut scenario, it's obvious that the first room should pay the most and the third the least. This split was agreed upon accordingly: $850 for the first room, $650 for the second, and $500 for the third.

Now, not every roomshare is going to be as clear-cut as this. But, when evaluating how to split the rent, always stick to value points you can physically measure to keep the criteria as objective as possible:

- Floor space
- Bed frame size
- Depth of storage
- En suite
- Desk space

The more a room offers, the higher the rent, and vice-versa. This exercise requires an in-depth visit with all the prospective tenants to accurately assess what each room should be valued at. Before signing a lease, you'll need to decide what each room is worth and agree, collectively. This decision process will end up looking like a boardroom fracas à la *Succession*[4] unless you get a grip on it *Godfather*-style.[5]

---

4. Armstrong, Jesse, creat. 2018. *Succession*. United States: HBO.
5. Coppola, Francis Ford, dir. 1972. *The Godfather*. United States: Paramount Pictures.

It's also one of the first exercises in getting along as roommates. If you cannot agree on who should take each room and what each roommate should pay, take this as a red flag and run. You'll have avoided living with idiots. They say life isn't fair but rent splits certainly can be.

#43: Don't assume your rent will always go up

Just because you've agreed on the rent doesn't mean that's the price forever. There is *always* room for negotiation. Put another way: there is always an option to ask for a rent reduction. This is the little secret people rarely talk about. The assumed expectation is that prices will always go up (inflation, rising costs, market rates…), but if you play your cards right, rent can go down. It's uncommon, mainly because most people don't ask. You also have to time it right and be a little lucky.

The one thing agents won't tell you is that when tenants pay on time and don't complain about trivial things, good agents will do anything to hold onto them. Sometimes, rents will stay the same year after year, which (in effect) is a rent reduction (as anything below the inflation rate is a rent reduction). Of course, you should pay your rent on time before broaching the topic with the agent. Wait at least six months. This builds credibility and shows your reliability as a tenant. Paying your rent late even once will give the impression you're a "troublesome tenant," and you'll forever be in their "undependable" books.

Paying your dues first will build goodwill and prepare you for a conversation regarding rent. It's like running a marathon. You sign up for one but can't do it right away unless you're prepared to fall to your knees in agony after the first mile. It takes months of training and preparation. Although, why you'd sign up for a marathon in the first place is beyond me. Hey … each to their own.

#44: Get all roommates to agree to ask for a rent reduction

Henry Ford famously said, "Coming together is a beginning. Keeping together is progress. Working together is success."[6] This applies to a roomshare. If one of the roommates isn't on board, you can forget about asking for a rent reduction. It won't happen.

The agent cannot afford to lose all tenants, so having everyone united is the strongest way forward. Agents don't want disgruntled tenants who refuse visits from potential new tenants. And the worst case for an agent

---

6. Muñoz, John P. 2010. "Coming Together, Keeping Together, Working Together." *Peoria Magazine*. March 29, 2010. https://www.peoriamagazine.com/archive/ibi_article/2010/coming-together-keeping-together-working-together.

is to have an empty property because they will be the sole provider of the mortgage. It's like a car. As soon as one of the wheels gets wobbly, it's undrivable. Unless you're Vin Diesel in *Fast and Furious*. That man could drive a unicycle powered by NOS and still win any race.

How to Ask for a Rent Reduction

Securing a rent decrease is the holy grail of renting. It's a painstaking quest, and so rarely achieved it's like folklore. The reality is that a rent reduction is not only possible but feasible when approached in the right way.

Remember that the longer you live in the same property, the likelier you will pay more rent each year. If you're not prepared, this will happen to you. Agents want (they'll say need) to keep rent increases in line with inflation. In fact, statistics show that rent is outpacing inflation. According to a study from Smart Asset, from May 2022 to May 2023, rents increased on average by 5.45 percent across the U.S., with states like California, Michigan, North Carolina, and New Jersey seeing rents increase over 20 percent.[7] When faced with this reality, all you can do is be prepared and follow my advice to ensure you can afford your rent.

#45: Build a business case justifying a rent reduction

You wouldn't go to the bank for a loan without a business case. Neither would you go to your boss asking for a pay rise without justification. The same applies when negotiating with your agent. Like the bank and your boss, the agent is the person you need to convince. It all starts with a strong business case.

I'm not talking about creating a PowerPoint with videos and animations. In this scenario, a business case is a smartly written email with strong points and reasons that make logical sense as to why the roomshare needs and deserves a rent reduction. Only you know how best to shape it. You can include reasons such as:

- The heating doesn't work as expected
- The Wi-Fi is too slow
- Construction outside is disrupting your sleep
- Repairs take weeks to be sorted

You can also use personal reasons:

---

7. DeJohn, Jaclyn. 2023. "Rents Increased by 30% or More This Year in Some U.S. Cities—2023 Study." Smart Asset. July 27, 2023. https://smartasset.com/data-studies/where-rent-increased-most-2023.

- You're on unemployment
- Your salary's been cut
- Bills are more expensive than expected

Any reason is valid as long as you justify it in a logical and precise manner that strengthens your business case. Saving the best for last: rents in your neighborhood have dropped substantially, and similar apartments are on the market for a lower rent than what you're paying.

This is your "pièce de résistance." The agent will automatically assume you're thinking of leaving. In fact, if you are seeing a similar apartment available for much less, why would you stick around? Even though you've signed a lease, it is smart to regularly check your local rental market. You'll either remind yourself how lucky you are to have secured such a brilliant home or realize what a sucker you are when you could have a better apartment with more amenities and space and pay less rent.

The reality is, you're a sucker if you just rent a place and let the agent increase the rent year after year. The competition to secure good, reliable, long-term renters is tough in big cities. Agents will do everything they can to keep decent tenants. Best-case scenario? They agree to a rent decrease, and you come out winning. Worst-case? Nothing changes; you pay the same, and the earth keeps spinning and you keep renting.

#46: Confidence (real or fake) and patience are key when asking for a rent reduction

Some roommates are less confident and don't want to be seen as "difficult." From their point of view, it's not worth the trouble of even asking. I mean, if they can afford the rent, why risk the status quo? Also, what if the agent decides to kick you out? The reason you sign agreements and contracts is to protect yourself from unscrupulous agents who decide to unlawfully remove tenants without a justifiable reason. The only scenario that can justify a tenant's removal before the lease is up is the lack of rent, which is also why paying your rent on time is important, no matter what. Until you start staging sit-ins and dirty protests, asking costs nothing. Patience costs nothing either except effort and practice.

If an agent usually replies immediately, but it's been a few days, and there has been no reply, this is good news. It means that the request for a rent reduction is being mulled over. You can be sure the agent has seen the email.

In any negotiation situation, being pushy is annoying. Whatever you do, don't follow up every two days asking for an answer. The agent will be ready in due course, as they can't ignore a request like that. If there's still no reply after two weeks, then a polite follow-up along the lines of:

> "Hey [insert agent name],
>
>> Just wanted to check the below was received? Many thanks!
>
>> All the best,
>> [insert name of lead tenant]"

That will be perfectly sufficient. Rent negotiation is a game of patience, so getting the agent to crack first is key to getting what you want. You also need to know when to give up and move on. It's like the first time you tell your partner you love them, and they don't reciprocate your feelings. After a month of not saying it back, you have bigger problems.

#47: Keep everything in writing when discussing a rent reduction

I can't stress this enough: always keep the rent reduction negotiations over email. Don't leave anything to chance. Stop "hoping for the best." Never negotiate over the phone. Things can be said over the phone that might be misconstrued, forgotten, or denied, and then it becomes a case of "they said this" or "they said that." As you can't legally record conversations without permission, stick to email. Otherwise, it would be like the FBI asking an informant not to wear a wire and verbatim everything.

On the rare occasion that picking up the phone or having a face-to-face meeting is necessary to move things forward, take extensive notes. Write them up with as much detail as possible and send them to the agent as a follow-up. In this email, ask them to clarify if any of your notes are missing details you may have forgotten.

The point is to ensure there is a written record of what is discussed and agreed to so that you can refer to it later in your negotiations. Memories are like colanders; they have plenty of holes.

#48: Stand your ground in your request for a rent reduction

It can be nerve-wracking if it's your first time asking for a rent reduction. Don't be intimidated. As long as you pay your rent on time, you'll be fine. An agent will value a good tenant paying a little bit less far more than an empty property waiting for a new tenant who is, possibly, a complete nightmare.

Don't be the first to stand down. It's like a Wild West cowboy duel. The first one to back down loses. And lastly: You have literally nothing to lose except a few moments of your time as you compose and send that email. There is no harm in trying, even if it goes nowhere. If anything, it will boost your confidence. Putting a new twist on an old saying, the email is mightier than the sword.

11

Getting Costsmart

When you find your perfect roomshare and are doing everything you can to get the paperwork sorted, it's tempting to let the splitting of the rent and bills slide and assume you'll easily figure it out later once you're all moved in.

Yet the cost of the day-to-day living in that roomshare is as important as how much rent you'll pay for your room. Without pre-agreements, you'll be setting yourself up for arguments. It would be like going to the grocery store and buying a bunch of ingredients without thinking about the recipe you'll cook, then going home and hoping you'll have a nice meal at the other end.

How to Approach the Cost of a Roomshare

#49: Know how much you're willing to spend on rent

Ask anyone, and they'd love a little bit more money. It's the one factor in life everyone feels would make them happier. And, to an extent, it's true. A higher income means you can afford a nicer vacation, a bigger home, and a better car.

Money gives you choice. More money and choices don't automatically mean happiness. Money can cause couples to break, families to tear, friendships to stop, and strangers to hate. No one can escape the reality that money and how much you possess shapes and determines your life. In the world of roomsharing, how much you earn is irrelevant. How much you're *willing* to spend is all that matters. You could earn over $100,000 a year and only want to spend $1000 a month on rent. This is your choice. On the flip side, you could earn $2000 a month and spend $1000 on rent, but you choose to spend more than the traditional "third of your salary on living costs" because you want to live in a nicer place than what a third of your salary could afford.

How much you decide to spend matters (not how much you earn). And you don't have to justify how much you want to spend to your roommates. All you need to tell them is how much you're committing to spend. This way, if there are increases, everyone will be on the same page about who wants to pay or not pay what. If the rent increases and a roommate moves out because it's above their financial threshold ... no hard feelings.

Everyone knows a budget can force someone's hand. Once you know this, you'll be happier with your own choices without feeling guilty. Just because you earn at a different level to those around you doesn't mean you should be forced to make financial choices you don't want to make.

#50: Check the status of all the bills before moving in

Before moving into any roomshare, the key questions to always ask are:

- How are the bills split?
- When are bills due?
- Are there any management fees?
- And most importantly.... How much are all the bills on average monthly?

I love surprises. I just hate surprise bills. Asking those key questions will avoid those. Talking of hating surprise bills, check that all the roommates' bills are settled before moving in. Asking for proof will feel like overkill and is absolutely critical. I've known many a roomshare where someone left, promising to settle their share of bills later, and ended up disappearing. Last I heard, governments don't have extradition policies to settle gas bills between stingy roommates. To avoid these nasty surprises, all you need is an open and frank discussion regarding which bills everyone is expected to contribute to.

A roomshare with a fair system to pay the bills in a timely manner is proof that all the roommates are solvent and organized enough in the first place to have created such a system. It also means they all care about the roomshare, which makes them likelier to want to keep it clean and tidy. Apps like Splitwise, Splid, and SettleUp are lifesavers. Splitwise's free version is enough to keep track of everyone's expenses and payments. If you ask how the roommates split the bills and the answers are vague, or they don't have a system; rather, they "figure it out," run like Forrest Gump. And if you offer to set up a system on their behalf and they don't think it's necessary, this is a sign that you should avoid this roomshare.

11. Getting Costsmart

#51: Always split the bills

If this feels obvious, good. That is the intention. Water, electricity, gas, and Wi-Fi are all bills that should be split equally between every individual in the roomshare, regardless of whether they're a couple. I've known single roommates argue that a couple should pay more "because they're a couple." Wrong. You're all using the same facilities and appliances, albeit differently. Even if Roommate A takes 20-minute showers and blasts the heating on. Or Roommate B takes five-minute showers and puts on an extra sweater in the winter. Roommate C stays at their partner's apartment for two weeks at a time. In this scenario, splitting the bills equally might seem unfair, but you can't accommodate lifestyle into how much is owed on bills. This would turn the bill-splitting process into a nightmare with plenty of room for making errors as to what everybody pays monthly.

You all agreed to live together, which means splitting bills equally, no matter how little or often utilities and appliances are used by the roommates. It's like splitting the cost of pizzas. You all pay the same amount for a couple of pizzas; some might be less hungry and leave the leftovers for others.

#52: Agree on the cost of communal items before moving in

I once lived in a six-person roomshare where every roommate lived so independently we never shared anything. Each of us bought our own staples, from toilet paper to soap to dishwasher tablets. One roommate never cooked, so didn't contribute towards kitchen-related costs. Another showered at the gym and didn't pay towards shower gel. My lowest point was leaning into my bedside cabinet and handing over toilet paper and soap to a date as she sauntered to the bathroom. When she came back empty-handed, I couldn't help but think I needed to get both items back before my roommates used them. Back then, I thought this was normal. Looking back, I laugh at how ridiculous it all was, and I hope this never happens to you…

Within two weeks of moving into a new roomshare it will become clear as crystal who does what and who cares about restocking essentials. Agreeing to "take it in turns to buy the toilet paper" will be forgotten when it's not at the top of people's priority list. This is normal because everyone has their own priorities, such as jobs, relationships, and hobbies. The ideal solution here is to agree that whoever notices you're running low, purchases some more and adds the cost to the bill-splitting app. Financially, this is the fairest way of ensuring everyone pays an equal share of the toilet paper (a symbolic item, as I could be easily talking about salt and pepper). The best scenario is every roomshare has its version of Monica from *Friends*. She's a pain who keeps everything running smoothly.

#53: Transparency is paramount when paying bills

Overcommunication is key. Pay the bills promptly and let everyone know how much is due. But who should pay them in the first place? In an ideal world, everyone's names are on the bills. This way, every roommate feels contractually responsible. The reality is this usually only applies to local taxes due on the home. When it comes to utility bills, companies normally only allow one name on the bill.

If you live with a Monica, she'll have taken care of it all. The problem is if you live with a Rachel or a Joey. There is no perfect solution here and many ways to deal with them. One of the easiest options is to pick a "lead bills" roommate whose name is on all the bills; they're responsible for paying and getting everyone else to pay their share. The only thing to remember (and it's worth repeating) is that if there's no planning ahead, you're living with idiots. Unless you want your roomshare to become a real-life reenactment of *The Purge*, overcommunicate, and plan to pay all bills on time.[1]

---

1. DeMonaco, James, dir. 2013. *The Purge*. Universal Pictures.

12

Staying Roomsmart When Idiots Can't Pay Their Costs

Roommates coming up financially short happens. It's awkward to explain that you can't afford rent or a bill. Being prepared is key to fixing this issue. This chapter will arm you with the tools you need for a conversation I hope you never have to have. Although you can be prepared, it will always be awkward. It's like no matter how many times you think you're prepared for your partner to eat the last scoop of ice cream, it's always a challenge.

Approaching Financial Issues

#54: When to worry and when not to worry when idiots can't pay rent

If you pay your share of the rent for your room directly to the agent, your roommates' finances are not your problem. You can sleep easy knowing it doesn't affect your living situation. Now, if you can get past the fact that I've just used an expression invented five centuries ago…

If you've all signed a contract for an overall amount and you then split that rent, meaning the agent receives the whole rent from a single account, and someone can't pay their share, it *is* your problem. The agent doesn't care who can or can't pay. They care about getting their money. And it doesn't matter where it comes from. You are all equally liable. It's a tough one because, when you move in with randoms, you obviously don't know each other well. Sometimes you become friends, and sometimes you don't. When it comes to money, there's no messing around. The reality of where you stand is clear. If someone has lost their job, you can't be expected to pay for their share of the rent. Just have an honest and open conversation as quickly as you can, establishing your boundaries regarding the situation. When a roommate can't afford their share of the rent, you need to know immediately. If you're in this tricky situation, you must let everyone know. That is the key: overcommunicating.

Everyone is more than capable of being a douche. So, the scenario where a roommate goes rogue, skips on rent, and moves out overnight isn't far-fetched. Anecdotally, it happens more often than you think.[1] With rising inflation and rent increases, 62 percent of Americans are worried about rental costs.[2] This doesn't mean over half of Americans will swerve paying rent; just that more than half are worried about paying it. Inevitably, a proportion of those will have no choice but to skip out. It's a hell of a burden to bear, and it's part of the risk when signing up for a roomshare.

When discussing this issue, nothing is more important (other than a wedding, funeral, job interview—insert equally dramatic life change). Cancel whatever plans you have that very evening (such as a date, a gym class, a drink with a friend, insert equally nice easily reschedulable life event), and get together as a group to discuss. Don't Zoom (unless you're on a work trip, vacation, meditation retreat, insert equally unchangeable life priority). When sensitive topics are discussed via text or video calls, intentions and cues can be misinterpreted. You need to be able to all look each other in the eye and come up with a solution together. If you're a tight-knit group, the problem will be quickly resolved. And, if the trustworthy roommate falling behind promises to pay you all back the following month, it may not be so bad. But life is rarely this rosy. Having a face-to-face conversation is key to ensuring discussions never descend into a scene straight out of *The Real Housewives of Beverly Hills*.[3]

#55: Solutions to explore when idiots can't pay their share of the rent

Assuming everyone wants to stay in the roomshare, one solution is requesting a temporary rent reduction. Some agents are understanding, and instead of causing a mass exodus because no one else can afford to stay, they may be happy with a temporary decrease until a permanent solution is found. If you choose this route, do it over email and explain (in

---

1. I love using the word anecdotally as it means I don't have to provide stats to back this up. I just know it's happened to lots of people I know. No point in asking me how many. It's anecdotal, remember?
2. Mayadeen, Al. 2022. "62% of Americans worried about paying rent in 2023." MR Online. August 16, 2022. https://mronline.org/2022/08/17/62-of-americans-worried-about-paying-rent-in-2023.
3. Dunlop, Scott, creat. 2010. *The Real Housewives of Beverly Hills*. United States: Bravo.

12. Staying Roomsmart When Idiots Can't Pay Their Costs

detail) the problem. Be clear and open about what kind of reduction you're looking for and how long. It's a big ask. The agent is completely within their right to tell you to shove it. You might get lucky and catch them on a good day, and you have a miracle on your hands.

Or someone else replaces that tenant before the rent is due, which is a smooth, alternative option. The agent will have to agree, but if you can get someone in to pay the rent, it will be like there was no problem in the first place. It'd be better to find a new roommate and say "good riddance" to the other one. On the flip side, it could mean you're welcoming an idiot. Like poker, it's high risk and high reward.

My least favorite option is asking to defer paying the missing share of the rent until you get it sorted. This is not ideal, as the full amount will still be owed. But if you love your home and want to stay, and none of the previous options are viable, then it's better than being forced to move.

It's a balancing act between wanting to stay in your roomshare and facing the reality that, financially, it may be unlivable. The problem grows as you end up with a larger share of the rent. You're literally kicking the can down the road, and that can is getting bigger and heavier the longer it rolls down. It's going to really hurt once you get to it again.

Another option is biting the bullet and covering that missing share of the rent. If you're desperate to stay in the property and nothing else works, as a *Mandalorian* would say, "This is the way."[4] But personally, I believe this is the worst option of all. It's like signing a deal with the devil, except you don't get any benefits. You're just setting yourself up for a life of financial hell.

The last option is to move out. Packing up and moving is a pain. It costs money. It's stressful. But these things happen for a reason, and you could end up somewhere better. Chances are there are plenty of options you've never considered because you weren't looking. It's like being fired from a job. It's awful until you end up at a better company with higher pay and your former colleagues are now the suckers.

---

4. Favreau, Jon, dir. 2019. *The Mandalorian*. Lucasfilm.

Part D

Finding Roommates

"Hell is other people."
—Jean-Paul Sartre

When People Do or Don't Make You Happy

The crux of the entire book is about finding the right people to live with. Yet finding the perfect roomshare is like putting together a team to win the Superbowl. You need an owner with resources (the agent) and a good stadium for training and games (the home). Most importantly, you need a great team who can work together well (the roommates). Once you have all these elements, you are set for success. Just like the NFL teams are picky when drafting, it's the process of choosing the right people to live together which determines the outcome.

No matter how stunning your home is, it will become a nightmare when the wrong people live together. You might get exceptionally lucky and love all your roommates. Or maybe you'll never see them, so it doesn't matter. But if you never see your roommates (this has literally happened to me), you may as well live alone. After all, everything starts and ends with people. And, for a roomshare to work, learning to pick the right people and avoid living with idiots is the most important step of this journey.

13

Attending a Roomshare Interview

You've found (what looks like) the perfect three-bedroom roomshare. It's a great location, has a living room, and the two people there seem nice. Now, you have an interview for the spare room.

There is a lot of demand for rooms in overpopulated cities like New York, Los Angeles, and London. They're like breadcrumbs to Central Park pigeons; as soon as one becomes available, hundreds pounce to gobble up whatever they can get.

The pandemic (temporarily) changed the renters' market. For a short while, renters were in a position of power. They could dictate lower rents, better specs, and larger rooms. People moved out of the city. Agents were desperate for renters, so they bent over backwards to avoid being tenant-less (and therefore income-less). Now that the world has swung back to its pre-pandemic behaviors, people are returning to urban areas, and more renters are competing for fewer properties than ever before. Viewings for rentals are now like scenes from *The Walking Dead* with survivors fighting for scraps.[1]

Stories abound of hopeful renters offering 50 percent over the asking price with six months' rent upfront. Some tenants are staying where they are because they can't afford to move. Other tenants are moving because they can't afford not to move. Some countries have imposed rent controls to protect tenants. In Scotland, agents were temporarily banned from increasing rents unless they could justify the higher costs.[2] In Paris, agents are legally required to stick to a mandated property value when renting out homes.[3] This doesn't address the actual problem of supply not meeting demand. Needless to say, picking the right roomshare to move into is

---

1. Darabont, Frank, dir. 2010. *The Walking Dead*. AMC.
2. Scottish Government. 2023. "Protections for tenants extended." Scottish Government. January 19, 2023. https://www.gov.scot/news/protections-for-tenants-extended.
3. The Local France. 2022. "France to limit rent rises to help households with cost of living." The Local. July 8, 2022. https://www.thelocal.fr/20220708/france-to-limit-rent-rises-to-help-households-with-cost-of-living.

13. Attending a Roomshare Interview

more important than ever because there's a good chance you'll be there for a while.

To complicate things, if two people are interested in the same room, you're battling "who will offer more" in front of the agent. Frankly, if you're not, I'd be careful about wanting to live there. If whoever is showing you around doesn't even care who wants the room and says, "It's a first come, first served situation," it's a major red flag (unless there is a valid logic). The reason is, if they don't take the time to get to know someone before they move in, there will surely be a ragtag of people living under the same roof with no consideration for compatibility. No respected employer would advertise jobs as "first come, first served." Unless it's volunteering to clean radioactive waste. Even then… You'll probably want to do a background check, right?

Picking the right people to live together takes skills in conversation, listening, and judgment. None of those things can be rushed. And it all starts with the interview. Remember one rule which you can apply to anything in life: don't be a dick. You never know when you might encounter these people again, either at work or socially (the world gets smaller the older you get). And, if the first viewing doesn't work out, you never know what the future holds. The roomshare you loved and didn't get might have a vacant room sooner than you think, and you could be first on their call sheet (this happened to me a week after I was told they were giving it to someone else). With this in mind…

Your viewing appointment is set and ready to go. The thing is, it's not just an appointment to see a roomshare. It's an interview. You're being judged from the get-go, from arranging the viewing to turning up early, late, or just being plain smelly. Don't overthink your outfit. Just don't turn up in rags or sweaty gym clothes. If you want the room, you must put on your best self. It's like a first date which could lead to happiness in the foreseeable future.

Of course it works both ways. You'll be interviewing the people living there, too. Sure, you need somewhere to live quickly before you're made homeless. You've looked at Airbnbs, which are all unaffordable, unavailable, or insert another perfect reason why Airbnb isn't viable, and your friends may not have a spare room. So you need to find a roomshare. And pronto.

Now, desperation doesn't mean you should accept the first offer coming your way—no matter how stressed or how much it may feel you have no other choice. There is always a choice. Just like in *The Matrix* when Neo had to choose between taking the blue pill and staying plugged in, or taking the red pill and finding out the truth.[4] The choice just has to be the right one … for you.

---

4. Wachowski, Lilly, and Wachowski, Lana, dirs. 1999. *The Matrix*. Warner Bros.

The Key Topics to Cover as the Interviewee When Visiting a Roomshare

#56: How fast is the communal Wi-Fi in the roomshare

I once saw an apartment where the lead tenant said they didn't have Wi-Fi because he didn't want to sign up for a long-term contract. Apparently, everyone living there had unlimited data on their phones, meaning they used their hotspots for internet access. It also meant no Netflix on the television. No Netflix on the TV??? If this sounds like a nightmare, it was for me, too.

The question, "Do you have Wi-Fi?" shouldn't even be one you have to ask. It should always be, "How fast is the Wi-Fi?" You need fast Wi-Fi. This is not just because you're paying for premium ad-free Netflix but also because you do not want any buffering. You need fast Wi-Fi to work from home. You'll want to video call your friends and family without worrying about losing the signal. If your roomshare isn't set up with fast Wi-Fi or you receive an evasive reply such as, "The Wi-Fi is okay," run a mile. The people living there are likely making do with slow internet because they can't be bothered.

And people who can't be bothered are the sort to take the blue pill.

#57: Test the water pressure in the bathroom

It may not be the most comfortable question, but it's necessary. Maybe it's awkward to ask, but you need to test the water pressure in the shower. You'll be using it every day; why wouldn't you try it out before moving in? The number of times I've moved in, forgotten to check the water pressure, and found myself with a trickle for a shower…

The problem is that low water pressure is often linked to a plumbing issue in the foundations of the building. This means that when you ask your agent to investigate, they'll just say, "There's nothing we can do." Suffering a low-pressure shower is like watching a terrible movie over and over again. Avoid it entirely.

#58: Check roommates' morning routines before committing

You say goodnight and set your alarm for seven in the morning. You'll get close to eight hours of beauty sleep if you can nod off quickly. Now, it's time to dream…

BEEP! BEEP! BEEP!

You can hear your roommate's alarm. It's four in the morning. You try and go back to sleep. Next, there's a CREAK. They're doing press-ups in their room. CLACK. Now, they're boiling the kettle. "Hello, and welcome to ABC News." Watching the news? Really? BANG. They're out the door at six. You've had four hours of sleep at best.

You might have all the key ingredients for a great roomshare: space, cleanliness, and a central location. However, if your schedules clash, you're setting yourself up for failure. One of the key tenets of a successful sports team is synchronicity. And it's the same with a roomshare. Living together will never work if you're out of sync with your roommates.

To clarify, being in sync doesn't mean getting up and coming home at the same time. It means coexisting positively. For instance, a roommate has friends over for dinner. You've been invited and decided to either skip it or opt for other plans. Regardless, you can trust that when you go to bed, you will sleep peacefully and not be disturbed by the guests. Or the roommate who does wake up at four in the morning does so so quietly you don't even realize that's their routine until they tell you about it over dinner. It's these subtleties of living together which make roommates compatible. Living together is like a cooking recipe. Everything has its place and works together to produce a flavorsome meal. As soon as a rogue ingredient gets in, it all goes wrong.

#59: Discuss the lifestyle vibe preferred by the roomshare (is it a "let's party all night" or a "let's relax with a glass of wine after work" scenario?)

I've lived with party animals and loved them. I've even started roomshares dedicated to throwing parties that would make Chuck Bass proud. But, as you get older, you may realize you prefer to relax and sleep than go out all night. At least I did when I hit my mid-thirties. I reached a point where I could no longer party so often and deliberately chose roomshares I knew would reflect this lifestyle.

You must be on the same page as your roommates regarding lifestyle choices. So, ask your potential roomshare what the vibe is outside of working hours. For instance, if drugs are your thing, and your roommates feel the same, you've found your tribe. No judgment here, but drugs aren't, and weren't, for me. I once took over a room without being told the roommates smoked weed. It annoyed the hell out of me. The smell lingers, sticking to your clothes and skin. Even though asking if anyone does drugs sounds like you're the shifty undercover cop, you'll want to know upfront so you know what you're dealing with.

#60: Meet all the roommates before signing anything

I've made the mistake of not meeting everyone and regretting it every time. It is hard to get everyone together, but if whoever you're living with can't even prioritize meeting the person who wants to move in, they obviously don't care. And do you really want to live with people who don't care about who they live with?

The roommates you meet can tell you what the others are like, and they'll likely say only positive things. Yet there's only so much you can gauge from someone's opinion about another human being. They can sing their praises until the cows come home, and their perception of that person could differ completely from how you see them when you eventually meet them. You'll share cooking utensils, a toilet seat, and a shower. You need to meet and spend a bit of time with every one of them before committing to living together. It doesn't have to be at the same time, which can be close to impossible when there are multiple roommates. A nice roomshare will make the effort. A video call won't cut it. There is so much subtlety in human behavior a face-to-face can pick up on.

As Prof. Scanlon explains, "Renting with strangers isn't new. You just have to try to suss them out."[5] You could be a brilliant judge of character, but you'll only be able to really gauge them by meeting them. It's like a candy bar. Someone can rave about how delicious Hershey's *Gold Peanuts & Pretzels* is, but only once you've tried it can you know for sure.[6]

#61: Your instinct will tell you if moving in is a good idea

Of course, if you already have a bad feeling at the interview stage, stay polite, walk out, and never look back. It's that "feeling" you get about something you can't quite explain. Scientists believe the limbic brain is responsible for this "gut instinct," and it's not something anyone can describe with actual words. You just know it. If something feels off on arrival, this will only get worse.

Conversely, if everything feels right, go for it. You might have spotted a few niggles here and there, and perhaps not everything is up to your "standards," but if your gut tells you it's right, go for it. It's like when you see someone, and your heart melts. You have no idea why, but it just feels right. I believe in love at first roomshare.

---

5. Scanlon, Kath. 2020. Phone interview. December 11, 2020.
6. I'm a Brit, my country doesn't even legally recognise Hershey's as chocolate. True story.

14

By the Way, Discrimination Is Legal in Roomshares

This was the most difficult chapter for me to write. Discrimination is horrendous. It's abhorrent and illegal in most countries around the world. As it should be. To clarify, an agent is not allowed to discriminate. So, when you're putting in an application to live somewhere, it is illegal for an agent to reject you based on ethnicity, age, or gender.

It gets complicated, and the law doesn't apply when you go beyond the front door and into the home itself. Once the decision on who lives in a home is out of the agent's hands, and the roommates themselves are deciding who to live with, they can do whatever they like. Full disclosure: I was shocked when I discovered that roomshares are exempt from the usual values and discrimination laws that apply to every other aspect of society.

When someone is being interviewed for a room, there is no adjudicator of "fairness." There isn't anyone making sure people aren't being discriminated against. Potential roommates can be rejected by the current roommates because they:

- Are too old
- Hold a certain religious belief
- Have an accent the roommates hate
- Are the "wrong gender"
- And so on and so on…

It can be any reason whatsoever, and this can be as ableist, sexist and racist as the roommates feel. The research I uncovered while writing this book threw me in a spin. I hadn't even thought it possible.

Facing Discrimination

#62: Discrimination in roomshares is hard to verify, let alone quantify

Part of the problem is the lack of information available. It's not like governments are openly advertising the fact they allow discrimination.

As Dr. Chris Martin asks, "Is it because the legislators thought that sharing a home is such a personal part of your life that they don't think anti-discrimination law should intrude there?"[1] In New Zealand, attitudes towards discrimination by agents are explicitly laid out in the law. Section 53 of New Zealand's Human Rights Act makes it unlawful "to deny any person directly or indirectly the right to occupy land or any residential or business accommodation by reason of any of the prohibited grounds for discrimination."[2] Yet, the very next one, Section 54, lays out the exception to the rule: "Nothing in Section 53 of this Act shall apply to residential accommodation which is to be shared."[3]

The same is said for Australia. It is illegal for an agent to discriminate against anyone when renting out a property, and not when it comes to roomshares.[4] The UK follows a similar principle that it's illegal for an agent to discriminate based on sex, race, disability, gender, pregnancy, creed, or sexual orientation when letting out a property.[5] There is a huge exception—age. It is perfectly legal for a UK agent to discriminate based on age.[6] If an agent wants to reserve the apartment "for people aged between 25 and 40," it's legal.[7]

Just like in Australia and New Zealand, things also get murky when choosing roommates for a property you live in. This is based on a little-known piece of UK legislation called Schedule 5, the "small premises exception" of the Equalities Act 2010.[8] It explains that when it comes

---

1. Martin, Chris. 2021. Phone interview. February 4, 2021.
2. Parliamentary Counsel Office. n.d. "Human Rights Act 1993." New Zealand Government. n.d. https://legislation.govt.nz/act/public/1993/0082/latest/DLM304632.html.
3. Parliamentary Counsel Office. n.d. "Human Rights Act 1993." New Zealand Government. n.d. https://legislation.govt.nz/act/public/1993/0082/latest/DLM304633.html.
4. Tenants' Union of New South Wales. 2021. "Factsheet 17: Discrimination." Tenants' Union of New South Wales. July 2021. https://www.tenants.org.au/factsheet-17-discrimination.
5. Spareroom. n.d. "Discrimination and Flatsharing." Spareroom. n.d. https://www.spareroom.co.uk/content/default/discrimination.
6. Spareroom. n.d. "Discrimination and Flatsharing." Spareroom. n.d. https://www.spareroom.co.uk/content/default/discrimination.
7. Spareroom. n.d. "Discrimination and Flatsharing." Spareroom. n.d. https://www.spareroom.co.uk/content/default/discrimination.
8. The National Archives. n.d. "Equality Act 2010." Legislation.gov.uk. n.d. https://www.legislation.gov.uk/ukpga/2010/15/notes/division/3/16/22/3.

14. By the Way, Discrimination Is Legal in Roomshares

to choosing who you live with, you can legally discriminate against all criteria except race. To help you visualize this, below are the examples used by the UK government, copied and pasted from their own website Legislation.gov.uk:

- A homeowner makes it known socially that he wants to sell his house privately. Various prospective buyers come forward, and the homeowner opts to sell it to a fellow Christian. The other prospective buyers cannot claim that they were discriminated against because the homeowner's actions were covered by this exception.[9]
- A single woman owns a large house in London and lives on the top floor, although the bathroom and toilet facilities are on the first floor. The ground floor is unoccupied, and she decides to take in a lodger, sharing the bathroom and toilet facilities. Various prospective tenants apply, but she chooses only to let the ground floor to another woman. This would be permissible under this exception.[10]
- A Jewish family own a large house but only lives in part of it. They decide to let out an unoccupied floor, but any new tenant will have to share kitchen and cooking facilities. The family choose only to let the unoccupied floor to practicing Jews as they are concerned that otherwise their facilities for keeping their food kosher may be compromised. This would be permissible under this exception.[11]

Similarly to the UK, the U.S. has the Fair Housing Act, which prohibits discrimination. However, when it comes to roomshares, this doesn't apply. Here's how it works for Americans....

#63: How the U.S. legalized roomshare discrimination

In a landmark ruling back in 2012, the U.S. 9th Circuit Court of Appeals confirmed that the Fair Housing Act would not apply to choosing roommates, in effect cementing the legality of roommate discrimination. In the judgment summary, Chief Judge Alex Kozinski explained that it "makes practical sense to interpret 'dwelling' as an independent living unit and stop the FHA [Fair Housing Act] at the front door."[12] In this case,

---

9. The National Archives. n.d. "Equality Act 2010." Legislation.gov.uk. n.d. https://www.legislation.gov.uk/ukpga/2010/15/notes/division/3/16/22/3.
10. The National Archives. n.d. "Equality Act 2010." Legislation.gov.uk. n.d. https://www.legislation.gov.uk/ukpga/2010/15/notes/division/3/16/22/3.
11. The National Archives. n.d. "Equality Act 2010." Legislation.gov.uk. n.d. https://www.legislation.gov.uk/ukpga/2010/15/notes/division/3/16/22/3.
12. Williams, Carol J. 2012. "Roommate-finder doesn't facilitate discrimination, court rules." *Los Angeles Times*. February 3, 2012. https://www.latimes.com/local/la-xpm-2012-feb-03-la-me-roommates-20120203-story.html.

Kozinski felt that the government and society's responsibility stopped as soon as you walked into the threshold of a home. So, whatever people want to do once inside their home is their choice.

Personally, I find this baffling. A crime is a crime wherever it is committed. In the street, in a bar, *and* at home.

The reason why discrimination is ostensibly legal when choosing your next roommate is because of the concept of "shared facilities." When agents let out a whole property, they don't have to live there. But these exceptions state that if you're going to be sharing facilities such as a kitchen and bathroom with other people, then you should be allowed to choose who you share them with. Most governments don't want to limit these choices in any way, which means roommates can base their decisions on any criteria, even if that includes gender, age, creed, race and big noses.

#64: *You can live and be friends with whomever you like*

You can decide not to befriend someone because they bite their nails. It's a particularly stupid example which makes the point loud and clear. No one can force you to do something you don't want to do, especially in the privacy of your own home. And if you decide to only live with vegan brunettes who recycle their Diet Coke cans, this is your choice.

This brings us to the next question: why do people feel the need to discriminate on such grounds in the first place? And why have governments effectively legalized roomshare discrimination? People want their home to be a place of comfort and relaxation. They want to enter their front door knowing they're safe. And this comes back to the concept of the "group dynamic." People prefer to share a home with others they feel comfortable with. As Andrea Shapiro explains, "If you're living with someone, particularly as a woman, I don't want to be forced to rent with a single man. I want to be able to choose who I'm living with. Choice is important because part of the conflict we often see is around not having real choice."[13]

Taking the example of women preferring to live with other women, the data backs this up. On the Diggz roomsharing service, 80 percent of matches for females are with other females. The large majority of women want to share a home with another woman. Meanwhile, for men, it's half and half. As Burstein explains, men are "kind of indifferent of the gender, but for females, it's more important to live with another female."[14]

---

13. Shapiro, Andrea. 2023. Phone interview. May 3, 2023.
14. Burstein, Rany. 2023. Phone interview. March 31, 2023.

14. By the Way, Discrimination Is Legal in Roomshares

Whoever you want to live with is a personal choice. The government will not stand in your way. If you don't want to live with someone who loves Coldplay, that's within your right. Does that make you a music snob? For sure. Does this mean you'll miss out on living with some amazing people? Absolutely. Is there anything Coldplay fans can do about it legally? Nope. It's the reality of the world we live in, and it's never going away.

15

How Old Is Too Old to Be Living with a Roommate?

In your twenties, no one expects you to live alone or own your own home. In fact, if you are in your twenties, own your apartment and live alone, everyone assumes it is family money. "Their parents must have helped" is the common justification. Although this deflects from the fact that some young people are simply more financially successful, in the majority of cases, the parents stepping in and helping their 21-year-old get on the housing ladder is a safe assumption. One study found that the "Bank of Mom and Dad" is the 7th largest lender in the U.S.[1]

As soon as you hit your thirties and you're still living with roommates and don't have a mortgage, you become the adult equivalent of the fat asthmatic kid at high school who gets picked last for the relay team. It's demotivating, and you'll do anything to avoid the embarrassment. Dr. Heath found that older adults, particularly women in their late thirties living with roommates, "no longer told their workmates about their living arrangements because they were perceived as being somehow odd."[2] It's like a celebrity claiming they're "all-natural" when the before and after pictures on a Google timeline clearly show they had a nose job, a tummy tuck, and their teeth done.

Historically, people only started living alone in big numbers from the 1900s onwards.[3] Until the twentieth century, only 1 percent of the world population lived alone, rising to 9 percent in 1950.[4] Put another way, in

---

1. Legal & General Group. 2019. "New Study Ranks 'The Bank of Mom and Dad' 7th Largest Housing Lender in the U.S. in 2018." Legal & General Group. February 27, 2019. https://group.legalandgeneral.com/en/newsroom/press-releases/new-study-ranks-the-bank-of-mom-and-dad-7th-largest-housing-lender-in-the-u-s-in-2018.
2. Heath, Sue. 2021. Phone interview. January 6, 2021.
3. Lepore, Jill. 2020. "The History of Loneliness." *The New Yorker*. March 30, 2020. https://www.newyorker.com/magazine/2020/04/06/the-history-of-loneliness.
4. Lepore, Jill. 2020. "The History of Loneliness." *The New Yorker*. March 30, 2020. https://www.newyorker.com/magazine/2020/04/06/the-history-of-loneliness.

15. How Old Is Too Old to Be Living with a Roommate?

1950, when your great-grandparents were in their prime, 91 percent of people lived with others in some way. For centuries, this was considered normal. In the last fifty years, buying your own home and settling down has become the norm in most Western societies. And with this, the stigma associated with roomsharing as you age increases. Once you hit your thirties, you're expected to be actively saving for a deposit or, at least, preparing to live alone. Then, once you reach your mid-thirties, it's "expected" to be living alone or in a long-term partnership.

Yet, according to Visual Capitalist, the median salary across the U.S. is $67,000 a year. However, to afford a mortgage, you must earn an average of $76,000, and the numbers vary wildly from state to state.[5] In San Jose, the house prices are so high that you need to earn over $330,000 annually.[6] People now rent into their thirties even though they might earn six figures a year simply because they have no choice.

Lee Chambers believes, "roomsharing is a very valuable alternative of aligning ourselves with a societal group who we can then now spend time with, live with and bond together with to form a unit which becomes a support network. It becomes a place that we can call home and share with other people. The fact that society says that that's not acceptable is sad."[7]

Let's break down some stereotypes. The stigma of older roommates needs to end. If Ed Sheeran can make gingers cool, we can make roomsharing for older adults cool too. And here's why...

Age Doesn't Matter

#65: Where and how you live is personal

No one truly knows someone else's situation. They may have had a divorce, and their ex-partner rinsed them of all their income, leaving them no choice but to live with a roommate. Even close friends hide their financial woes. Falling on hard times can happen to anyone. Just look at Jeff Bezos. Poor guy divorced his wife, costing him over $38 billion.[8] He must

---

5. Koop, Avery. 2022. "Mapped: The Salary You Need to Buy a Home in 50 U.S. Cities." Visual Capitalist. August 1, 2022. https://www.visualcapitalist.com/mapped-the-salary-you-need-to-buy-a-home-in-50-u-s-cities.
6. Koop, Avery. 2022. "Mapped: The Salary You Need to Buy a Home in 50 U.S. Cities." Visual Capitalist. August 1, 2022. https://www.visualcapitalist.com/mapped-the-salary-you-need-to-buy-a-home-in-50-u-s-cities.
7. Chambers, Lee. 2021. Phone interview. February 15, 2021.
8. Neate, Rupert. 2019. "Amazon's Jeff Bezos pays out $38bn in divorce settlement." *The Guardian*. June 30, 2019. https://www.theguardian.com/technology/2019/jun/30/amazon-jeff-bezos-ex-wife-mackenzie-handed-38bn-in-divorce-settlement.

have really had to cut down his expenses with only $118 billion left in the bank.[9]

If living with someone means that person can financially return to their "normal" life, i.e., going out with friends, visiting family, jetting off on vacation, then living with a roommate is smart economics. Some people go into debt to maintain their lifestyle and, thus, spiral into financial instability. Making the right choice for your situation is the only choice worth making.

#66: Roomsharing can cure loneliness

For a lot of people, living alone sucks. Personally, I absolutely hate it. I hate it more than I hate olives. And I *really* hate olives. In fact, the only time I ever lived alone was because I was forced to do so after a break-up. My partner moved out of our home, but there was still a mortgage to pay. It was a one-bedroom apartment, so there was no space for a roommate. Our mortgage conditions wouldn't let me rent it out, and I couldn't afford to live elsewhere while paying for the mortgage. I lived by myself for nine months until the property was sold. Every second of those nine months, I hated waking up alone, cooking for one in my tiny kitchen, and watching TV on the couch alone. And worst of all, I hated not having anyone to talk to about my day when I got home.

Conversing and socializing are two of my favorite things to do. When I had roommates I liked, I loved nothing more than catching up at the end of the day and making plans to hang out. I'd even suffer a roommate's terrible B.O. just for the company (well, not for too long … even I have my limit). But living alone, eating alone, and watching TV alone? Night after night? Week after week? For some, it's paradise. For me, it was hell.

The statistics make it clear that living alone is corrosive to your mental health. Harvard studies demonstrate there is a correlation between living alone and loneliness.[10] And the worst thing about loneliness is the detrimental effect it has on your physical and mental health. According to the Center for Disease Control, social isolation "significantly increased a person's risk of premature death from all causes, a risk that may rival those of smoking, obesity, and physical inactivity," and "was associated with about a 50% increased risk of dementia."[11] In contrast, "loneliness among

---

9. Bezos was worth this much at the time of writing this book. He's probably worth over $1 trillion now by the time you read this.
10. Molinsky, Jennifer. 2018. "Are More Older Adults Sharing Housing?" Joint Center for Housing Studies of Harvard University. August 20, 2018. https://www.jchs.harvard.edu/blog/are-more-older-adults-sharing-housing.
11. U.S. Centers for Disease Control and Prevention. 2021. "Loneliness and Social Isolation Linked to Serious Health Conditions." CDC. April 29, 2021. https://www.cdc.gov/aging/publications/features/lonely-older-adults.html.

15. How Old Is Too Old to Be Living with a Roommate?

heart failure patients was associated with a nearly four times increased risk of death."[12] From anxiety to heart disease, there's no denying that living alone increases and exacerbates depression and ill health. I'd even prefer to live with my in-laws than be alone. Maybe…? Nah. Living alone isn't as bad as living with your in-laws.

Wanting company is one of the reasons more and more older people are choosing to share their homes with others. Even the rich are in on the action of companionship. As LA-based luxury estate agent Matt Adamo explains, if you're part of the super-rich and living in the mansions of Beverly Hills, those living alone "don't want to be alone because they'll actually have assistants live with them. And those assistants become their best friends or their family."[13] When even the rich spend their money to ensure they're not lonely… You know living alone is bad.

Living with others can be a mental health boost on a par with watching a new episode of *The Kardashians* on Disney+ (it's a great show, no one can deny it).[14] As Lee Chambers explains, during the pandemic, many people found that "moving into a roomshare was beneficial to their mental health, giving them people to bond with, to eat with and to really connect with on a deeper level."[15] The pandemic revealed that "social connection has been highlighted in just how important it is."[16] Mental Health America states that 71 percent of people turn to friends or family in times of stress.[17] After reviewing 148 studies (308,849 participants), MindWise Innovations concludes that people with "stronger social relationships had a 50% increased likelihood of survival."[18] A good roomshare is like a hot cup of cocoa in the depths of winter—a layer of warmth for your heart.

#67: Living with others is more common than ever before

From 2022 to 2023, roomshare-finding service Diggz saw the sharpest rise in older users using its platform. In fact, those looking for roomshares in their 40s increased by 24 percent, and those in their 60s by 58

---

12. U.S. Centers for Disease Control and Prevention. 2021. "Loneliness and Social Isolation Linked to Serious Health Conditions." CDC. April 29, 2021. https://www.cdc.gov/aging/publications/features/lonely-older-adults.html.
13. Adamo, Matt. 2023. Phone interview. March 31, 2023.
14. Seacrest, Ryan, creat. 2022. *The Kardashians*. Disney+.
15. Chambers, Lee. 2021. Phone interview. February 15, 2021.
16. Chambers, Lee. 2021. Phone interview. February 15, 2021.
17. Mental Health America. n.d. "Connect with Others." Mental Health America. n.d. https://www.mhanational.org/connect-others.
18. MindWise Innovations. 2017. "The Importance of Social Connection." MindWise. July 24, 2017. https://www.mindwise.org/blog/uncategorized/the-importance-of-social-connection.

percent.[19] According to the Joint Center for Housing Studies of Harvard University, older renters (those 55 and over) who contributed to the rental housing growth from 2004 to 2019 now represent one-third of all renter households (over 13.2 million households), shattering the myth that renting is exclusive to younger generations.[20] Dr. Martin explains that roomsharing "is something people are doing longer into their lives, and it's happening more and more often."[21] Even for those aged 65 and over, roomsharing is increasingly common. According to Dr. Jennifer Molinsky, Director of the Housing an Aging Society Program, part of the Harvard Joint Center for Housing Studies, 2 percent of people aged 65+ live in shared households.[22] This is "driven by the affordability" and the fact that just having "somebody else in the house" provides a "feeling of security."[23]

In fact, Molinsky points to the fact that the U.S. is in "an unprecedented situation" and "the number of people eighty and over" is "set to double."[24] And "this is an age when people do tend to have more affordability challenges" because "their rent keeps going up," but their income usually goes down "in older age."[25]

Molinsky predicts that "we're on the cusp of something we've never seen before. This is where a lot of interest comes from. Many people are saying, 'Well, what are the options?' And they're realizing, 'Maybe staying in my current single-family house isn't so great, living alone. Still, I can't afford the assisted living or the retirement home complex, or the active adult lifestyle.'"

So, the next time you spot a snotty, entitled teenager, just think… One day, they might be your roommate shoveling snow off your porch, changing the lightbulb in your kitchen, and sitting down with you to catch up on the latest drama with the Kardashian family.

#68: People are living at home longer and moving into roomshares later

If you were born after the *Titanic* movie came out, you're living at home longer than previous generations.[26] Dr. Martin found that

---

19. Burstein, Rany. 2023. Email interview. April 17, 2023.
20. Molinsky, Jennifer. 2020. "Ten Insights about Older Households from the 2020 State of the Nation's Housing Report." Joint Center for Housing Studies of Harvard University. December 17, 2020. https://www.jchs.harvard.edu/blog/ten-insights-about-older-households-2020-state-nations-housing-report.
21. Martin, Chris. 2021. Phone interview. February 4, 2021.
22. Molinsky, Jennifer. 2023. Phone interview. April 5, 2023.
23. Molinsky, Jennifer. 2023. Phone interview. April 5, 2023.
24. Molinsky, Jennifer. 2023. Phone interview. April 5, 2023.
25. Molinsky, Jennifer. 2023. Phone interview. April 5, 2023.
26. It was released in 1997.

15. How Old Is Too Old to Be Living with a Roommate?

"the number of young adults (18–25) renting has actually gone down in recent years. The sense is that they're not moving out of the parental home at the same rate as people did 10 or 20 years ago. So it's all shuffling up the line a little bit; people are getting into rental housing later and getting out of rental housing later."[27] That means that the post-Titanic generation hitting their thirties will have only been roomsharing for five or seven years before society expects them to have now bought their own place. Previous generations in the 1950s and 1960s could purchase a house on lower incomes with smaller deposits and cheaper mortgages.

According to a study by Richard K. Green and Susan M. Wachter, "In 1949, mortgage debt was equal to 20% of total household income; by 1979, it had risen to 46% of income; by 2001, 73% of income."[28] Fast-forward to the 2020s, 64 percent of Americans live paycheck to paycheck.[29] Even though the mean annual salary is $71,456, more than half of Americans are not saving money. Of the 36 percent of Americans not living paycheck to paycheck, average saving levels are down to 3 or 4 percent.[30] In other words, the average American has only $2572.4 in savings. In theory, someone earning $71,456 can afford a $300,000 house.[31] But if a person puts down a 10 percent deposit and only saves $2572.4 a year, it will take them 11.67 years to save $30,000. And this doesn't factor in legal fees, agency charges, and moving costs. Even if inflation were low and 11.67 years later, someone finally scrapes together a 10 percent deposit ($30,000), a house priced at $300,000 in 2024 will be more expensive in 2034. So, they'll need a bigger deposit.

Side-note reality check: inflation has always existed and will make things more expensive as time progresses. Trying to get your salary to outpace inflation yearly is like playing whack-a-mole. You'll never win.

---

27. Martin, Chris. 2021. Phone interview. February 4, 2021.
28. Green, Ricard K., and Wachter, Susan M. 2005. "The American Mortgage in Historical and International Context." *Journal of Economic Perspectives.* 2005. https://doi.org/10.1257/089533005775196660.
29. Dickler, Jessica. 2023. "64% of Americans are living paycheck to paycheck—here's how to keep your budget in check." CNBC. January 31, 2024. https://www.cnbc.com/2023/01/31/share-of-americans-living-paycheck-to-paycheck-jumped-in-2022.html.
30. de Querol Cumbrera, Fernando. 2024. "Personal savings as a percentage of disposable income in the United States from June 2015 to June 2024." Statista. August 5, 2024. https://www.statista.com/statistics/246268/personal-savings-rate-in-the-united-states-by-month.
31. Higuera, Valencia. 2024. "How Much House Can I Afford with a $70K Salary?" The Mortgage Reports. May 2, 2024. https://themortgagereports.com/70827/70k-per-year-salary-how-much-house-can-i-afford.

#69: Shared living lets you live better

The financial benefits of sharing are undeniable: Wi-Fi, streaming services, and utilities are cheaper. In 2016, 9.7 million adult homes were cost-burdened. Being cost-burdened is defined as spending more than a third of your income on housing costs. Almost half of people aged 65+ living alone fall within that bracket compared to 20 percent of married or partnered homes.[32] When a quarter of adults 65+ spend half of their income on housing compared to 12.9 percent who are roomsharing, why wouldn't you get a roommate?[33]

As you get older, you're no longer willing to continue living like an impoverished student. Once you hit your thirties, gone are the all-night ragers. Gone are the $2 meal deals you can heat up in the microwave and cook in a few minutes. Instead, you spend more on food, on wine, on clothes. You even make the effort to buy better plates, glasses, cutlery and cooking utensils.

Prof. Tuffin found that people in their early thirties were "pleased" to be sharing because this meant that rent was "affordable" on "a two-bedroom property, and they got on really well with the other person and that meant that they were only having to pay half the rent."[34] The older a roomshare gets, the finer it becomes. Just like wine gets better with age, the difference is an older roomshare can afford to splurge on those fine wines.

#70: Sharing with others is becoming the norm no matter your age

Roomsharing is a choice and is gradually becoming a necessity. Within this context, roomsharing is becoming progressively accepted in wider society. Lee Chambers even hopes that the pandemic has accelerated that change in perception to remove the stigma of older roomsharing entirely.[35]

The financial realities of our modern world mean that many people will have to share a home with strangers if they want to live in a decent neighborhood and have access to good-quality facilities. Roomsharing

---

32. Molinsky, Jennifer. 2018. "Are More Older Adults Sharing Housing?" Joint Center for Housing Studies of Harvard University. August 20, 2018. https://jchs.harvard.edu/blog/are-more-older-adults-sharing-housing.
33. Molinsky, Jennifer. 2018. "Are More Older Adults Sharing Housing?" Joint Center for Housing Studies of Harvard University. August 20, 2018. https://jchs.harvard.edu/blog/are-more-older-adults-sharing-housing.
34. Tuffin, Keith. 2021. Phone interview. January 19, 2021.
35. Chambers, Lee. 2021. Phone interview. February 15, 2021.

15. How Old Is Too Old to Be Living with a Roommate?

is like pooling people's wealth so everyone can benefit from a better life. It opens the possibility of living somewhere nicer for cheaper, which is a smart way to live.

Would you rather rent a tiny studio in Manhattan for $2500 a month with no concierge, no pool and no gym just to live alone? Or spend $2500 a month renting a room in a ten-bedroom and 12-bathroom mansion in Long Island with pool, gym and movie theater?[36]

---

36. Assuming at least ten people live there, sharing the cost of a cook and a cleaner would be cheap too...

16

Establishing a Group Dynamic That Works

When members of Congress and the Senate have strict rules to control their behavior while working together and still manage to get into massive arguments, it's a miracle so many randoms can live together peacefully in roomshares up and down the country. This comes down to the "group dynamic" concept when choosing roommates. The group dynamic is a cohesive set of unspoken rules and behaviors that ensure a harmonious living situation for everyone living under the same roof and sharing facilities.

If you have four 25-year-olds who love to party together every weekend, get drunk, smoke weed, sleep in, and watch TV while eating cold pizza, they're not even going to consider interviewing a 45-year-old divorcé and father to two young children. The group dynamic wouldn't work. Why? Because the lifestyle of the 45-year-old is so far removed from that of the 25-year-olds. They don't want young children hanging around while they're recovering from a hangover. They don't want to keep the music down on a Monday night because the 45-year-old has a big presentation at work the next day. And neither would the 45-year-old want to live with them in the first place. The likeliest scenario is that they wouldn't even apply to view the roomshare.

Of course, not every 25-year-old wants to party and play loud music all the time. There are swathes of people in their 20s who would love to live with an older person with children. They know the home will likely be clean and tidy. They'll never have to worry about strangers being brought back after a wild night out (or perhaps they will if the older roommate is a 25-year-old at heart). It's likelier the 45-year-old has more disposable income and is a good cook who volunteers to delight your palette with fine cuisine every night simply because they enjoy it.

Group dynamics are intrinsically linked to personality and circumstance. People who roomshare successfully do so thanks to a healthy group

16. Establishing a Group Dynamic That Works

dynamic. As soon as you introduce an idiot who threatens that, the roomshare breaks down. This is why whoever you choose to live with needs to fit with your lifestyle, tastes, and living preferences.

When choosing whom you live with, you don't have much time to vet them as roommates. This brings us to the problem of appearances and impressions. It's hard to judge who would be the "best fit" to join your roomshare. The only information you have to interpret is the in-person interview and periphery interactions over email, text, and phone. In *Talking to Strangers,* Malcolm Gladwell explains that we all "default to truth."[1] Humans take other humans at face value. If you meet a stranger who is to share a home with you and they tell you they're tidy, you're going to believe they're tidy. Your first instinct won't be to cross-reference their statement by interviewing their previous roommates to establish the "truth." Committing to that level of due diligence is time-consuming and emotionally draining.

The human instinct to default to truth is a gift and a curse. Most of the time, people are telling the truth. It's far easier and quicker to assume everyone you meet is honest. Nothing will ever get done if everyone is suspicious of everyone else and wants to check every fact. In addition, would you really want to live with roommates who are suspicious of you before you sign a lease? On the rare occasion that you find out after moving in that your new roommates did lie (or bent the truth slightly), it's easier to forgive and forget than harbor resentment for the duration of your time roomsharing with them. Especially when it's a "harmless" lie.

Regarding easier choices, humans are quicker to trust people who are similar to them. As Prof. Tuffin explains, when deciding whom to live with, "People want to live with people like themselves. Mirrors of their own beliefs, certainly age and so on. So, of course, the reason for that is that they assume that means that there's less likelihood for conflict, disagreement and problems down the track."[2] He's completely right: we identify closely with those who look and sound like ourselves and feel safer living with people who are similar to us. It doesn't mean it's "right" in an ethical sense, it's just what happens. After all, this comes back to the concept of compatibility as the key to the group dynamic. You don't want to live with someone out of sync with your lifestyle. That creates tension. Your home is a sanctuary. Once you've closed the front door, you want to be at peace with your roommates.

When picking roommates, shortcuts in the decision-making process are inevitable. If someone has a similar background, this immediately

---

1. Gladwell, Malcolm. 2019. *Talking to Strangers.* London: Little, Brown, p. 51.
2. Tuffin, Keith. 2021. Phone interview. January 19, 2021.

makes it easier to understand each other. It's not necessarily better, it's just what humans instinctively do. This is why the hard-partying 25-year-olds are likelier to prefer someone similar in age who also likes to party. This person, by default, has a likelier chance of fitting in with the group. It's human nature to assume this, paving the way for a successful group dynamic. This is the cornerstone of a successful roomshare. Everything must fit together for an easy living environment, and it starts by making sure roommates are compatible.

Modern technology is also geared up to facilitate a better group dynamic. Diggz, for instance, will use an algorithm to match compatible roommates. As Burstein explains, the software will match roommates "having similar budgets, similar interests if you're teaming up to find a place or if you're interested in living in the same areas, same neighborhoods, move dates, pet alignments."[3] Get these right, and you'll be off to a good start.

The only caveat is that when choosing someone new to live within a roomshare, the fleeting roommate interview isn't enough to gauge whether the dynamic will flourish or flounder. You must remember the reality of any situation, a truth repeated throughout this book: You never *really* know someone until you start living with them. It's like picking a juicy apple at the grocery store. On the surface, it looks delicious, but it's only once you bite into it that you know it's not rotten inside.

Steps to Take to Set Up a Successful Group Dynamic

#71: Have a WhatsApp group for the roomshare

Communicating with your roommates is a crucial part of living together. Get it wrong and, at best, you'll get frustrated and, at worst, anarchy. Imagine going to the bathroom, doing your business, and then realizing your roommate used the last of the toilet paper and didn't tell anyone. World War Three has started.

Healthy communication is mission-critical. It's like Calpol for angry roommates, and the right way to administer the Calpol? WhatsApp. Meta's private messaging service already has almost three billion users worldwide exchanging 140 billion messages every day.[4] Here's why:

---

3. Burstein, Rany. 2023. Phone interview. March 31, 2023.
4. Persuasion Nation. 2024. "60 WhatsApp Marketing Statistics No Marketer Should Miss" Persuasion Nation. April 19, 2024. https://persuasion-nation.com/whatsapp-marketing-statistics.

16. Establishing a Group Dynamic That Works

- Email is too formal and slow
- Androids and iPhones can use WhatsApp
- As if Facebook Messenger is still a thing
- Instagram is better for 1–1 messaging
- Telegram is yesterday's news
- When was the last time you used Snapchat??

In the same way that every home needs band-aids, hot water, and a TV connected to Netflix, a group WhatsApp is a necessity. Ask the people you'll be moving in with if they all have WhatsApp. It only takes one roommate to hate WhatsApp, and trouble beckons.

In my 18 years of living in roomshares, nothing has worked better to communicate between roommates than a WhatsApp group. Sure, there was a time before the Internet when people communicated via telegrams, letters, and landlines. There was also a time before cars and planes. Enough said. Now for the appropriate WhatsApp etiquette.

#72: Don't ever criticize anything over a group chat, as it can be misconstrued

They say perception is reality (no matter how frustrating this is, I've always found it accurate). So, maintain a friendly tone when messaging the WhatsApp group. This doesn't mean you're "banned" from asking questions and favors. Just re-read any message before pressing send so you don't accidentally (or intentionally) write anything rude or passive-aggressive.

> *"Hey, which selfish idiot drank my OJ?"*
> ✓sent at 6:04 a.m.
> *"Who tf took my last bread roll this morning?"*
> ✓sent at 8:06 a.m.
> *"Thanks [INSERT NAME IN CAPS] for taking TOO LONG in the shower and making me LATE again for work. Reminder everyone: We agreed to spend only 5 minutes in the shower before work. Thank you! :)"*
> ✓sent at 9:01 a.m.

Let's not kid ourselves, even if the above is true, the sender is a douche. By the way, the examples are real messages I've seen in WhatsApp groups. And worse, they make the guilty party a martyr (even if they did unload a smell in the bathroom so bad you were forced to wait until you got to work to do your personal business. And yes, this happened to me, too).

There will be important reminders to pay bills and rent, but chasing people for money should be done privately. What you can do is, when someone has paid, thank them publicly on the group. It's the closest you can get to being passive-aggressive without actually being so. It will remind the overdue ones to pay ASAP.

#73: Engage in the WhatsApp group and keep it fun and interesting

Everyone knows you're being taken for a fool when someone claims "not to have seen" an important message. This will also tell the roommates that they don't care or want to care about the roomshare, and that they don't even want to live there anymore.

Some messages may seem inane and a waste of time. They probably are; it wouldn't be the first time and it certainly won't be the last time you get them. Everyone has their breaking point. If you're like me and reach it quickly (even quicker when hangry), temporarily mute the group and answer the relevant ones when you have the headspace. The key here is to stay engaged or, at least, pretend to be engaged to maintain a healthy group dynamic.

Use GIFs and emojis. Share funny articles, memes, and important roomshare updates. You'll want to make people want to open the group chat and stay engaged. Communication doesn't work if half the roommates don't bother checking the messages. People will want to be involved when it's worth their time and will want to avoid it if it feels like hard work.

#74: Talk to difficult roommates in person

There will always be someone in the group who breaks etiquette. Not everyone is perfect like you and me… Screw it, I'll say it. In the past, I have been an absolute dick. It's hard to keep calm sometimes. Whenever you do feel like you're about to lose your shit, get some fresh air. Go for a walk. And then chat with people in person. Their behavior is usually symptomatic of something else, and you'll only know for sure by talking face-to-face. Sometimes it *is* just them being a douche.

When you chat, the psychological trick to avoid being punched in the face is never accusing anyone of anything. As Donna Dawson explains, "When you say 'I feel,' instead of saying 'you never' or 'you always' do such and such, when you go on the attack, the other person is busy defending themselves. They're not really taking in what you're saying. So they're just thinking about the next retort they wanna make. But when you say I feel, I feel this, this isn't going right, because I'm feeling a bit, imposed upon, nobody can invalidate your feelings. Your feelings are your feelings. So it's the way you put stuff across that's important."[5]

---

5. Dawson, Donna. 2023. Phone interview. April 14, 2023.

Rip off the band-aid as quickly as you can with a heart-to-heart. If you can cry, this is even better. Nobody can argue with tears, real or crocodile.

Beyond the Texting

#75: If a roomshare is meant to work out, it will work itself out

At the end of the day, the old saying, "Where there's a will, there's a way," still stands. If the communication isn't working between roommates, it's likely something else is afoot. Perhaps they just don't like you. Or you don't like them. And this is okay. You don't want to live with them anyway, so it's best to just move out. Got some pent-up anger towards your former roommates? Give them all the middle finger emojis on the WhatsApp group as you leave. Trust me. It *will* make you feel better.

The Personal User Guide by Peter van der Bel

One of the many fascinating conversations I had while researching this book was with renowned psychology professor Sam Gosling, author of *Snoop: What Your Stuff Says About You*.[6] At the end of every interview for this book, I asked interviewees if they could recommend someone who might have some insight to share. Gosling recommended Peter van der Bel. He described van der Bel as an entrepreneur, which he most certainly is. In fact, van der Bel has been so successful he's been able to dedicate the last decade to one of his passions: personality research. Based in The Hague, the Netherlands, van der Bel founded the Center for Applied Product Personality Research (CaPPr), which aims to look "for ways to integrate pictures into psychological concepts."[7]

This particularly interested me as personality is at the heart of roomsharing. Compatible personalities are crucial for a successful group dynamic. For clarity, compatibility doesn't have to mean similarity, although similar personalities tend to get on better with each other. Compatibility means living successfully with others (the crux of a successful roomshare). The problem is no one anywhere in the world has an objective

---

6. Gosling, Sam. 2021. Phone interview. February 23, 2021.
7. The Center for Applied Product Personality Research. 2024. "About Us." The Center for Applied Product Personality Research. 2024. https://cappr.org/about.

system for rating each other's personalities and checking for compatibility. In fact, when choosing a roommate, it would be weird to make everyone bring a list of personality traits rated out of five stars. How weird would it be really though? It's what we do in other aspects of our lives.

When booking an Uber, all riders check the driver's rating, and if the driver is rated below 4.5, they think twice before confirming. Similarly, with vacations, before booking a hotel, you look at the reviews, ratings, and prices. The same applies when shopping on Amazon. Before proceeding to the checkout, you always check the item's rating and how it compares to everything else on offer.

Anyone who doesn't apply this due diligence is not maximizing their spending. In other words, when it's so easy to check the quality of a product before a purchase, one would be a fool for not doing so. Yet, applying these same principles to who you share a bathroom with doesn't happen.

No one comes to a roommate interview equipped with a review, rating, and shopping basket to pop you in. Roommates will believe whatever you say. On rare occasions, an agent contacts your references usually to check if you lived where you claimed and if you paid your rent on time. They're not going to conduct a review of how you are as a tenant. Even if they did, your roommates never will. Yet, *where* and *how* you live is as important, if not more important, than choosing a job. You certainly look up a company's reputation and speak to employees before accepting one.

We live in a world where complete strangers agree to live with each other based on trust and instinct. Logically, it's weird (dare I say dangerous) that people don't commit to rigorous interviewing and background checks before ever agreeing to live together.

Shared living goes beyond splitting the rent. Roommates share a toilet, living room, cooking utensils and a Netflix password. You see them every day. You hear everything they do. You can't avoid them (even if you try). Humans go about their lives trusting their roommates and hoping their personalities will suit. Personality is key and is (obviously) a massive area of psychology.

Tests like the Birkman Colors code people in green, blue, red, and yellow personalities according to their behavioral traits.[8] However, this research is niche and not mainstream. If people in a roomshare are going to assess the personalities of new potential roommates the way psychologists do, to do so accurately they'll have had to study, taken an exam, and earned a degree or a certificate in the topic. Which is completely

---

8. Birkman. n.d. "Birkman Colors." Birkman. n.d. https://birkman.com/resources/articles/birkman-colors.

impractical and unrealistic. Most people will never go into this much depth for a roomshare.

This is where Peter van der Bel's research comes in. He created a *Personal User Guide,* a "brief user manual for a person."[9] This is based on the Big Five personality traits:

- Openness to experience
- Conscientiousness
- Extraversion
- Agreeableness
- Neuroticism

Taking van der Bel's test is simple: a word is displayed, and you have a choice of pictures to associate with it. Minutes later, you're provided with a thorough guide to your personality. I've done it myself, and the results sparked my other half to claim they were "uncannily accurate." Whether this is a good or a bad thing, she refuses to comment...

Although it isn't intended for roommates, the user guide's application can help determine compatibility. The purpose of the *Personal User Guide* is literally in the title: it's a guide. It can "help you to get to know each other better, build a good relationship and get a lot done faster."[10] If everyone completes their guide and shares it at the interview (before signing a lease), it will provide transparency and clarity on the potential group dynamic, which would never be possible through a quick meet-and-greet.

As van der Bel explains, you "should not only look at the big deviations between people, but also how you are compatible. So, let's say you are both extroverted, then your blind spot can be that you become too noisy in the literal and the figurative sense. And that might eventually drive you crazy. I try to produce suggestions where you differ or are complementary, but I also provide suggestions when you are similar to evade blind spots. Because when you're both very conscientious, you might eventually think everybody else is conscientious. So, you become short-sighted in a way."[11]

When van der Bel was running his own company, he knew he had to pick the right hire or face the huge cost of removing them. As he explained, "When I hired people, it was not a one-off €300 like when I bought a microwave, but it was at least €3000 on top of the monthly cost of their salary, but I didn't receive any user manual like I did for the microwave."[12] These

---

9. Personal User Guide. n.d. "What Is a Personal User Guide?" PersonalUserGuide.com. n.d. https://personaluserguide.com/how-it-works.
10. Personal User Guide. n.d. "What Is a Personal User Guide?" PersonalUserGuide.com. n.d. https://personaluserguide.com/how-it-works.
11. van der Bel, Peter. 2021. Phone interview. February 25, 2021.
12. van der Bel, Peter. 2021. Phone interview. February 25, 2021.

principles apply to roomshares. If you know what your roommates are like before moving in, you can make a more informed decision before committing thousands of dollars and months of effort to make living together work.

It will take a lot before the renting world accepts a concept like *The Personal User Guide*. But why should they? People are, by nature, unpredictable, so no tool or test will entirely figure us out. As Donna Dawson puts forth, "We can never get it 100% right. In some respects, we have to become lucky. You know we have to follow our guidance, we have to ask the right questions, but at the end of the day, we have to keep our fingers crossed too that this person [the new roommate] is as they appear to be."[13] If roommates started using *The Personal User Guide* the same way they use Uber ratings, the world would be a better place. Like anything in life, nothing is certain. At least this user guide can provide more information on what someone is like before you take the plunge and commit to living with them. It minimizes having FOMU (Fear of Messing Up) in new roomshares. To find out more about van der Bel's *Personal User Guide*: https://personaluserguide.com/how-it-works.

Developing Friendships

In our interview, Dr. Sophia Maalsen perfectly encapsulated the concept of friendships in a roomshare when she said, "A good way to make friends is to live with a stranger who then becomes a friend. And the quickest way to ruin a friendship is to live with one of your friends."[14] In theory, friends are the ideal roommates. You know them already, and you trust them. So, why ruin all this by moving in together?

It was discussed in *Chapter 3: Your Choices as a First-Time Roomshare,* unless you became friends by living together first (such as in college), when moving in for the first time with a friend, you will witness them do things you never would have thought possible. They'll have habits you'll hate. It can, of course, work out brilliantly, which is great. It's just not worth the risk.

On the other hand, when roommates become friends, they become the best of friends. There's no hiding from each other. It's the most beautiful of friendships and can only happen if the roommates make an effort to become friends. You wouldn't wake up one Saturday morning and say, "I'll run a marathon today." It takes months of effort. Just like friendships, work is involved.

---

13. Dawson, Donna. 2023. Phone interview. April 14, 2023.
14. Maalsen, Sophia. 2020. Phone interview. December 22, 2020.

If you've followed the advice about cooking together, celebrating holidays, and general roomsharing etiquette, you'll have done your best to develop genuine friendships with your roommates. Developing a friendship is an organic process. At the end of the day, if you like another person, you'll make the effort to become friends. If you don't like someone, pretending to be friends can go a long way towards harmony. A roomshare should be a home with friends. A home you feel welcome to return to. Getting to a place where you feel welcome and comfortable takes effort from everyone.

#76: New friendships are always possible

In Marisa Franco's TEDx Talk *The Secret to Making New Friends as an Adult*, she comments that "friendship does not happen organically in adulthood" and that "one study found that people that think that it happens based on luck are actually lonelier five year later, whereas people that see it as happening based on effort are less lonely five years later."[15] You can make new friends no matter your age. Being 20, 40, or 80 years old doesn't matter, and when meeting new people in a roomshare, you have the opportunity to develop new friendships.

Franco's research leads her to conclude, "If you want to make friends, you must assume that people like you. The reason is when researchers told people, 'Hey, you're going to go into this group, and based on your personality profile, we predict that you will be liked.' This was completely bogus, a total lie. But they found that when people went into this group of people, they became warmer, open, and more friendly because they made this assumption. And so indeed, it became this self-fulfilling prophecy called the 'accepted prophecy.'"[16]

Which is how you should approach your roomshare. It's akin to a *Star Wars* Jedi mind trick, except you don't need any training or power.[17] Simply assuming people like you will make it easier to cement new connections and friendships into your life.

#77: Engage with your roommates

Professor Clark explains that "one of the best predictors of becoming friends is very dull. It's proximity. We become friends with people who

---

15. Franco, Marisa G. 2023. "Marisa G. Franco: The Secret to Making New Friends as an Adult." Ted.com. February 2, 2023. https://www.ted.com/talks/marisa_g_franco_the_secret_to_making_new_friends_as_an_adult/comments/transcript.
16. Franco, Marisa G. 2023. "Marisa G. Franco: The Secret to Making New Friends as an Adult." Ted.com. February 2, 2023. https://www.ted.com/talks/marisa_g_franco_the_secret_to_making_new_friends_as_an_adult/comments/transcript.
17. Lucas, George, dir. 1977. *Star Wars*. 20th Century Fox.

are proximal to us."[18] In this context, living with someone "speeds everything up, you're seeing the person every day and thus have the opportunity to be supportive of one another frequently."[19] When you cross paths with a roommate, engage with them—ask how they are. Sociologist Rebecca G. Adam's research found that "for friendship to be fostered organically, you need to have this unplanned interaction and the shared vulnerability."[20]

In Franco's book *Platonic*, she explains that "when you find something that's repeated over time, what happens is something called the 'mere exposure effect' sets in. The mere exposure effect describes our tendency to unconsciously, completely consciously, like people just because they are familiar to us."[21]

Those impromptu conversations and interactions are a critical part of a successful group dynamic. They strengthen the bonds of friendship in a roomshare. Of course, if you run into your roommate and want to punch them in the face, you have a different problem on your hands....

#78: *Friendships thrive when you open yourself up to them*

Saying no is easy:

"No, I don't have time to try that new vanilla latte. I'll just get an Americano and go home."

"No, I don't want to join your poker club. I don't know how to play poker."

"No, joining the running club isn't for me. I prefer to go swimming and get some alone time."

Saying no to making friendships is easier than trying. Everyone wants a simpler life, right? Ironically, this type of thinking will make your life harder. Not making any effort with the people you live with guarantees your isolation from them. Personally, I have lived in 13 apartments in 14 years, roomshared with more idiots than I care to remember, and I wished I could forget the idiots I can remember.

Taking it a step further from Franco's assessment, my biggest lesson from all these experiences is that you need to *want* to like the people you live with before you can *actually* like them. It sounds so obvious when you write it down and read it back, but so many people take one look at

---

18. Clark, Margaret. 2023. Phone interview. May 17, 2023.
19. Clark, Margaret. 2023. Phone interview. May 17, 2023.
20. Franco, Marisa G. 2023. "Marisa G. Franco: The Secret to Making New Friends as an Adult." Ted.com. February 2, 2023. https://www.ted.com/talks/marisa_g_franco_the_secret_to_making_new_friends_as_an_adult/comments/transcript.
21. Franco, Marisa G. 2023. "Marisa G. Franco: The Secret to Making New Friends as an Adult." Ted.com. February 2, 2023. https://www.ted.com/talks/marisa_g_franco_the_secret_to_making_new_friends_as_an_adult/comments/transcript.

16. Establishing a Group Dynamic That Works

someone and immediately think, "I'm not going to like this person." This attitude will make you think every roommate is an idiot. Being open from the start and willing to try to be nice and sociable will pay dividends.

Life is better this way, no matter how irritating your roommates can be. Many people have annoying habits. There is no denying that out of the 8,000,000,000 human beings on this earth, at least 4,000,000,000 are idiots. You just have to find one or two of the non-idiot 4,000,000,000 and learn to get along.

17

What to Do When a Roommate Leaves

You've had enough laughs, drinks, and memories to last a lifetime. You've literally found your perfect roommate. The problem is, unless you decide to become partners in business or love (or both?), you will have to say goodbye at some point. Sometimes, this hurts. Sometimes, this just makes sense. Sometimes, this won't make any sense at all. The only guarantee is that it will happen.

How to Handle a Roommate Leaving

#79: Be prepared to regularly interview new people

Living with roommates is a revolving door. People's health, jobs, and relationships evolve, so their priorities change, and where they live changes accordingly. It's a killer, isn't it? You have a compatible roomshare with roommates you like, and you're loving life, and then someone decides to move out. It feels like a break-up, and the only thing you can do is be happy for them. There's no point in being angry or annoyed, as you'll risk ruining your friendship.

Heraclitus, the Greek philosopher, is credited with saying "Change is a constant."[1] This is true for roomshares. Someone's circumstances will change and, voilà, they'll leave. Even though they've been there a while, their notice period is probably only a month, and they're likely to be too busy leaving to help find a new roommate. And they probably don't care. It's no longer their problem...

---

1. He actually said, "Life is flux," but this has evolved over the centuries; Mark, Joshua J. 2010. "Heraclitus_of_Ephesus." Ancient History Encyclopedia. July 14, 2010. https://www.ancient.eu/Heraclitus_of_Ephesos.

17. What to Do When a Roommate Leaves

This is the reality of living in a roomshare with randoms. Even if you have become friends, people look out for number one. Themselves. They'll never say it out loud, but it's what everyone does. Never take personally someone's leaving.

A perfect roommate is like a great relationship that doesn't work out. You had your time together, but once it's over, accept it with grace. The best you can hope for is a continuing friendship and (maybe in the future) a return stint as your roommate. Great roommates are not easy to find, but when they are found, hold onto them whether or not you're still living with them.

Or throw a massive tantrum and break some plates when they tell you they're leaving. I probably would. Once you've calmed down you can take comfort in the fact you've lived with a perfect roommate which proves they exist, and they're not some unicorns that only live in your imagination.

18

Interviewing People for Your Roomshare

When the time comes and a roommate does leave but you want to stay in the roomshare, you must be equipped to deal with being on the other side of the equation: deciding who gets to live with you. The following will prep you for this.

Advertising your Spare Room

#80: Make sure to advertise the roomshare accurately

Be honest with yourself. What kind of person are you looking to live with? Here, you can dream big! Do you prefer someone social and active? Quiet and clean? Loud and messy? As Rany Burstein explains, "Do you want someone that's going to be friendly, or do you want a stranger there that just pays the rent?"[1] The advert should be as detailed as possible so potential roommates know what they're interviewing for.

When someone is coming for a viewing, check with them first what kind of living situation they're after. Donna Dawson explains that a roomshare is "like a marriage. You're sharing the same roof; your needs are the same in terms of eating, drinking, using the bathroom, getting enough sleep, and keeping the right hours. It's about running alongside each other."[2] Personally, I like my home quiet, clean, and tidy. Once, I had a potential roommate who wouldn't stop talking, was overly hyper, and asked me if it was okay to have friends over for "drinks and parties" in the middle of the week. I knew this was the wrong roommate for me...

Your ideal advert should appeal to your dream roommate, so craft it accordingly. Detail your space and the dynamic of the roommates already

---

1. Burstein, Rany. 2023. Phone interview. March 31, 2023.
2. Dawson, Donna. 2023. Phone interview. April 14, 2023.

living there. As Burstein explains, "There's no ideal roommate in general, but there's an ideal roommate for you."[3] The advert is the first step in a complicated filtering process to pick the right person.

Before scheduling visits, make sure that you space them out. Too many interviewees in a single evening can easily blur them all. Leave at least a ten-minute window between visits to write your thoughts on every person you see so you can make an informed decision later. It's also buffer time. You'll also need the toilet, food, and downtime for your brain (not just your vocal cords). In the first round of visits, it's unlikely all roommates will be available. However, you will want the finalists to meet everyone before committing. After all, you may love all the candidates equally, but your roommates might have a preference. And a roomshare is only as happy as the least happy roommate.

#81: Be wary of latecomers to the roommate interview

Potential roommates turning up late and not apologizing are a big no-no. They probably have a great excuse:

"The line at the grocery store was so much longer than I expected."
"A meeting at work ran over, and I couldn't get out of it."
"I was on a date that was going so well I lost track of time!"

Whatever their reason, they didn't plan enough to show up on time. This shows a lack of respect for you and is a bad sign of what they will be like as roommates. Lateness for a first appointment should never be tolerated. If they're late showing up to visit, imagine what they'd be like day-to-day. You'll never be able to trust them to show up when they say they will.

#82: First impressions count

Don't let anyone ever tell you otherwise. Study after study confirms that first impressions impact how people are perceived.[4] Interviewing for a roommate is like interviewing someone for a job. The interviewee (the potential roommate) needs a place to stay (a.k.a. the company), and the interviewer (the current roommate) needs someone to fill the room (a.k.a. the role). If these first impressions are good, hooray! If they seem likable, polite, and kind, these are good signs. Are they asking the right questions? Do they seem approachable?

---

3. Burstein, Rany. 2023. Phone interview. March 31, 2023.
4. Dobrin, Arthur. 2013. "The Power of First Impressions." *Psychology Today*. February 5, 2023. https://www.psychologytoday.com/gb/blog/am-i-right/201302/the-power-first-impressions.

First impressions are made in thirty seconds or less, even before someone has said a word.[5] As Dawson explains, "Our minds tend to take shortcuts when we're summing people up. Because it's just easier. It just saves our brains for more important, more urgent issues."[6] From how someone dresses to how they walk, style their hair, trim their nails, and smile, those cues will usually tell you everything you need to know about someone before you meet them. You're judging a book by its cover, so it should look good. If your gut tells you it won't work out, it's usually right.

#83: Quiz potentials on previous roomsharing troubles

Asking about past problems will cause any red flags to surface. As Dawson explains, "Asking them about their negative experiences living with somebody else might tell you a lot about them."[7] For instance, "If they start saying things like, oh, you know, I wouldn't put up with any crap. I would go there with all guns blazing, you know, really tell them and give a piece of my mind. Then you know straightaway well that's not gonna work."[8]

Asking if there have been any issues with past roomshares is as awkward as asking a first date how much they earn. It's brash and unsubtle, and your agenda is clear. An ingenious approach would be asking a question like "anything you're looking to avoid having in your next roomshare that's been bothersome in previous ones?" Framing it like this allows the potential roommate to explain themselves without judgment.

To remove all doubt from the impression you're getting from a short interview, check references for all incoming roommates. This will feel like overkill and rarely done for multiple reasons. The main one is: can anyone really be bothered?

Interviewees are taken at face value, while their references may tell a different story. As Dawson explains, references "will give you a lot of information because you know, beyond the charming exterior, some people know about how this person really lives."[9] How people seem and who they actually are can be two sides of the same coin…

---

5. Prossack, Ashira. 2018. "How to Make a Great First Impression." *Forbes*. April 30, 2018. https://www.forbes.com/sites/ashiraprossack1/2018/04/30/how-to-make-a-great-first-impresson.
6. Dawson, Donna. 2023. Phone interview. April 14, 2023.
7. Dawson, Donna. 2023. Phone interview. April 14, 2023.
8. Dawson, Donna. 2023. Phone interview. April 14, 2023.
9. Dawson, Donna. 2023. Phone interview. April 14, 2023.

What to Do When It Goes Wrong

#84: If a visit doesn't feel right, then cut it short

This is the most important advice: you'll know within thirty seconds whether someone is right. If they're not right, there's no point in dilly-dallying. If you're one of those who breaks off a relationship by saying, "You're not right for me," you can apply this same logic with potential roommates. If you're like me and you're scared to get hit in the face, so you skirt around a topic, the second-best solution is to say you've had an emergency come up. Any old excuse which has nothing to do with them suits perfectly:

- The Migraine: You suddenly have a piercing migraine. Apologize and cut the visit short. If they follow up, say you've decided to cancel all visits until further notice, and you're taking the room off the market.
- The Interview: There's a last-minute job interview you have to prepare for. This is ideal as it makes you sound like a rushed professional.
- The Deadline: A work deadline suddenly comes in. You feel bad, but the visit must be short because you need to work on a presentation.
- The Call: You get a message from a family member or a friend saying it's "urgent, need to talk." You have no idea what it's about, but you have to reschedule the visit, and you'll keep in touch.
- The Drugs: If they mention they like to smoke weed, say, "This is a no-drugs apartment." If they say they'll do it outside, explain you're uncomfortable with anything related to drugs. They'll see you as an uptight square and find somewhere else.
- The Booze: If they mention drinking alcohol, say you're allergic and can't be near any. This will only work if you hide any alcohol before they visit. It will quickly scare them off…

Anything you can come up with which won't hurt their feelings is ideal. At the end of the day, if it doesn't feel right from the start, there's no point in pretending it could work in the long run. Remember the golden rule: don't be a dick.

You never know when you might bump into these people or how they might affect your life in some way, shape, or form. As long as you remain polite and courteous, everything will be fine. To ensure they don't check in, explain that you're cancelling all visits until further notice and taking the room off the market. This is the simplest and easiest way to stop incoming enquiries from persistent idiots who can't take a hint. Once you've found the right roommates, it's time to ensure you have a winning formula for a successful roomshare.

PART E

Rules of Roomshare Living

"I can't take this long-distance relationship anymore. Fridge, you're coming to my room."

—Anonymous

Rules (Agreed and Unsaid) Make Shared Living Livable

The problem with being a human being is that we're human beings. We're flawed, selfish, and liars dealing with everyone else's flaws, selfishness, and lies. This is why roomshares can be a source of such discontent, discord, and horror stories when living with idiots.

Eating dinner naked, leaving the front door unlocked, and not flushing when it's a number two are all behaviors a typical roommate would never do—unless they're trying to prove a point or they're just an idiot. They tie back to the "unwritten rules" of acceptable behavior for society to run smoothly. I am not going to list all the preposterous things you shouldn't do. By virtue of picking up this book, you're looking for advice on how to better live with others. Anyone who has ever lived with other people will have Jerry Springer–worthy anecdotes to share. *Living with Others* is about helping you get to a place where you can co-live contentedly with your roommates. This is where rules come into play.

In principle, everyone loves to bend or break the rules to their advantage. Yet, rules keep the world together (almost). Without rules, chaos ensues. Having "roomsharing rules" comes from the same principles governing how you act in the street, at work, and in public. You can't just shut your front door and think of home as your own universe where you can do whatever you like. Some people advocate pre-agreeing to a list of rules before moving in together. Donna Dawson explains that "pre-emption is always the best way. You need to write up an informal contract that says, if somebody doesn't abide by the rules, they get a verbal warning, then a written warning, and then there's a meeting to consider whether this person can stay there."[1]

In theory, this would work brilliantly. Realistically... If I were given a list of rules before moving in somewhere, I would run a mile. Most people would. Call it human instinct, call it bananas, we're all (mostly) rational adults who can (for the most part) behave appropriately. As soon as you formalize rules, it's not a friendly living arrangement; it's a glorified prison. This is also why roomshares can break down. People irritate people, and when irritation is suffered in silence out of politeness, it provokes tension.

This is as much about unwritten rules as it is about clear communication. Everyone sharing a living space needs to be on the same page regarding what is and isn't acceptable. It sounds straightforward, but as we all know, it never is. There's a difference between communicating and making sure it is understood. Lee Chambers explains, "Often we think that we communicated, but the comprehension hasn't been received."[2] In other words, unless you have had a clear conversation with your roommates and ensured everyone understands, you risk misunderstandings and arguments. Miscommunication has been at the root of human conflict since our ancestors could grunt. Whenever you discuss an issue, topic, or plan for getting together as a roomshare, ensure everyone understands the what, where, when, who, and why.

Part of me would love nothing more than to advocate for a no-rules lifestyle as soon as you shut the door. The problem is all roomshares would descend into iterations of the *Lord of the Flies*.[3] Still, it doesn't have to be this violent or chaotic. Like Eeyore from *Winnie the Pooh* once said: "A little consideration, a little thought for others, makes all the difference."[4]

---

1. Dawson, Donna. 2023. Phone interview. April 14, 2023.
2. Chambers, Lee. 2021. Phone interview. February 15, 2021.
3. Golding, William. 1954. *Lord of the Flies*. New York: Penguin.
4. Milne, A.A. 2024. "The Wit and Wisdom of Winnie-the-Pooh." *The Guardian*, Oct. 14, 2016. https://www.theguardian.com/books/booksblog/2016/oct/14/the-wit-and-wisdom-of-winnie-the-pooh.

19

Cooking

Eating together is one of the best ways to bond with your roommates. In fact, the word "companion" comes from the Latin "panis," which means "bread" and the act of sharing a meal.[1] Food is the way to anyone's heart; via this bonding, your roomshare will be easier and nicer. There's something magical about preparing a meal to share with colleagues, romantic partners, friends, and roommates. Everyone knows humans are social creatures by nature. When you bond over a lovely meal, you let your guard down, sowing the seeds of friendship one could never cultivate in a video chat or over text.

In the past, I lived with two chefs who cooked a big weekly meal for everyone and were delighted to share their kitchen tips and tricks with me. That was one of the greatest roomshares I ever had. I was so grateful for everything they taught me and the dishes they plated up week in and week out. All I had to do was wash up. I felt like the luckiest roommate. This weekly cadence of eating together is important to sustain. It's easy to lose track or cancel, then suddenly, a month goes by, and you haven't spent any time with your roommates. When everyone is so busy at work or with friends and partners, prioritizing who to spend your time with is hard. Everyone needs to eat—doing so together is a great way to catch up. You don't need an appointment in the diary to make it work, either. If you're cooking a cheap, simple meal, you can offer some out to your roommates (easily done via WhatsApp). They'll be grateful for the offer, thus strengthening your bond.

Let's put the shoe on the other foot. Stop what you're doing if you're always cooking and your roommates turn up and munch on the leftovers without saying thanks. If you're not getting the gratitude you deserve, then you're living with idiots, and you need to get out.

I've also lived in roomshares where cooking together never happened. We all cooked and ate separately; our paths never crossed. We hadn't

---

1. "Breaking Bread with 'Companion." n.d. Merriam Webster. n.d. https://www.merriam-webster.com/words-at-play/history-of-word-companion.

bonded, and our schedules never coincided. We didn't even try to spend time together. The reality was, none of us could be bothered. We were more interested in our own lives and didn't care for each other.

Sometimes, this is exactly what you want in a roomshare: soulless, friendless, with four walls and a roof over your head, living with randoms. But, my goodness, how depressing is that? I'd rather be getting tickled to death. At least I'd have company.

When It Comes to the Kitchen

#85: Always contribute and express your gratitude when a roommate cooks

If you're on the receiving end of someone's culinary generosity, there is only one rule: *always contribute.* No matter how much the roommate may insist you don't need to get anything for the meal and doing the dishes is enough, there are plenty of things you can do (and you must insist). Here are some examples:

- Contribute financially:
  They'll probably refuse but always offer. You can be sure that whatever you pay will be cheaper than going to a restaurant.
- Wash the dishes:
  If they're cooking, you're cleaning. Even if they insist you don't need to, take the initiative and wash the dishes. Deep down, no one *really* wants to do the dishes….
- Replace the ingredients:
  Did your roommate use a whole bunch of pasta and refuse any money? Replace it with the same brand. Your roommate will be grateful for the kind gesture; it sends a message that you loved their cooking and paid attention to what they used (secretly, you're really hoping they'll cook the dish again).
- Buy a plant or flowers:
  If you prefer doing something more heartfelt, greenery always works. Nothing that costs more than the price of a beer at the local bar. It will do wonders for your roommate and be a constant reminder of how grateful you are for their cooking. If they decide to place it in the communal area, it will also brighten up the roomshare. Win-win for everyone.

Cooking is one of the kindest things human beings do for each other. It's why restaurants are so popular, and chefs are celebrated. The sensations you garner from a great meal are impossible to replicate. Be thankful your roommate likes to cook and remind them of your gratitude!

#86: Offer to cook for your roommates (periodically)

I hesitated to include this one because I hate cooking so much. I consider myself well-raised, so I'll always offer to cook, no matter how reluctantly. Most people have a signature dish they can whip up with their eyes closed.

I usually opt to contribute financially or do the dishes. Cooking will send my stress levels through the roof. It won't be half as good as whatever my roommates cook, and I'll constantly worry about being judged. For me, cooking is like walking over hot coals with bare feet—and there is no payoff.

#87: Avoiding your roommate's awful cooking

I once lived with an amateur chef (the previous chefs mentioned were professionals) who refused to take no for an answer even when I insisted I was happy to cook my own food. At first, it was lovely, but he used so much oil that had I kept eating his meals, my arteries would have clogged up and I would have had a heart attack on the sofa at 32. The recipes were hit and miss, with more misses than hits as he loved experimenting and going "off-piste" like his hero Anthony Bourdain.

Here are some excuses I came up with:

- I'm on a diet
- I have IBS
- I had a big lunch

Any excuse that's not personal will do. Diplomacy is in your best interest because telling the blunt truth will hurt your roommate's feelings. The last thing you want is a bitter roommate stinking up the kitchen and moping around the living room.

The Fridge

How you deal with your food in the fridge depends on its size and how many people you live with.... The last thing you want to do is label your food like you're in kindergarten. Yet, I've been in many a roomshare where labelling your food is the norm because so many roommates "accidentally" (a.k.a. deliberately) take someone else's butter, orange juice, yogurt, or whatever else they wanted....

#88: *Make sure the fridge is big enough for you to buy your own refrigerated staples*

The size of the fridge is key. Too small, and it will be anarchy. The rule of thumb is to provide at least one whole shelf per roommate, and if you can't do this, trouble brews. Also, people have awful memories. When sharing shelves, accidentally eating your roommate's food because you forgot it wasn't yours could start a food fight (literally and figuratively). Safe to say, the bigger the fridge, the better your life. Especially when everyone uses butter, salt, and bread, in theory, it makes sense to buy them communally, right?

Wrong. You should buy staples for yourself and yourself only. These are items you'll be using regularly and probably have a brand preference. Attempting to buy them communally is like trying to convince a free-living, hairy hippie to go to a spa for a massage, wax, and mani-pedi. It's going to create arguments which will sound like:

> "Who needs to buy the butter?"
> "I bought it last time!"
> "I like the expensive stuff!"
> "Well, the cheap brand is exactly the same!"

It may seem foolish to have four different types of butter, but if you each have your own shelf, that won't matter.

#89: *Avoid big weekly shops which fill up the fridge*

When you sign up for a roomshare, you automatically sign up for small shopping trips. It's just basic respect not to overload the fridge with your food, preventing others from putting their shopping anywhere. It's worth repeating the point: make sure the fridge is big enough before moving in (especially if there's no space for a mini fridge in your room). The more people living in a roomshare, the harder it is to stick to one shelf each. A big shop for a dinner party might be required and putting your food on other people's shelves is likely inevitable. It'll be fine if you ask them first and they're reasonable. If only two of you share a home, things are easier. Whatever you didn't buy is theirs. Remember, if it's only a small fridge, just be considerate with how you pack your food. The one shelf each rule still applies, but it can be constrictive. Still, buy your own butter, milk, and bread, regardless of whether you have one or ten roommates.

Non-Fridge Food

Non-fridge staples for your cupboard should be handled the same way as with the fridge. Before moving in, check that there's enough room so you each have a cupboard to fit your condiments, salt, pepper, olive oil, and canned goods. Similarly to refrigeration etiquette…. We all use different levels of olive oil, salt, and sugar. Even thinking about buying those communally will be a springboard for arguments. You have more important things to worry about, like what's new on Netflix. In the same way you wouldn't let randoms use your Netflix profile as it will screw up your recommendation algorithm, stick to buying your own staples and keeping them in your own cupboard. If your roommates need to borrow some, fine. You'd be a [insert your own appropriate put-down for someone being mean] if you refused. You want to avoid having a roommate who never buys their own. I hope it doesn't come to this for you, but when you're living with a bunch of randoms, like over a third of Americans, you're bound to end up living with idiots who will do just that at some point.[2]

I first started keeping my staples in my room as a student. Even though we all had our own shelf space (there were six of us sharing a big kitchen), I saw how quickly my olive oil, bread, and (most importantly) chocolate chip cookies would disappear soon after purchase. I had no idea who was responsible, and I didn't want to accuse my roommates individually (although I had my suspicions…. I know it was you, Ben!). I resolved to keep all my staples in my room. The result was a happier (and fatter) me living with clueless roommates who started buying their own staples (and cookies) again.

---

2. Fry, Richard. 2018. "More adults now share their living space, driven in part by parents living with their adult children." Pew Research Center. January 31, 2018. https://www.pewresearch.org/short-reads/2018/01/31/more-adults-now-share-their-living-space-driven-in-part-by-parents-living-with-their-adult-children.

20

Working from Home

Since the pandemic, working from home is now de rigueur, so a dedicated space to work from is essential to your well-being. As Lee Chambers explains, "All of a sudden, a roomshare is no longer just a roomshare. It's a co-living space, and the people who you live with have become your colleagues, as well."[1] Now, having your own office space is unlikely. Chambers states, "Domestic properties are not generally built for us to work from."[2] In a way, you're literally trying to fit a square peg in a round hole. At the bare minimum (assuming you're in a roomshare with a living room), discuss where you could all sit to work alongside each other. Have designated desks (sofa or armchair) so that you each have some distinctive space solely for your working hours. You might prefer working from your bed, but that won't do your posture any good. Only a good quality chair will help protect your spine. And here's what else you can do to make that peg a little rounder…

Setting Up to Work from Home

#90: Invest in fast communal Wi-Fi or buy a dongle (actually just buy a dongle)

The first and most important priority is ensuring fast Wi-Fi for you to work as well as you do at the office. If multiple people work from home simultaneously (not uncommon in a roomshare), having Zoom calls and downloading documents will be slow and painful and make you want to throw your laptop at the wall. Either upgrade your Wi-Fi or buy your own Wi-Fi dongle for uninterrupted service. It might feel drastic (even selfish) to purchase your own, and that's the whole point. I'd do anything to

---

1. Chambers, Lee. 2021. Phone interview. February 15, 2021.
2. Chambers, Lee. 2021. Phone interview. February 15, 2021.

seamlessly stream Friends in the background while pretending to work from home. Especially on a Friday. No one *really* works on a Friday. Do they? So yeah, make sure everyone is on board with fast Wi-Fi so you can stream your favorite TV to your heart's content, while also making sure you have your own private Wi-Fi through your dongle for those work calls with your bosses.

#91: Overcommunicate about important calls and take them from your bedroom

Pre-pandemic, taking video calls using headphones in an open-plan office was the norm. Everyone was used to it. At home? Conducting meetings in the living room while everyone else tries to work is obnoxious.

Assuming your roommates are office-based and using technology like Slack, Zoom and Microsoft Teams, they're likely to also have video calls. The solution: take your meetings in your bedroom with a virtual background (to avoid commentary regarding where you're working from), or in a dedicated area of your roomshare that won't disrupt your roommates. To improve the experience, invest in high-quality, noise-cancelling headphones. Otherwise, you'll want to punch your chatty roommates in the face whenever you have an important call.

As to the number of calls you might have, setting up a shared calendar will help you know what you're all up to, but you can't realistically add every single work meeting there. Some meetings are more important than others, so proactively telling your roommates when you have one coming up is considerate for all parties. Whether it's a presentation or interview, the worst thing to happen is your roommates start cooking, making coffee, or playing loud music, blissfully ignorant you're in a critical meeting. When you have no choice but to run a meeting from home, give your roommates a heads-up. If they're not so considerate, hope and pray that they don't walk around naked behind you because they're "hungover and forgot."

#92: Exit the roomshare at least once a day

A way of screwing up relationships with roommates is spending too much time with them. Everyone needs time apart, no matter how well you get on with someone, whether they're your best friend or someone you met last week. On top of that, remaining in your roomshare for too long will have an adverse effect on your mental health, as well as your physical health. The side effects of staying at home are well documented, with mood swings, sleep troubles, and weight gain.[3]

Is there a local coffee shop with fast Wi-Fi from which you can work and make calls? It's healthy to get out for some fresh air once a day. Of course, whether fresh air in a big city actually exists is another debate for another book. The important thing is a change of scenery. Sat with tea or coffee and working from a café provides you with space away from your roommates. After all, you signed up for a roomshare, not a WeWork.

One of the easiest ways to clear your head is by walking. This isn't just to take a mental break from work. Walking has a myriad health benefits, such as improving circulation, losing weight, and sleeping better.[4] Even at the height of the pandemic lockdown, people were allowed to leave their homes for a walk. You need to ensure you spend time outside every day, no matter how busy you are.

So, whatever you do, get some fresh air for at least thirty minutes a day. Prioritize this like you prioritize brushing your teeth and going to the toilet. You commit to these basics, so why should going for a walk be any different?

#93: Switch off from work

Remember that work is not, nor should it be, your whole life. A healthy balance between work and leisure needs to be achieved for the sake of everyone's mental health. It's harder to do when you're working from home, as at the end of the day you need to "leave work."

And when you're just sitting on the sofa watching TV in the same spot where you've just spent eight hours working on your laptop, the lines get easily blurred. Just because your office laptop is less than three feet away doesn't mean you need to keep responding to emails and messages. No matter how short and quick they are (especially the yes or no questions). It's a slippery path. You start responding because it "takes two seconds, and the adverts are on," and the next thing you know, you've worked another two or three hours. The only winner is your employer.

There needs to be a boundary between work and home. This could be shutting off your laptop at six in the evening or working in a dedicated office area that you then "leave" to relax and unwind on the sofa or in

---

3. Walk-In-Lab. 2020. "How to Cope with the Negative Health Impacts of Staying Indoors." Walk-in-Lab. June 8, 2020. https://www.walkinlab.com/blog/cope-negative-health-impacts-staying-indoors.
4. Arthritis Foundation. n.d. "12 Benefits of Walking." Arthritis Foundation. n.d. https://www.arthritis.org/health-wellness/healthy-living/physical-activity/walking/12-benefits-of-walking.

your bedroom. Whatever boundary works for you is good enough. When you're office-based, most contracts don't pay you overtime like in the service industry. You're working for free when you check your messages out of hours. Even if you love your work and it fills you with pleasure to work that hard, having a clear mental break to come back to it fresher and more energized will reap dividends in the long-term. Otherwise, you'll end up like Jack Nicholson in *The Shining*.[5]

---

5. Kubrick, Stanley, dir. 1980. *The Shining*. Warner Bros.

21

Having Friends Over

Having friends coming to your home is part and parcel of living. You'll want to do it at some point or at least have the option to, and your roommates will too. It's an unwritten social contract between roommates that occasionally someone will have a friend coming to visit or crashing overnight. Like everything in life, there's a terrible way to go about it that will alienate everyone involved, and there's a better way to go about it that will strengthen your friendship with your friends and roommates.

The Etiquette of Having Friends Round

#94: Give your roommates notice that a friend is coming over (especially if more than one)

Similar to discussing work, a shared calendar between roommates for social topics clarifies each other's schedules. If only a shared calendar were foolproof and always accurate. You can't assume your roommates will check it regularly or even take the time to update it. Even if they did, they'll want to know with enough notice (minimum 48 hours, ideally a week) that you're planning on having friends over, particularly if those friends will be staying the night. Asking your roommates on the day itself whether a friend can stay will annoy them. It doesn't give them time to digest. They may have planned a relaxing dinner in front of the television. You may not have received any notice yourself. Your friend is stranded and would stay in a hotel but can't afford the bill... This sounds like a "them" problem, but let's assume you're kind and generous, and your roommates greenlight it. The friend better buy a nice bottle of wine for the hassle. Unless your friend is Ryan Gosling, then all is forgiven. What kind of wine should your roommates buy for Ryan? Also, why didn't you say earlier your friend was Ryan Gosling? Even a Ryan Gosling look-a-like is good enough...

21. Having Friends Over

#95: Prepare for your friend crashing over properly and set a two-night limit

When you're young and single, having a friend crash in your bed or giving them a sleeping bag and some pillows for the floor feels enough. After all, you won't be spending much time sleeping anyway as you'll be too busy chatting and having fun. As you get older, things get trickier as you get stuck in your routines and home comforts. What if Wednesday is face mask night? Face mask night is sacred, after all! And as you're older and have more disposable income, can't your friend stay in a hotel? Probably, but you haven't seen them in ages, and them staying with you is the best chance to catch up properly.

Either way, when you have a friend staying over (which was planned, right?), fix up a blow-up mattress. They're not expensive and more hygienic than a sofa. You could, *in theory*, use the sofa to crash on. But it's not like the covers for the sofa get washed every week ... or ever? Your friend will be grateful for the comfort of a blow-up mattress, and your roommates will appreciate not having strangers sleeping on the same sofa they use to watch TV.

More importantly, plan the arrangements with your roommates so they know what's going on—discussing routines, alarms, bathroom times, etc. It's dull, I know. It's called Adultland, not Disneyland.

Talking of being an adult.... It's your friend so they're your responsibility. If your friend is messy, clean up. Your roommates will only care that the mess exists, not who caused it. This includes ensuring the living room is clean and tidy when your friend isn't sleeping. As soon as they wake up, you tidy up, pack the mattress and their belongings away. You'll want to leave the communal areas as clutter-free as possible. Don't expect your friend to clean or know where to put anything unless your friend is the reincarnation of Mother Theresa, can read people's minds, and intuitively knows what to do.

Remember the golden rule: stick to a two-night policy. Even if they were the holiest of the holy and the best-behaved guests in the history of guests, and your roommates are away so you have more freedom, do you really want your friend to crash with you longer? Two nights, and you're onto a winner. It's like my mother-in-law says, "Guests are like fish. After two days, they start to stink."

22

Living with Pets

Although 66 percent of U.S. households own a pet, they are contentious if mishandled.[1] As a rule, roomshares aren't the best homes for pets. A lot of agents don't allow pets and even when they do it's hard to predict how other roommates will react to you bringing in one.[2] Plus, the likelihood of someone being allergic is high, as 10 percent of the population has a pet allergy, with twice as many people allergic to cats as they are to dogs.[3]

Assuming you're not allergic and love animals, if the roomshare is living with a pet, great! This can be lovely as they bring joy, fun, and companionship. You get the benefits of having a pet without the parental and financial responsibilities. This can be a deciding factor on whether you want to move in at all.

Either way, your only option is to fully embrace the fact you'll be living with a pet now, as any unhappiness or displeasure may be perceived negatively by the rest of the roomshare. Pets are like needy, annoying roommates. They take up space, food, and energy while creating a mess someone else must clean up. Think carefully before getting one.

Still want one? You must ask your roommates first, especially if you're getting a hamster. They are noisy AF at night. Remember that acquiring a pet for a previously pet-free roomshare can be a minefield. Some roommates might be too polite to refuse. Others may chime right in and want to get involved. You won't know how your roommates really feel until you bring it home. With all that in mind, if you're *still* keen on getting one or already have one and plan on bringing it into a new roomshare...

---

1. Megna, Michelle. 2024. "Pet Ownership Statistics 2024." *Forbes*. January 25, 2024. https://www.forbes.com/advisor/pet-insurance/pet-ownership-statistics.

2. The Humane Society of the United States. n.d. "Information for renters with pets." The Humane Society of the United States. n.d. https://www.humanesociety.org/resources/information-renters-pets.

3. Griffin, Morgan, and Key, Alison Powell. 2024. "Are you allergic to cats?" WebMD. May 20, 2024. https://www.webmd.com/allergies/cat-allergies.

22. Living with Pets

#96: *The pet is your responsibility and yours alone*

You should never expect someone you're living with to be a pet sitter. Relying on others to care for your pet is the first step towards a toxic roomshare; you do not want to be the source of any toxicity. If you have a fish, it's the "kind thing to do" for a roommate to feed them while you're away. With a dog, sometimes your roommates might be eager to co-parent when you're busy. If so, you're onto a winning roomshare.

Ultimately, you need to take responsibility. Help from roommates should be considered a bonus, and you always need a plan when you're stuck. Pet hotels exist for a reason. We would already have world peace if every human being were so generous that you could always rely on free pet sitting. This extends to the pet's sleeping area, which should be checked before you get one. When your room is too small or set up in a way that a pet can't sleep there, decide where its sleeping area should be with your roommates. Especially if it's a dog, make sure everyone is happy where they'll be sleeping. Even something as small as a goldfish needs somewhere to go, and a fish tank takes up more space than you think. If there's plenty of space in your room, great. Problem solved. However, most rooms are small, so the communal area is the likeliest place for your pet to spend the night.

When I re-read this chapter, I've made it sound like having a pet is more of a hassle than it's worth. Arguably, that's true. They drain your money, time and space. You get nothing back except companionship and love. Even those aren't guaranteed (particularly if you have a cat). At the end of the day, if having a pet brings you joy, go all in. Your life is short, and a pet's life is even shorter. So if it doesn't work out, it won't be forever.

23

Decorating a Roomshare

Love a cozy home? Like displaying pictures and hanging posters? Painting is as easy as breathing for you? Even if all of the above is the case, decorating in a roomshare is not straightforward. So many factors are at play that need to be broken down into different buckets depending on your situation. It all depends on who you're living with, how long you intend to stay, and whether you're even allowed to decorate. You read that part right.... Your agent might have strict rules around what can and can't be done to the property. Which you'll be fully aware of because you read the contract in its entirety right? ;-)

Regardless of what the contract says, I'm here to help. Why does that last sentence make it sound like I'm an agony aunt?

Navigating Decoration Choices

#97: Avoid buying heavy furniture
(in fact avoid buying any furniture)

The worst thing you can do in any roomshare is buy items like a sofa, fridge, or antique table. I could list more (wardrobes, washing machines, beds), but you get what I mean, right? They are bulky, expensive, and difficult to transport. It's like taking hold luggage on a cut-rate airline. Everyone knows it's a terrible idea and will cost you more than the flight. Actually, everyone knows you shouldn't book a budget flight in the first place.

A decent roomshare should have all the basics you need. Until you have a home of your own that you need to furnish from scratch, stick to buying stuff you can easily carry in moving boxes. It will save you a world of pain. If anything major is missing (wardrobe, bed or fridge or insert equally bulky item), convince the agent to buy it, with their incentive being that it will be re-used for future tenants. You'll benefit from these purchases without the financial burden. Although, if you can convince an

23. Decorating a Roomshare

agent to do this you should be hired to convince the world's richest countries to spend the money to end world hunger because having the skills to persuade an agent to spend any money is a gift from God.

#98: Don't decorate much if you're there for the short-term

I would qualify short-term as 12 months or less. If this is the case, investing in sprucing up your home can be hard. The problem is just because you're there for a short while doesn't mean it should feel like a nondescript hotel. You'll need home comforts and personal items to make it feel like living in your own space. Putting up frames and posters is easy and can be done quickly with command strips.

Regarding short-term rentals, find the nicest option you can afford so you don't need to decorate. You'll want to enjoy being at home and move out without worrying about packing and moving too much stuff. A good agent will always hear you out. You need some paint to refresh your room? The agent should supply. Want some more shelves? More frames? Reassure the agent that a lick of paint will make it look like there was nothing there in the first place if they want them taken down after you leave.

The point is … no matter how short-term your stay there is, everyone has stuff with them that has sentimental value they'll want on display when living in their home. Otherwise, you may as well live in a hotel. Actually, I'd love to live in a hotel…[1]

#99: Go wild with the decor if you're there for the long-term

When you know you'll be staying somewhere for over a year, then you can really make it your own. It all comes back to putting your own stamp on your home. No need to impose your tastes on others, but little reminders here and there of your existence, particularly in your room, are important for your mental well-being. Decorating the roomshare is also a brilliant opportunity to bond with your roommates. You don't need their permission to decorate your own room, but it's a conversation starter and a way to get to know them better. You can then switch the focus to the communal areas. Get them on board. If they've been living there a while, they likely had a hand in decorating the living room. This requires a delicate approach. It's similar to how you need to get buy-in from colleagues when you want to do things at work that will impact their own workload. If you think a poster in the hall is awful, don't outright declare you hate it. In 99 percent of cases, one of the roommates chose it.

---

1. Fresh sheets. No dishes. Bathroom cleaned daily. The dream!

Diplomatically, enquire under the guise of curiosity:

- "Whose frame is this?"
- "When was the last time the living room was painted?"
- "Whose lamp is this?"

Always discuss in person, too. Any other method of communication has a high rate of failure. If on the roomshare's WhatsApp group you ask who put the 1980s Arnold Schwarzenegger poster up, someone will inevitably interpret it as, "Oh, you don't like Arnie! Urgh, such a [insert appropriate put-down]!"

In person, you'll be able to gauge body language and adjust your attitude accordingly. If it's a nice and healthy roomshare, the roommates will be open to changes and improvements.

Most people think of decorating as a chore. It's only a chore if you make it one. It can also be a fun excuse to dress up in crap clothes, put some music on and hang out with your roommates. After all, the intention is to make the place look nicer. Who would be against that? Scrooge would be. Lucky he's just an old Dickens character then and not one of your roommates…

24

Weekends

Anyone expecting a lie-in on the weekend has never lived in a roomshare. From drunk roommates with the middle-of-the-night munchies to the fitness addicts making smoothies at dawn, uninterrupted sleep is a pipe dream best left to "reality"[1] shows like *Summer House*.[2] The only guarantee for a restful and quiet weekend is to live alone in the middle of nowhere surrounded by acres of trees. Even there, birds will twitter outside your window first thing in the morning.

When your roommates are around, they will make noise, whether it's a Monday, a Friday, or a Sunday. We're humans. We're noisy. We chat. We cook. We shower. We watch TV. We can't all be mutes just because one of us is sleepy... It's called living in society. Your roommates are away? Vacation? Business? Doesn't matter. You have the place to yourself! Paradise! You'll be able to sleep in. Read a book in peace. Even have a nap in the middle of the day! That's until your neighbor decides to drill some shelves at eight in the morning on a Saturday. Then they're having a house party, so you can't get your beauty sleep. Urgh. Living with other humans is just painful isn't it...

How to Handle Weekends

#100: Never interrupt a roommate with a closed bedroom door

The first rule of a roomshare is: you do not open a roommate's closed bedroom door. The second rule of a roomshare is: you DO NOT talk about your roommate having a closed bedroom door! Third rule of a

---

[1]. I added "quotation marks" because no matter what producers say I'm convinced all "reality" TV is scripted...
[2]. Clifford, Sean, creat. 2017. *Summer House*. Bravo.

roomshare: someone yells "I'm home!," heads into their bedroom, closes the door, and the conversation is over. Fourth rule: only two roommates in a roomshare.[3] Aside from being a fan of *Fight Club*, there really is a rule within a roomshare about closed bedroom doors. As Prof. Tuffin explains: "Everyone understands and respects what a closed bedroom door means."[4] Do they, though?

Closing your bedroom door in a roomshare is the equivalent of a "Do Not Disturb" sign in a hotel. A roommate's privacy is sacred. On the rare occasion you want or need to talk with them while their door is closed, WhatsApp first. Tell them you noticed their door is shut and didn't want to interrupt, so you're sending them a message instead. If I was in my bedroom and had my door closed and someone knocked, or worse, opened it without knocking, I would transform into the angry Hulk in a heartbeat.

#101: *Wear earplugs and an eye mask while sleeping*

Whether you care or not, you'll want to know what your roommates are up to at the weekend. This serves two purposes:

- Builds rapport
- Gives you info so you can work around your roommates' plans to maximize your rest

Speaking of rest, to increase your chances of a good sleep, you'll need to invest in high-quality customized earplugs and a comfortable luxury night mask. You want to become so insulated from any noise that there could be 200 people raving outside your door, and you'd sleep like a baby. The reality is that your roommates will get hammered. If you drink, you'll be smashed, too. It's called living your life. The only situation when this is a problem is if it happens every weeknight and weekend and disrupts your routine (especially if you prefer a quiet life). In this case, you're clearly in a "party roomshare," which should have been addressed before you moved in. Having weekends that work for you is crucial to your well-being. If you're unable to relax and recharge, move out. Your roommates won't change, and I don't blame them. If you've just moved in, you won't be high on their priority list to appease.

---

3. The actual lines from the *Fight Club* movie are: "The first rule of Fight Club is: you do not talk about Fight Club. The second rule of Fight Club is: you DO NOT talk about Fight Club! Third rule of Fight Club: someone yells 'stop!', goes limp, taps out, the fight is over. Fourth rule: only two guys to a fight." Tyler Durden. n.d. "Fight Club Quotes." IMDB. n.d. https://www.imdb.com/title/tt0137523/characters/nm0000093.

4. Tuffin, Keith. 2021. Phone interview. January 19, 2021.

#102: Don't hog the television

No one likes a hogger. Particularly when the hogger monopolizes the television. Televisions are social connectors for people to bond while watching the same show or movie. It only works when everyone is happy (or not too unhappy) watching the same thing. If you can't agree on watching television together, then watch whatever you want in your bedroom. It will be a better viewing experience than the communal television as it won't be interrupted by chatter, phones, and toilet breaks. A shared television experience should be like a good meal with people you love. You bond and create memories. Forcing others to watch something they don't enjoy is like force-feeding the lactose-intolerant a four-cheese pizza. Neither of you are going to like the crappy aftermath.[5]

---

5. Literally and figuratively.

25

Big Occasions

A big occasion means different things to people depending on where you're from and how you grew up. Easter could be huge for you, whereas the summer solstice could be massive for your roommate. Another might think Sundays should be blessed with a great meal and prayer. In this chapter, I'll only discuss the big occasions that universally apply to all roomshares because big occasions are worth marking. Living together makes it easy to think you don't need to make as much effort. On the contrary, those big occasions have an even bigger significance *because* you live together.

Yes, it takes effort and time. Yes, it takes commitment. Yes, this is what's needed to have a successful roomshare. If you're unwilling to make the effort, put in the time, and commit, you should reevaluate living in a roomshare in the first place. You spend at least a third of your life at home, and if you're not enjoying your roomshare, you need to find one where you can.[1]

Big Occasion #1: The New Roommate

Moving in or having a new roommate is the perfect excuse to go out and celebrate. What better way to kick off your journey of living together? Whether it's a dinner party, welcome drinks, or a big night out with dinner and cocktails, the arrival of a new roommate should be celebrated with all your roommates. No exception. It's a great way to bond and quickly understand how your new roomshare operates. A welcome celebration will reveal the group dynamic, things you couldn't gauge from the interview. You'll see who's organized, who's lazy, and who's always late.

#103: Planning fun with roommates should be easy

Organizing an informal get-together should be straightforward. You chat on the WhatsApp group, pin down a date, and get on with it.

---

1. Sleep alone accounts for seven to eight hours a day.

Celebrating the new roommate is a symbolic get-together, so everyone should be included. Schedules will conflict, but seeing whether the roommates make the effort tells you a lot about how much they respect and welcome you.

If a moody roommate is never available, that will shine through immediately, and you'll know not to bother much with them. Now, I know the bigger the roomshare, the harder it is for everyone to come, but if you're trying at least, it will go a long way to making everyone feel included. If it turns into a big hoo-ha and nobody can agree, this could be symptomatic of a wider issue. When the same roommates are never available, they clearly don't want to hang out with everyone else, which is fine (in principle). It just means you shouldn't expect to be best friends. However, if it does end up being a complete non-starter and no one is available or you have a massive argument, rest assured that this is okay too. It happens. However, this evokes the wonder that you might not want to stay. If it's this difficult to have a fun night out, it begs the question as to whether the group dynamic is going to work.

Big Occasion #2: Birthdays

Inevitably, your birthday will come around. You may choose to ignore it and treat it like any other normal day, thus not telling your roommates. But if, like me, you love your birthday, then this isn't an option.

I don't want to get emotional here, but having a birthday is the perfect excuse to see your nearest and dearest and check in with how everyone is doing. Hopefully, you're including your roommates within that circle. Birthdays come around so fast, and the older you get, the faster they come. They also remind you that you're still around and can celebrate life with those you love. Like a cheesy birthday card once said, *"Birthdays are healthy for you. The more you have them, the longer you live."*

#104: Offer to celebrate your roommate's birthday

As soon as someone moves in, find out their birthday and keep track of it in your shared calendar (or your own if you don't have a shared one). When their big day arrives, a quick birthday text will do wonders for your relationship. They may not want to do anything and ignore it completely, but small gestures make all the difference. Whether they'll admit it or not, everyone likes someone remembering their birthday unprompted. Cards are a cheap way to do this.

Always offer to celebrate a roommate's birthday. They may not want to, but if they're a loner who hates birthdays, it's unlikely they'll be living in a roomshare in the first place. Even if you can't make it on the day your roommate is celebrating, offer to celebrate another time, another way. The offer will be appreciated. On the flip side, when you're living with idiots, don't worry about mentioning your birthday. Focus on celebrating with people you love (all the while finding a home you actually want to live in).

Big Occasion #3: Christmas

You can hide from birthdays, but you can't hide from Christmas. Unless you're a Grinch, who would want to? Particularly when you live in the U.S. or UK (whose celebrations light up entire streets), it's crucial to mark the occasion. After all, Christmas will be on television, the radio, podcasts, and social media. Christmas is in your face the moment Halloween is over. Sometimes, advent calendars pop up at Walmart in September! For (a minimum of) eight weeks a year, you'll be blasted with music, food, decorations, and festive greetings wherever you go. And this will happen no matter your faith, race, or creed. You may as well embrace Christmas. The rest of the world will be celebrating whether you like it or not. And come on. Even a Grinch appreciates a smile and a Christmas chocolate…

#105: Buy a Christmas tree for your roomshare

Nothing beats the real deal. No fake tree can ever compete with the natural Christmas tree smell, look, and feel. Ideally, you'll want to buy a tree together as a roomshare on the 1st of December, and you can start decorating it that day. Everyone's schedules are different, and some roommates might not care to make the time. This shouldn't phase you. If no one volunteers, nominate yourself to organize it all. Even if some roommates complain it's a waste of time and money, everyone will appreciate the tree once it's set up.

If there's no room for a real tree, or if one of your roommates is allergic (unfortunate and rare, but it happens), purchase a fake one. You'll have a tree to decorate and space underneath for presents. Deep down, everyone appreciates it, no matter how much of a Grinch they claim to be. As for the cost, Christmas trees don't need to break the bank. In an ideal world, you're all happy to split the cost evenly. In the unlikely event you have an idiot who refuses outright, just absorb their share. It's Christmas and not worth arguing over. The most important aspect of having a Christmas tree is that it adds a festive flair to your home and brings you together as roommates. It's a conversation starter. It's something to experience collectively as a roomshare. Each roommate can add a decoration to the tree and feel like it's "theirs" too. Talking of decorations….

#106: Get into the Christmas spirit

String tinsel along walls, place mini Christmas trees on shelves, and a wreath on the door. Anything Christmassy works. It will be one of the greatest activities you can do together where everyone can chip in. It will make the roomshare feel like a family of friends.

Whether or not people are going home for Christmas, organizing a Secret Santa is a great way to encourage the Christmas spirit. If no one is taking the initiative, then do it yourself. Everyone loves receiving gifts. There are apps and websites to organize everything on your behalf. All it takes is for people to register their details.

In most cases, you and your roommates will spend Christmas with your respective families or loved ones. In which case, make sure you put a date in the diary for a meal or a celebration beforehand. It doesn't matter if one of your roommates refuses to have anything to do with Christmas (there is always one). They don't have to join in. If they're such a Debbie Downer, they'll move out soon anyway. What's important is spending time with the people who want to live and celebrate together.

#107: Celebrate Christmas Day itself

Remember to wish your roommates a Merry Christmas on the day. If you happen to be spending the actual day with your roommates, make sure you celebrate it with a meal, games, and festive movies. Start celebrating on Christmas Eve, continue on Christmas Day, and finish off on December 26th.

What else can you do?

- Vote on which movies to watch
- Schedule the cooking and everyone's responsibilities in the kitchen
- Stock up on alcohol
- Play games (Cards Against Humanity, Sequence, Monopoly)

Whatever Christmas means to you, it's an opportunity to celebrate friendship and family. Some people may gripe, others claim to hate it, and a few will ignore it, but no one can escape the festive season. Now, gifts aren't the point, but the spirit of Christmas is. It's a time when people need to appreciate friends and family. Life is short, so gift out your hugs and smiles before arthritis kicks in and Botox makes your face look like a sheet of metal.

Big Occasion #4: New Year's Eve

Some hate it, some love it. Depending on where you stand, it's either the most fun night of the year or the worst night of the year. Just like Christmas, you can't avoid it, so you may as well embrace it.

#108: Agree on what to do for New Year's Eve

If you know you'll be around on December 31st, discuss with your roommates what they're thinking of planning. Dinner at home? Night on the town? Movie trilogy marathon? There are so many options, but the important thing is for the roomshare to agree on the course of action. This will avoid any miscommunication and concern for last-minute plans. More importantly, New Year's Eve is always messy, and no matter what you organize, you must clean up afterwards to avoid out-of-town roommates being angry when they come back to a massive mess. Do not make your roommates clean up because you and your friends over-indulged. If you're hosting, the easiest thing would be to book a cleaner to come around on the 1st of January. It will save a world of headaches.

You can also go for the easiest option: head out of town and skip everything. As long as you agree with your roommates that the roomshare will be clean and tidy when you're back, being away for New Year's Eve can be the most fun and/or the most relaxing choice. Imagine the movie *Four Christmases* being only ten minutes long because, at the airport, Reese Witherspoon and Vince Vaughan fly off on vacation and skip all the drama.[2] It could be just like that for you.

---

2. Gordon, Seth, dir. 2008. *Four Christmases*. Warner Bros.

26

The Roomshare Taboos

Taboos are the things no one talks about. They're awkward, avoided, and most roommates pretend they don't exist. The reality is they can't be avoided, so I wanted to address them once and for all.

Taboo #1: Envying Someone Else's Roomshare

Former U.S. President Teddy Roosevelt is quoted as saying, "Comparison is the thief of joy."[1] I couldn't agree more, and it happens to everyone. You'll be invited round to someone's home for drinks, and it's twice the size of your place, immaculately kept, centrally-located, and there's a balcony! A balcony in the heart of the city! You'll get "Home envy." You'll start questioning your life choices. You realize the person living there is your age (or younger), yet their living situation is much nicer... You start panicking and think you've made mistake after mistake in your career choices and you're so far behind from where you should be. It's a downward spiral into a bottomless pit of despair. This will happen time and time again, no matter how old, successful, and big or swanky your own home is.

#109: Don't compare your living situation to others

The grass is always greener on the other side. This is a fact of life. With whatever you have, you'll find reasons to want something you don't have. Especially when a peer already has it. This doesn't just apply to wanting a bigger place, a more central home, or a balcony. There will always be someone else with more. Comparing yourself to what others have is toxic and

---

1. Goodreads. n.d. "Theodore Roosevelt > Quotes > Quotable Quote." Goodreads. n.d. https://www.goodreads.com/quotes/6471614-comparison-is-the-thief-of-joy.

demotivating. Scrolling through Instagram and believing that everyone else's life is so much more fun and interesting than yours blinds you to the fact that your own life is actually great. The healthiest thing you can do is be happy for those around you who have nice things. You can admire, desire, and cook up a plan for how to acquire something similar, sure. Just don't lose sight of what you already have. It's not bad to be inspired, ambitious, and want more. But if you *like* your home, you should be grateful for what *you* have.

On the flip side, not only will there always be someone better off than you, but there will always be someone worse off than you. Also, that person who has the perfect home? You don't know their life story. They're only showing you a part of their lives. That dinner party that makes you envious of their home is like a real-life version of social media. It's a glamorized version of the truth. Someone on Instagram may be boasting about their new home, but you have no idea what the real story is. Maybe their parents are rich and gave them a head start. Or their grandparents or parents died young, leaving them with an inheritance. Most of the time, this is why someone my age has a better place.[2] Admittedly, they might have a higher-paying job and can afford luxury vacations in Aspen and Cancun. But do they enjoy their work? Are they complaining about the long hours and how boring it is? Miserable people who hate their jobs compensate for their misery with incredible vacations and homes. They're filling the void their work creates with luxuries their money can buy. A diamond can only go so far in making someone happy. Although, to be fair, I wouldn't mind earning millions while holding down a boring job. That sounds right up my street.

Taboo #2: Subleasing Your Room

I always get confused between subleasing and subletting, so for the avoidance of doubt:

- Subleasing: a current tenant leases a room (or the whole property) to someone else (a.k.a. a subtenant) in a formal long-term or short-term agreement.
- Sublet: a tenant agrees for another tenant to sign a temporary agreement with the agent while the original tenant is away.

In an ideal world, you can do whatever you want with your room. After all, you're paying for it, so why not? For instance, you're going away on a

---

2. Anecdotally. I have no idea of the "real" stat.

26. The Roomshare Taboos

two-week vacation, why not sublease your room to cover your costs? Or perhaps you have a generous friend who has a spare room you can stay in while you rent out your place to save some money to buy yourself something nice? If you lived alone, it'd be hunky dory. Advertise your place on Airbnb, vacate for the bookings while away for work or stay with friends and family, and let the cash roll in. As always, the reality is a lot more complicated.

Firstly, subleasing is probably banned in your contract. Of course, this doesn't stop people from doing it anyway.... After all, how likely is it the agent will ever find out? Secondly, unless subleasing was informally agreed on before you moved in, it's a delicate subject if your roommates don't want strangers rocking around while you're away. Thirdly, letting complete strangers move into your room for weeks carries inherent risk. Your belongings could get stolen or broken, or squatters could take over your property.

I've lived in roomshares where subleasing was rife, and I've lived in others where the roommates were horrified at the idea. If you're strapped for cash and going to the blood drive isn't an option, convincing your roommates to let you sublease your room should be treated the same way you convince your boss you deserve a raise. It will take some persuasion and a solid business case, and don't expect approval straight away. You also need to be self-aware enough to know when to ask... If your boss is in a terrible mood, you're going to wait until they seem to be in good spirits. The same principle applies to roommates. Read the room first!

#110: Casually bring up subleasing with your roommates

Put some feelers out there. Casually mention while cooking that a friend of yours subleased their room which paid for their luxury vacation to the Bahamas. Assess how your roommates react. Positive? Push further. Negative? Fall back.

If the immediate reaction from your roommates is to snuff out the idea, then just be aware it will take time. Don't lose hope. As Mark Cuban once said, "Every no gets me closer to a yes."[3] You'll have to be subtle about it. In passing, mention you're finding it hard to save money for that vacation you want to go on. Say you would take on a second job if your main one weren't so hectic. Don't talk about subleasing yet. However, this will make your roommates aware you're looking for ways to make extra cash.

This plants the idea that there's an alternative (and legal) way of

---

3. Dickey, Amy. 2014. "5 Quotes from Billionaire Mark Cuban That Will Inspire You To Work Your Ass Off." Elite Daily. September 9, 2014. https://www.elitedaily.com/life/motivation/quotes-from-billionaire-mark-cuban/727103.

supplementing your finances and will pave the way for when you return to the topic. It's a well-known psychology trick made famous by Daniel Wegner. He came up with the "white bear effect," where you tell someone not to think about white bears, and all they think about are white bears.[4] It's like the movie *Inception* by Christopher Nolan: plant the seed of an idea in their heads and let them conclude that subleasing is a great idea that they came up with.[5]

#111: Invite a friend over who successfully subleased their apartment

Get them over when you know your roommates are around so they can hear first-hand about the successes of subleasing. People are always reassured when they meet others who have had successful experiences. The psychologist Robert Cialdini termed this "social proof" back in 1984 in his book *Influence: The Psychology of Persuasion*. In his words, "One means we use to determine what is correct is to find out what other people think is correct."[6]

If it sounds like a manipulative tactic taken straight out of HBO's show *Succession*, great. Logan Roy would be proud as it's for a good old-fashioned capitalist cause: making more money.

#112: Ask if a friend can take your room as a test

Companies like Airbnb or CouchSurfing.com wouldn't exist if every single guest organized parties and damaged property. Most guests are perfectly pleasant and polite. There lies the problem: "most." No matter how much money companies invest in algorithms and artificial intelligence to block people likely to draw bad press, we're human beings. By nature, we're unpredictable. Especially when trusting strangers not to soil your bedsheets or steal your television.

So, if it's the fact that strangers might be living in the property for a weekend that horrifies your roommates, then they might be more persuaded if it is somebody familiar. Friends, family, friends of friends, whatever the connection back to you is, at least your roommates will feel a level of trust there. Maybe this person has been over before and already met your

---

4. Association for Psychological Science. 2010. "The Psychological Science of 'Inception.'" Association for Psychological Science. August 12, 2010. https://www.psychologicalscience.org/news/releases/the-psychological-science-of-inception-2.html.
5. Nolan, Christopher, dir. 2010. *Inception*. Warner Bros.
6. Briggman, Salvador. n.d. "Review of Influence: The Psychology of Persuasion by Robert B. Cialdini." Salvador Briggman. n.d. https://salvadorbriggman.com/review-of-influence-the-psychology-of-persuasion/.

roommates, but they just need a place to crash for a few weeks. Your roommates don't even need to know that your friend is paying you rent. It's rare when the stars align for a friend to need somewhere to crash the exact week you'll be away. So, you might have to be flexible to make it work. Assuming it goes well, your roommates might then be more open to the idea of subleasing… If it doesn't go well, you can forget bringing up the topic again.

#113: Move to a roomshare open to subleasing

If you've tried everything and your roommates are still a blocker, just drop it altogether. As *Frozen*'s Queen Elsa says, "Let it go."[7] And if you're still set on subleasing, move to a roomshare open to subleasing. Once you decide to move, you don't have to inform your roommates. View as many roomshares as you like until you find somewhere great, and then ask them in the interview if they're open to roommates subleasing their rooms. In this scenario, honesty is the best policy.

When you do instigate the move, stay alert to the timings. You wouldn't quit your job until you've signed a contract with a new employer, right? It's the same with roomshares. It's happened to me and my friends. You find a property, agree to move in, set a date, tell your nearest and dearest, and then serve notice at your current place. Then, for whatever reason, it falls through, and you're now officially "homeless." Only once you've signed a tenancy contract, have a move-in date, and have the keys in hand can you celebrate a new life as a cash-generating tenant.

Taboo #3: Lies in a Roomshare

As kids, our parents insisted we tell the truth, the whole truth, and nothing but the truth. Then, as you get older, you realize… Is telling the whole truth and nothing but the truth really in our best interest? You see your boss with an embarrassing leather jacket and pants that are two sizes too small. Do you really think giving them fashion advice will endear them to you? No. Of course not. It will only make them self-conscious and dislike you.

When you enter the workplace, it's like entering a roomshare with randoms. Telling small lies here and there is perfectly socially acceptable. In fact, it's recommended for the sake of polite society. The group dynamic is sacred, and if a lie here and there is needed to protect that, it's worth the deception. Within reason, of course…

---

7. Buck, Chris, and Lee, Jennifer, dirs. 2013. *Frozen*. Walt Disney Pictures.

#114: When the truth has no effect on your living situation stick to truthfulness

Being truthful on general topics of conversation won't (or at least shouldn't) get you cancelled by your roommates:

- "All politicians are awful."
- "I love *Below Deck*."
- "Radiohead is the best band in the world."

These opinions define who you are. They're markers of your personality. Whether your roommates agree is a different matter. Nobody should tiptoe around or hide who they are. Showing your personality and being open with your opinions is the best way for others to get to know you so you can develop real friendships. No one can be friends with every single person they meet. Even Jesus Christ had haters and still he wanted to spread the love. There will always be people who don't like you or who disagree with you. You can only control who you choose to spend time with. By spending time with people you like, your personality can shine freely and breezily.

#115: When the whole truth negatively impacts the roomshare, tread carefully with what you want to express

Supposedly, we're lied to between ten and two hundred times a day.[8] Your colleagues, family, and friends are all guilty. We even lie to ourselves once or twice a day.[9] Whether it's, "Oh, that new shirt looks great," or, "Of course, I'd love to babysit my niece for a whole weekend," when really the shirt is a crime against fashion and your niece is a spoiled brat who does nothing but scream and demand candy. Lying is second nature and necessary to make relationships run smoothly, especially with roommates. Call it lying or simply "omitting the truth," it's a necessary part of living with others.

If you tell a roommate their coat looks horrendous, they'll grow self-conscious and probably cry (I know I would). Donna Dawson puts it another way and explains that it's "none of your business whether your roommate is overweight or has terrible dress sense. They're not there to share your material values."[10] It's not your job to tell a roommate to dress better or lose weight. It's your job to be supportive. As Dawson explains,

---

8. TED. n.d. "The Truth About Lying." TED. n.d. https://www.ted.com/playlists/222/5_talks_on_the_truth_about_lyi.
9. TED. n.d. "The Truth About Lying." TED. n.d. https://www.ted.com/playlists/222/5_talks_on_the_truth_about_lyi.
10. Dawson, Donna. 2023. Phone interview. April 14, 2023.

"We all take criticism badly even if on some level we learn from it. It still hurts."[11]

Some people are "straight-shooters." Either their brains are wired in a way that makes it impossible to avoid lying, or they cannot comment beyond their unvarnished perception of reality. Recognizing when it's appropriate to tell the truth and when it's better to lie (or at least say nothing) is an underrated social skill that is key to maintaining healthy relationships. It's like when you start dating someone and hold things back until you're comfortable with them and have a strong foundation to be completely open with each other. Especially on a first date when you're getting to know each other. On date number one, you're not going to tell your date you have a strange mole and you're really worried about it, are you? Unless the date is a skin doctor. I'd jump at the chance of having free medical care.

#116: *When you have to speak the truth, consider the consequences*

There are scenarios where telling your roommates exactly what's on your mind is needed. They might have blind spots and didn't realize how their behavior affects you and others. Things like leaving dirty dishes out is selfish and unsanitary. Hogging the television, bathroom, and kitchen are all things that make it difficult for you when you're at home. By definition, a roomshare shares all communal areas equally and fairly, and there's a way of going about ensuring that's the case that's respectful for all involved. When roommates are not playing by the normal rules and make you want to smash their face in, then being truthful and addressing the issues head on is required.

The problem with new roommates is you can't tell them outright, "Your dirty dishes make me want to vomit all over my shoes." Although this may be true, you'll be forever stained with the "douche" brush.

You also can't let an uncomfortable situation fester, or it will get worse. In *Never Split the Difference,* (former) FBI Negotiator Chris Voss advises that asking open questions is the best way to get out of any difficult negotiation.[12] Make the other roommate feel like they're the center of attention by asking without judgment or passive-aggression.

Tactics include never beginning with "why" but rather using calibrated questions that start with "what" or "how." Never be accusatory. Do

---

11. Dawson, Donna. 2023. Phone interview. April 14, 2023.
12. Voss, Christopher. 2017. *Never Split the Difference: Negotiating as If Your Life Depended on It.* London: Random House Business Books.

not get angry or emotional. If you come across dirty dishes, you can ask your roommate:

- "Do you know who left these dishes in the sink?"

When it's just one roommate (and it's obvious they left the dirty dishes):

- "I don't remember leaving these dishes in the sink, do you?"

If the roommate doesn't volunteer to clean up, you can follow up with:

- "Is everything ok? Do you need help cleaning them?"

Voss is hailed as one of the best negotiators the FBI has ever seen, so if it doesn't work, don't blame me, blame Voss. After all, this *is* a negotiation. Your roommate is exhibiting behavior which affects your quality of life. There's no room for compromise or bandwidth to "meet in the middle." Either they stop their harmful behavior, or you move out. Using the techniques outlined by Voss should get you where you want to be—a functioning group dynamic with roommates whose behavior doesn't make you want to bang their head against the wall.[13]

Taboo #4: Mental Health in a Roomshare

There used to be a time when conversations around feeling low often ended up with the person you were sharing this with telling you to "chin up" or "suck it up and smile." Nowadays, the world is more aware that mental health is as important as physical health, if not more so. This change in attitude is to be celebrated. Especially in the workplace where HR departments encourage employees to discuss their mental health and employees feel empowered to share their stories. Has this state of affairs reached roomshares? Debatable.

#117: Expect mental health issues in a roomshare

When you're in a roomshare, mental health problems will bubble up. Professor Patrick Shrout of New York University says, "In America, 20 or 30% of the population has in a year some significant distress. And, often, it's called mental illness as if it's chronic. But, if you think about physical health, you can get a cold, and you get better, and, that doesn't mean that you're a sickly person."[14]

---

13. I highly recommend reading *Split the Difference*. It's a great book for this purpose and will help in your day-to-day life with roommates, colleagues, and family and friends. It's a brilliant handbook for working together with others in any situation.

14. Shrout, Patrick. 2023. Phone interview. April 28, 2023.

26. The Roomshare Taboos

I spent my 20s in a haze of partying and short-term relationships. If one of my roommates were having a tough time, I never would've noticed even if they told me they were depressed. If they had, I would have shrugged and replied: "Let's have a drink! That will make you feel better!" Back in the 1990s, mental health was never talked about openly like it is nowadays. People had problems for sure, they just never mentioned them. Living in a roomshare means you'll be exposed to people who potentially have issues. As Prof. Shrout says, "Almost any roommate is gonna have days where they act like someone who's depressed or anxious."[15] While stuck with a roommate during the pandemic, I came to realize how tough it can be to live with someone who is suffering mentally. Mental health problems take various shapes and forms. In this particular case, my roommate lost his job due to the pandemic. He insisted he was fine and made plans for the future. But when you live with someone, no matter how great a game they talk, their actions show you what's really going on. This roommate would:

- Sleep until the afternoon
- Talk about big ideas and never follow through
- Have unexpected mood swings
- Cancel and forget plans
- Always complain
- Rarely shower

I thought he was just a douche until my other half made me realize he was depressed. There's no silver bullet when dealing with mental health. It's a moment in time, and it's tough. Hard as it is for the person suffering, it's also tough on the people living with them. When the person you live with is depressed, your own worries and anxieties can amplify. You think:

- How can I help?
- What can I do?
- Should I listen?
- Can I advise?
- How do I make their life better?

And this is where the conversation gets tricky… Choosing between what's best for your roommate and what's best for you. Sometimes, these two things don't align. Roommates can feel like family, for sure. Even with your own family, you can only do so much to help. The main thing is not to be an ostrich and pretend that mental health problems won't surface in a roomshare. You're living with human beings. We all have problems. It's how you deal with those problems that matters.

---

15. Shrout, Patrick. 2023. Phone interview. April 28, 2023.

#118: Be present (if you want to be and it's appropriate) for a roommate in distress

When you've had a long day at work and you're stressed, unloading your problems to someone can have a positive impact on your mental health. When it goes beyond simple conversation, the lines blur between feeling better and needing to see a professional. There's only so much a roommate can do. If you've developed a real friendship with your roommate and love them for who they are, being there for them with a glass of wine, juice, water or whatever is sometimes just enough.

Elizabeth Day discusses how to deal with problems encountered by your friends beautifully in her book *How to Fail* stating, "The best way to respond to this is not to proffer unsolicited advice but to respond with support and kindness. Your friend has to make their own choices and mistakes, and as long as they are not physically or emotionally at risk, your role is not to step in and show them how it's done. The truest advice is given only when asked for, because the act of asking means your friend is willing and ready to receive it."[16]

One hundred percent agree with Day. When a roommate is depressed and hasn't asked you for any advice or help, don't offer. If they open up and explicitly tell you they're suffering, simply being there will help.

#119: Protect your mental health from challenging roommates

When Prof. Tuffin studied mental health in roomshares, the testimonies were unanimous. The roommates didn't mind others having problems as long as those roommates "didn't bring the [mental health] issues up if they [all] had to sit down together and share a cup of coffee."[17] In other words, someone's mental health problems must be "invisible."[18] Which, as Prof. Tuffin explains, is another "way of saying they weren't that tolerant of it."[19] Although Tuffin's study was small and isn't representative of what every roommate in the world thinks, it does bring up an important topic: setting boundaries for yourself. When you're new to the roomshare, do not feel guilty about wanting to protect your own mental well-being. When you live with another person's problems, their issues will negatively affect you (if you let them).

As Professor Clark explains, "Mental health issues can be a major burden, no matter what the relationship is. You've got to be responsive to

---

16. Day, Elizabeth. 2019. *How to Fail: Everything I've Ever Learned from Things Going Wrong.* London: Fourth Estate, p. 215.
17. Tuffin, Keith. 2021. Phone interview. January 19, 2021.
18. Tuffin, Keith. 2021. Phone interview. January 19, 2021.
19. Tuffin, Keith. 2021. Phone interview. January 19, 2021.

each other's needs. And if they have a professional exam the next day, you should be quiet. That's not too much to ask. Or you know they're sick, and you make them soup. That's great and it may not be too much for them to ask for. Yet taking care of and coping with another person's persistent mental health issues is hard. It will probably be more than what people bargained for."[20]

When your roommate is suffering and they're not doing anything to help themselves, you do have to protect yourself. There's a reason why, on a plane, the advice is to put the emergency oxygen mask on yourself first. It's not because the airline transforms passengers into selfish pricks once you get into your seat. Unless you make sure you can breathe when you're in danger, you can't help anyone else.

It's human nature to want to help and be kind, but if this is having an adverse effect on your mental health, that has to be a red flag for your own life and influence whether or not you should move out and find a healthier roomshare. Taking on the troubles your roommate has in addition to the ones you might have is a huge undertaking that can have a massive emotional and physical toll. Your mental health is like a saucepan of water on a stove. Heat it too much too quickly, and it will boil and spill. Weird analogy, but you get the point….

Taboo #5: Children in a Roomshare

This will be a short section: roomshares and children are two worlds that should never overlap, just like you wouldn't make a cocktail out of coffee and wine. It just doesn't work. Right? Or is that another weird analogy…

If you're lucky enough to be expecting children, move out of the roomshare and find somewhere nice to live as a family before they enter the world. Kids need a safe space to grow up surrounded by family. You might think that newborn babies will never remember anything anyway and that you can save money for the first 12 months of their life as it will have no long-term impact. That's factually wrong. Babies ingest information from their surroundings as soon as they're released into the world (some even think this process begins in the womb). Science hasn't quite understood exactly what they can and can't understand. What *has* been universally agreed is that the environment a baby is raised in influences how they are as humans for the rest of their lives.

The language, accents, and mannerisms children are exposed to from the day they're born have an impact (in the womb babies can feel stress

---

20. Clark, Margaret. 2023. Phone interview. May 17, 2023.

and hear accents), which is why it's so important to be raised in a loving and caring home. For children to be exposed to randoms moving in and out is toxic and unfair. A roomshare is not a place for kids, end of story.

Taboo #6: Death in a Roomshare

When I was studying at Trinity College Dublin, Ireland, a girl named Sarah moved onto campus into an apartment with five other girls. They shared a kitchen, bathroom, and living room. They met for the first time on moving day. Three weeks after moving in, her boyfriend of two years, Tom, couldn't reach her. Her roommates hadn't seen her either, but everyone was busy with college, so it didn't seem unusual. Tom grew worried and contacted campus security. Her bedroom was locked, so they broke down the door. Sarah was lying facedown on the floor next to her bed. A diabetic seizure had gone unnoticed, and she had died alone on the carpet. She'd been dead for four days.

Stories like Sarah's are horrific and symptomatic of a problem with roomsharing with randoms; people don't know each other and often don't take the time to get to know each other, thus creating toxic group dynamics. This doesn't mean Sarah would have lived if she'd had a better bond with her roommates. But the fact that she lay undiscovered for four days brings home the point that a roomshare is never just a place to sleep, wash, and eat.

Roomshares are homes where people can form friendships and look out for each other. If your roomshare is not like this, it's not a home. It's a self-service motel. If you move in somewhere after a great roomshare interview and realize you made a mistake, find somewhere else to live. It's a hassle, but the short-term pain will be nothing compared to the long-term suffering you'll endure by staying. Your home is your sanctuary, and you need to set yourself up for success so that it feels like one when you walk through your door. Less *Bates Motel*[21] and more *Hotel Transylvania*.[22]

---

21. Cipriano, Anthony, Cuse, Carlton, and Ehrin, Kerry, creat.. 2013. *Bates Motel*. A&E.
22. Tartakovsky, Genndy, dir. 2012. *Hotel Transylvania*. Sony Pictures Releasing.

Part F

Rules of Hygiene

> "There should be a B.O squad that patrols the city, like a Smell Gestapo. To sniff 'em out, strip 'em down, and wash them with a big, soapy brush."
>
> —Jerry Seinfeld

A Smelly Armpit a Day Keeps the Roommate Away

I once had a roommate whose body odor was so awful, I proactively avoided him. He rarely showered, and it was three minutes tops when he did. He would work out in his bedroom and rush to meet his friends. You guessed it.... He didn't shower in between. It was embarrassing. I didn't know how to approach this issue with him. Taking the coward's route, I avoided him as much as possible and stopped breathing whenever I walked past him. The smell was so bad the police could have bottled up his B.O. and used it as a spray to disperse crowds instead of water guns. When he moved out, it took six months for the lingering smell to dissipate from his bedroom.

As the saying goes, "cleanliness is next to godliness," and this could not be truer than for communal living. Being unclean is the death knell for a successful roomshare, from dirty dishes to dirty toilets to dirty people. If you ever end up living in a roomshare with dishes piling up in the sink, clothes strung everywhere on the floor, and smelly people who rarely shower and clip their nails in the living room while watching TV, buy a nuclear-proof decontamination suit. And you think I'm joking ...[1]

---

1. Or just move out as soon as you can. Much simpler.

27

The Communal Areas

It's the bane of a roommate's life... A dirty plate on the living room table with no owner. Do you clean it up? Or do you make a point and leave it because it's the responsibility of the person who left it there? When it's only two of you, it's obvious which one of you is messy. There's no hiding. When you live with more than one person and you're not Sherlock Holmes, it's impossible to figure out unless you personally witness in flagrante the mess created and left behind by the inconsiderate roommate.

The more people you live with, the easier it is to get away with being gross because you hide behind the fact that it could be any of the other roommates. Communal areas in roomshares are like showers in a public pool: no matter how often you wipe and clean all surfaces, they quickly become dirty and disgusting again.

Keeping Your Home Clean and Tidy

#120: Secure a cleaner for your roomshare

According to Diggz, 64 percent of roommates see cleaning as a priority.[1] The problem is that no one really likes to clean, and there's nothing worse than letting a home get so dirty it starts to smell... That's no longer a home, it's just a bed in a trash can. Some roomshares think a cleaning rota is the solution. In theory, they're perfect. In practice, they never work. Ever. Someone will be away, another will forget, and the person assigned to "clean" that week doesn't do the job properly. Rotas are a disaster. The rows I've had about who last cleaned the toilet... This can be avoided if a regular cleaner attends the property. Thankfully, you can choose from plenty of cleaning services, including Tidy, MaidPro, and The Maids. You just need to find one which works for you.

---

1. Diggz. 2023. "16 Questions to Ask Potential Roommates—Your Complete Roommate Questionnaire." Diggz Blog. March 30, 2023. https://blog.diggz.co/16-questions-to-ask-potential-roommates-your-complete-roommate-questionnaire-a858823ce75d.

27. The Communal Areas

The main crux of the problem is getting everyone on board with the idea of paying for a cleaner, which is almost as hard as agreeing to what movie to watch on Netflix. All it takes is one person to disagree, and it falls apart. A roommate claiming a cleaner isn't necessary is an idiot. Excuses include:

"We have our own cleaning rota."
"A cleaner is too expensive."
"No one can be home to let them in."

I call hogwash on any reason not to have a cleaner. Rotas fall apart when a roommate claims they're too hungover, busy with work, or have family in town. They "forgot" to clean and will do "double" next time. Hog… Wash.

After living in roomshares in Dublin, Los Angeles, and London over the last two decades, my cardinal rule is to have a cleaner. The only question you should ask yourself is how often they should come around.

#121: Figure out a schedule for the cleaner

Difficult schedules are undeniable. You might have a work commitment, be travelling, or have an appointment for something impossible to rearrange. It happens. But, in a world where working from home is perfectly acceptable (and last I checked, weekends are still a thing), finding a slot for a cleaner is merely a question of priorities. If you can't find the time between yourselves to pick a slot for a cleaner, you have bigger problems.

I don't recommend having your cleaner come in while you're not home. I do know some people who happily leave their cleaner a key. Personally, I am traumatized from my childhood when our cleaner of 15+ years was caught stealing money and cutlery. Ever since, I've always been home for the cleaner. I also agree that, within a roomshare, it shouldn't always fall on the same person to stay home to let them in. These things can be done fairly. Of course, if one of you always works from home on a particular day, it may be "fair" to have the cleaner come around then. As long as it *feels* fair to everyone, this is all that matters.

#122: Don't doubt the need for a cleaner

The trend of having a cleaner is on the rise. Almost half of millennials in the U.S. have one,[2] and, in the UK, under 35s are twice as likely to

---

2. Jordan, Aimee. 2018. "Busy millennials confess: We hired a house cleaner and it's worth it." *The Minnesota Star Tribune.* April 12, 2018. https://www.startribune.com/busy-millennials-confess-we-hired-a-house-cleaner-and-it-s-worth-it/479412903.

hire a cleaner compared to older generations.[3] Despite the trends, there will be naysayers. After a couple of months, someone will pipe up and say, "The cleaner didn't do this." or "They didn't do that." It's true, some cleaners are better than others. In a big city, cleaners come and go like bad relationships. Once you have a good one, cling to them for as long as possible. What the naysayers forget, because they're idiots who focus on the negative, is that having a cleaner avoids conflict. Arguments like, "I took the bins out last time, so it's your turn to clean the toilet!" or "I took the hair out of the shower last week, so it's only fair you clean out the fridge" are avoided. It's emotionally taxing to argue about cleaning and entirely avoidable. Having a cleaner lets you focus on having a great relationship with your roommates. And if things aren't being cleaned or done properly, blame your cleaner instead of each other. Especially when you split the cost per roommate, having a beautifully clean home is the same price as a beer at your local bar.

To keep the peace and free up your time, get a cleaner, even if it's the *only* advice you take from this book. It will save you hours of work and make your home feel clean, a crucial part of feeling happy.

P.S.: I promise I won't cry myself to sleep at having worked over four years to get this book into your hands, and then for you to take away only that one piece of advice to get a cleaner.

---

3. Poulter, Sean. 2016. "Return of the cleaner." *Daily Mail.* March 31, 2016. https://www.dailymail.co.uk/news/article-3516617/One-three-families-pay-cleaner-35s-drive-trend-hiring-domestic-help.html.

28

Bathroom

We've all been there. You come home, desperate for the toilet, and an idiotically oblivious roommate is singing their heart out in the shower. So frustrating. Bathroom etiquette is the source of so much frustration in a roomshare, second only to dishes. Getting it right is crucial to avoid roommates falling out over how long it takes to brush their teeth.

Bathroom Manners

#123: Overcommunicate on bathroom times

When you move into a roomshare, discuss when everyone needs the bathroom in the morning and stick to this schedule like your life depends on it. The problem is when you have to modify this routine…

If you're working from home, then handling when you need the bathroom is an easier task. But, when you're heading into the office, and your commute is time-sensitive, you need the toilet and shower at a specific time, so you must communicate with your roommates in advance if you need the bathroom outside your normal hours. Particularly if there's a crisis in your stomach that will have dire consequences for your dignity, let alone your living space, if you do not go to the bathroom. This will feel like overkill, but the more roommates you live with, the harder it is to manage. Overcommunication is key, so ensure your roommates are fine with you using the bathroom at a different time.

#124: Always flush the toilet

Even if it's the middle of the night (unless you're all eco-warriors who don't flush when you go number one), flush the toilet to get rid of whatever comes out and scrub as necessary. There is *nothing* worse than finding someone else's floating leftovers.

Some worry the noise will wake the other roommates, but this is called "living in a roomshare." Noises in the middle of the night are inevitable. Annoying neighbors, hungry roommates, overfull bladders. It's far better to wake up to a clean toilet than a yellow bowl from a number one, or worse...

If there are recalcitrant roommates who think not flushing the toilet at night to be quieter is fine, have an in-person conversation with them.[1] Talk through their opinion and understand where they're coming from. Channel your best FBI agent alter ego in the negotiation process (à la Chris Voss). They may refuse to budge even when you carefully explain why it's more hygienic to flush and disrespectful to other roommates if you don't. Fingers crossed, they'll see sense after a healthy discussion and agree to flush. If the problem persists and they won't listen, you always have three options: kick them out, move out, or stay the course. I think we all know which one is preferable...

#125: *Be quick and adaptable in the bathroom*

Tick tock, tick tock, tick tock. Bathroom hoggers are the worst and deserve to be hated. Whenever you're in the bathroom, this goes through the minds of your roommates as they wait for you to finish. They have to unload their bladder, brush their teeth, and shower for work, too. Be quick unless you know for sure no one else is around, in which case you can treat yourself to a spa-like routine. With roomsharing comes the inevitable adjustment of your personal routine. It's like herd living. Just because you've always done things a certain way doesn't mean this will work everywhere you go. Adapt or move out. Having to change your normal ways just because you're in a new living situation is part and parcel of sharing a living space. It teaches you to accept and accommodate others' requirements.

That's not to say you should bow down to every single thing your roommates want to do. You'll always need your non-negotiables (such as a face mask, teeth brushing and flossing). Make sure you're aware of your limits so that when they're crossed, you'll know when to have a conversation with your roommates about compatibility and whether you even want to stay in that roomshare. If your roommates can't understand the need for a good skin routine, they're not worth living with anyway.

---

1. Or worse, they refuse to flush after a number two to save the environment the water.

29

Individual Behavior

As you read along, if this chapter starts to feel pointless and obvious, you are part of the minority of people who act right. Because, after decades of roomsharing, I can affirm that most never adhere to the advice laid out in this chapter. This is a worrying statement and a situation I would have never believed until I faced it time and time again in countless roomshares in multiple countries and cultures. I know you should always look out for number one, and I agree this should be the case in your career. At home, though? It's a springboard for disaster.

Personal Decorum

#126: Wash every day

I feel like an annoyingly nagging parent as I write this, but please, please, please wash every day. Whether it's a bath or shower, do it daily. It's mandatory. Skipping the bathroom by opting for a posh wash, dry wash, a sailor's wash, or whatever you call it when you use wipes to "feel clean" is not enough. Trust me. It won't take long before you stink up a room, and everyone calls you the one with terrible body odor behind your back. Ideally, they'll tell you to your face so that you'll do something about it.

There are only two scenarios when wipes are acceptable: festivals and camping. Everyone is in the same boat with little or no access to running hot water, so embrace the stink. But, at home and going into the office? No way.

It's federal law for a property owner to abide by the "implied warranty of liability," which means every tenant (across the U.S.) is legally entitled to a safe and habitable home which includes plumbing and heating.[1] The same is true for most Western countries. For instance, the UK's *Landlord*

---

1. Folger, Jean. 2022. "Guide to Tenant Rights." Investopedia. September 8, 2022. https://www.investopedia.com/guide-to-tenant-rights-5097213.

and Tenant Act requires owners to provide running water and a working boiler.[2] Federal law is in place to make sure you can keep clean. Although there's no law forcing anyone to shower, there's an unwritten social contract that choosing not to makes you a social pariah.

If you haven't yet had a stinky roommate, you're lucky. I've had my share, and it's nauseating (literally). Whether or not you want to discuss the issue with them directly depends on your personality and theirs, as well as how comfortable you are with them. Good luck if you have no qualms discussing it directly and no fear of being punched in the face. They probably don't know they stink and you'd be doing them a favor.

In most cases, the roommate will apologize and shower straight away. They may not like you for a while (the messenger *always* gets shot), but it's better than them stinking everybody out. In the small portion of cases where they deny their stink and claim they shower daily (when they clearly don't and are just in denial), find somewhere else to live. No roomshare is worth staying in if an idiot is going to squabble over keeping themselves clean. Life is far too short to deal with that kind of stubbornness.

#127: Use shower gel (please, for my own peace of mind about your personal hygiene)

Some people are "old school" and love a bar of soap. But, in a roomshare? Gross! You have no idea where that soap has been. If you thought the show *Girls Gone Wild*[3] was dirty, imagine a show called *Soap Gone Wild*. Shower gel is the key. Ideally, you'll want to buy one only you use, and inevitably, a roommate might dip in and out of it if they're running low with their own products (or they just prefer yours). There is the option of bringing your own shower gel back and forth from your bedroom every time you shower. Is that really practical, though? Of course not.

Ideally, you buy your own beautifully smelling luxuriant shower gel, knowing only you are using it daily. After a while, you'll notice you're running low sooner than expected. Your instinct will be 99 percent correct: your shower gel is being used by one or more of your roommates.

Obviously, you can't confront them. You'll face denials and aggression, leaving a sour taste to your roomshare. You have two choices: buy shower gel communally and split the cost, or hoard your own in your bedroom and take it in whenever you shower and bring it back to your room after you finish. That's the simplest way to get around the predicament.

---

2. Alan Boswell Group. 2021. "What Is Section 11 Under the Landlord and Tenant Act 1985?" Alan Boswell Group. April 30, 2021. https://www.alanboswell.com/news/landlord-and-tenant-act-1985.

3. Francis, Joe, creat. 1997. *Girls Gone Wild*. GGW Brands LLC.

29. Individual Behavior

#128: Dealing with the passive-aggressive roommate

> *"You leaving those dishes in the sink, are you?"*
> *"Do you really think it's a good idea to leave your shoes out in the hallway?"*
> *"I barely slept because SOMEONE stumbled in drunk in the middle of the night."*

Recognize any of these? Classic passive-aggressive roommate behavior is the hardest to deal with. It's frustrating and infuriating because it's so hard to uncover at the interview stage. At first, you think they're lovely and friendly, but then the mask comes off, and they're the Devil incarnate.

You can put your tough love hat on and call them out on it, hoping they'll change. They won't. In fact, they'll probably get worse. All you can do is figure out how much you're willing to tolerate, and when it gets to the point where you can't take it any longer, move out.

Moving in with a passive-aggressive roommate is unlucky, but the sooner you realize this, the quicker you can decide whether you want to make it work. The likeliest scenario is that there'll be a better roomshare elsewhere.

#129: Handling the neat-freak roommate

If someone openly tells me they're a neat freak, I will volunteer to live with them immediately. They're exactly who you want in a roomshare. They'll be cleaning, dusting, and tidying everything up! It's fantastic.

You'll still want a cleaner to avoid the arguments we previously discussed, like who last cleaned the toilets, mopped the floors, and so forth. Chances are that the neat-freak roommates will be critical of the cleaner and end up redoing everything anyway. The year I lived with a neat freak, it was the cleanest roomshare I ever had. I never had to worry about dirt around the stove or hair in the shower. Everything was taken care of before I even had time to think about it. Loved it.

Sounds too good to be true? These things always do. It's not all clean floors and a roomshare that smells like roses; the problems arise with the attitude accompanying a neat-freak roommate. It will be rare for them to relax. You'll start worrying about spilling a crumb on the floor if they notice and admonish you for being so careless. You start getting scared if you accidentally molt on the sofa, and they point out you're losing your hair. A neat freak can also obsess over locked doors, lights being turned off, and fluffed cushions.

This harks back to the discussion about mental health in a roomshare. Roommates tolerate mental health problems to the extent that it doesn't affect them, so you'll have to make a judgment call yourself on what you're willing to accept. When living with other people, as long as neatness behavior is contained strictly to cleanliness, I will tolerate everything and anything till the cows come home. I'd prefer to live with someone obsessed with keeping all surfaces clean than a slob who never does the dishes. It's not even the lesser of two evils. One is paradise and the other hell. And you can guess which one is which.

30

Washing Your Dishes

Dishes are like bosses. Everyone has them, and nobody likes them. However, getting this relationship right is one of the keys to roomshare success.

Washing Up Protocol

#130: Deal with dishes fast

The quicker they're dealt with, the better for everyone. If you have a dishwasher, having roommates say things like, "They're not my dishes, so I'm not touching them," is a sign you're living with idiots. What are we? Four years old? Don't get hung up on who loaded and emptied the dishwasher or whose turn it is. You have a dishwasher. This is equivalent to having running water when you live in the Sahara.

Assuming you also have pots and pans which are too big to fit in the dishwasher, don't make your life harder than it needs to be. Soak and clean everything as soon as you finish cooking (even before you start eating)—no matter the size of the dish and no matter what you cooked. From sauces to rice to eggs, when you soak them in soapy water long enough, it's a piece of cake to clean everything off. The worst thing you can do is let the dirty dishes dry, and then you have to scrape and scrape and scrape. It will take three times as long and three times the effort. Avoid all this by soaking your dishes in soapy water.

#131: Never leave your dirty dishes overnight

If, like me, you want to digest your food and relax before washing the dishes, then you can get a head-start on cleaning up while the food is cooking (e.g., when you need to leave a dish in the oven for an extended period of time). Another option is to tag team with your roommates. When you're cooking for someone else, get them to clean while you're cooking. It will go a lot faster that way.

If it's just you cooking and you're the only one eating, there will often be a mountain of dishes in the sink waiting to be cleaned after you finish. It's tempting to leave them while you digest and watch some television. But suddenly it's 10:30 p.m. and perhaps you can just do them tomorrow? There's nothing worse than waking up to dirty dishes. Actually, there is. It's waking up and cleaning someone else's dirty dishes just so you can have breakfast. Out of respect for your roommates, wash everything before you fall asleep. As Benjamin Franklin might say, "It takes many good deeds to build a good reputation, and only one dirty dish to lose it."[1]

#132: In a small roomshare wash all dishes. In a large one wash only yours

If you only have one roommate, don't get hung up about not cleaning their dishes. It's obvious whose dishes are dirty, and not cleaning your roommate's dishes could actually be seen as passive-aggressive. When it's just the two of you, washing each other's dishes is a basic courtesy.

It becomes a problem when your roommate never, ever washes the dishes and expects you to do them. If this happens, have a chat. Find out what's going on. Are they allergic to washing up liquid? Are they suffering from an eye condition that makes them blind to dirty dishes? Get their side of the story first. It's the adult thing to do. Counter-intuitively, the "washing all dishes" rule doesn't apply in large roomshares (three or more people). You do not want to be known as the chump who cleans everyone else's dishes.

The larger the roomshare, the harder it is to figure out who's making a mess and leaving dirty dishes. If every roommate denies leaving that particularly filthy and smelly plate in the sink for the last three days, you know you're living with a liar (and a lazy and dirty one at that). You might one day feel benevolent and just clean everything. You'll feel better in the short term. Will you get any gratitude from anyone else? Unlikely. The person supposedly allergic to cleaning dishes won't want to own up to the fact they let you clean their dishes while they stood idly by and watched TV instead (or whatever else they preferred doing while avoiding their chores). And by cleaning their stuff, you're setting a false expectation that you'll happily do it again. Let's face it: you have better things to do than

---

1. The original expression is "It takes many good deeds to build a good reputation, and only one bad one to lose it." Eccles, Robert G., Newquist, Scott C., and Schatz, Roland. 2007. "Reputation and Its Risks." *Harvard Business Review*. February 2007. https://hbr.org/2007/02/reputation-and-its-risks.

clean up after your roommates. Picking your nose, staring into space, pondering the existence of aliens. Even thinking about your ex. Literally anything and everything is better than cleaning up after your roommates.

#133: When dishes are a real problem, put yourself first

If keeping dishes clean is a problem, start the conversation. Make it open and friendly so your roommates don't feel ambushed. Perhaps over a dinner you're preparing for them? Whatever you do, never accuse anyone of being a cleaning slacker. This will descend into chaos and arguments à la *Real Housewives of Salt Lake City*.[2] The roommates will deny and deny, and you'll come across as the douche. If it's reached the point where you feel you have no choice but to keep your own dishes in your room to ensure you do have clean dishes when you want to cook, you know you must move out. Keeping your clean dishes in your room is ludicrous, yet very real. If your roommates consistently use others' dishes and refuse to wash up even after being confronted about the problem, you're left with no choice. When living with people like that, you're in an unwinnable situation. Unless you like doing all the dishes… Do you? Then this is paradise. Also I have plenty of dishes myself that need some TLC. Get in touch if you want to clean them.

---

2. Dunlop, Scott, creat. 2020. *The Real Housewives of Salt Lake City*. Bravo.

31

Drying Your Clothes

Ideally, you have access to a dryer, but realistically, you're more likely to dry your clothes on a folding frame in your roomshare. Even if you do have a dryer, you likely won't want to use it for delicates such as silks, shirts, and dresses. Don't rely on there being a folding frame in the roomshare or being able to borrow one from a roommate. This is like praying for Jesus to turn your water into wine because you can't be bothered to go to the store and buy your own. Besides, using someone else's folding frame is gross and unreliable. Plain and simple. When was the last time it was given a wipe-down? What if it's being used? Waiting for someone to clear the folding frame before you can hang your own clothes is a pain. They're not expensive. Just pop on Amazon and get one delivered.

The Art of Drying Your Attire

#134: Allocate an area of the roomshare to dry your clothes

If your room is big enough and you're working in an external office, then drying your clothes in your room (ensuring the bedroom window is open during the day to air the clothes out) works well. Your clothes will dry nicely in time for your return. In the likelier scenario that your room is too small or you're on the ground floor and can't leave the window open, you'll have to dry them in a communal area. The question is… Where?

Discuss with your roommates where drying your clothes would be best to minimize disruption. They may already have a system. Supposing they don't, find a convenient area near a radiator or window (ideally both). Tip: invest in a dehumidifier to control moisture levels and prevent mold.

In one apartment I shared with four people, I had to dry clothes in a little alcove along the hallway. This was so impractical that I ended up drying my clothes in my room, even though it was too small.

31. Drying Your Clothes

The reality is that, in a roomshare, there won't be anywhere particularly great to dry your clothes. Just figure out what works best for everyone and take it from there. You'll wash your clothes and sheets weekly, as will everybody else. So, depending on the size of the roomshare, it's likely that drying clothes will be a permanent eyesore. It's annoyingly inevitable. Unless you all go to the laundromat every week (which is what most people do in New York City), for as long as you're living in a roomshare, clothes will be drying around you. Just be grateful everyone *is* regularly washing.

If you have a solution to not have clothes drying out all the time, I'm all ears. We can patent the idea and sell it. We'll make a fortune.

Part G

Romance Kills the Roomshare

"Happiness is having the apartment to yourself for a night."
—Anonymous

The Multiverse of Roomshare Romances

As a kid, the first thing your parents teach you is, "Never talk to strangers." If a stranger offers you a ride in their car, call the police. If a stranger offers you a piece of gum, call the police. If a stranger told you, "Hey, when you grow up, you're going to spend half your salary on a place that isn't yours to live with strangers like me," you'd think they were out their mind and you'd call the police. As soon as you turn 18, everything changes.

You go to a stranger's home, meet them for ten minutes, and agree to live there permanently. That's not even questioned. In fact, you're paying, on average, a great deal of your income for the privilege, and there are more renters in the U.S. than there have been in over 60 years.[1] This is the reality of the typical, modern professional. Move to a big city. Find a home. Share with randoms. Date randoms. Trust they don't rob, maim, or kill you. When you put it like this, it's absolutely insane. Yet, not only is it the norm, but also it's expected. So, when getting ready to live with people you don't know, the best thing you can do is find a neighborhood you like, a home with a living room, and a bedroom you're happy with, living alongside people who seem normal. Then, just hope for the best.

To prepare you, this section is about the different scenarios you might find yourself in when you've found love (or lust). This section could be a

---

1. Summerville, Abigail. 2017. "There are more renters than any time since 1965." CNBC. July 20, 2017. https://www.cnbc.com/2017/07/20/there-are-more-renters-than-any-time-since-1965.html.

whole book in itself—a multiverse as depicted by Marvel if you will. This is because there is a multiverse of living situations with millions upon millions of possibilities for romance. To avoid this book being as lengthy as an encyclopedia, only the "headline" romances will be addressed, as they cover the majority of scenarios you might find yourself in.

As you read through, the overarching lesson to remember as you navigate your roomshare romances is that nothing is permanent. Romance in a roomshare is a journey. There are twists, turns, dead ends, and everything in between. It's like walking through the Amazonian jungle. There will be pitfalls, surprises, and some nasty moments, and this is your guide to navigating that journey so you can be better prepared for whatever is thrown at you. And trust me, you'll have a lot thrown at you…

32

Dating in a Roomshare

Romance and roomshares aren't great bedfellows (pun intended). You can't help who you fall in love with, so if it's one of your roommates, it can be a beautiful experience. As soon as you develop a relationship, this usually means the end of your roomsharing journey in the traditional sense. Most of the time, dating your roommate ends in disaster, leading to only one scenario: moving out.[1] It's likely you (or both of you) will move out when it goes awry. Once you've dated and broken up, staying under the same roof is too awkward. Of course, if you're part of the 1 percent where dating your roommate works out... Score! Even better, one of you can move into the other's bedroom and pay half the rent you were paying prior. Double score!

Assuming the relationship works, you will leave the roomshare (eventually). You'll want a place of your own for privacy. Whether this is good or bad, only time will tell... After all, half of all marriages do survive intact.

So, You're Falling in Love

#135: Prepare for your roommates to meet your dates and vice-versa

You've moved in, and there's no romantic spark with any roommates. Great, at least you know romance with a roommate won't be the reason for a premature departure. Assuming you're single, you'll be out there socially trying to meet "the one" (or the "one for the night," depending on your preference). Your date will eventually come over. Which means they will meet your roommates. If you're planning an

---

1. No one has yet conducted actual research on how many roommates get together and then break up. But I'm 99 percent sure this is accurate.

actual evening at home, speak to your roommates beforehand so they know what to expect and act accordingly. The last thing you want is your date to stumble on one of your roommates cooking dinner in their shark onesie. They'll likely be as embarrassed as each other. Or they might not be. Everyone's different, right?

Is your date joining you back home unexpectedly? Assuming you followed all the advice regarding cleanliness, at least you'll already be "date-ready." The only thing you can do is make your date aware you live in a roomshare so they're prepared. Beyond this, there's not much else except wishing you luck. How your date behaves will tell you a lot more about a potential future together, and nothing I can write will help you prepare for that.

Of course, it won't just be you inviting dates around. Your roommates will, too. Whether they're long-term partners or one-night stands, this is a reality of living in a roomshare. In an ideal scenario, you'll know ahead of time that your roommate is bringing someone around. But in most cases, you won't. After all, your roommate doesn't need your permission. It's their home as much as yours. The likeliest scenario is you'll have no idea someone is coming around. You don't need to sequester yourself in your room, but... Do you really have to watch the TV in the living room?

Roomsharing is give and take, so if your roommate doesn't get lucky often, it's only kind to give them privacy when appropriate. Don't avoid the toilet if you need to go. And don't cancel your takeaway just because you're worried about the interruption. It's still your home, too! Just give them privacy where you can. It's a nice and kind thing to do. The cringe first encounter with their date is always going to be like that: awkward. And it's okay! If your roommate is with them and you're introduced, just nod and say, "Hello, nice to meet you." Don't:

- Make corny jokes
- Speak ill (no matter how lightheartedly) of your roommate
- Reference your roommate's past partners

Love and connection are hard to find, so giving your roommate the best possible chance at success is the right thing to do. Yes, I believe in love and know how hard it is to find. Everyone deserves a chance at love. As their roommate, you'll have a tiny part to play in whether or not that love will blossom. Unless you hate your roommate. In which case... Have as much as fun as you're willing to have. And send me the stories. Would love to read them.

32. Dating in a Roomshare

*#136: Expect a roommate's partner
to become an unofficial roommate*

As Beyoncé would say, love "Got me looking so crazy right now."[2] It's true. Love will make you do things you never thought you would ever do. If one of these things is staying with each other all the time, it only becomes a problem when a couple outgrows a roomshare without realizing it. I'm all for love, but a roomshare is an agreement between a set number of people, so when someone else is thrown into the mix without a formal arrangement, tension will bubble, and World War Three will be around the corner.

If love is in the air, the couple is probably inseparable. Their partner comes to yours five to seven nights a week, returning to their place just to change. Having another human being present hikes up the utility bills, and you're now subsidizing the cost.

The only way to move forward is by having an open conversation with your roommates about costs and etiquette. You might be surprised at how easily a solution can be found. Or not… Either way, talking about it is the first step. Of course, if roommates don't want a partner moving in, but someone is in love (could be you or your roommate), the happy couple needs to realize that the partnership has outgrown the roomshare. It's time to find a private place for the relationship to flourish. Self-awareness is key and requires maturity from all parties involved. It's just what happens when love is added to the mix. The best you can do is wish them the best "'Cause, baby, you got me."[3]

---

2. Knowles, Beyoncé, Harrison, Rich, Record, Eugene, and Carter, Shawn. 2003. *Crazy in Love*. Columbia Records.
3. Knowles, Beyoncé, Harrison, Rich, Record, Eugene, and Carter, Shawn. 2003. *Crazy in Love*. Columbia Records.

33

Living as a Couple in a Roomshare

In this scenario, you and your partner have found an ideal two-bedroom apartment with a balcony, two bathrooms, and a big living room. The kitchen is to die for with wide surfaces perfect for cookie-baking and delicious Sunday roasts. Ideally, you'd take the whole place and use the second bedroom as office space with a guest bed.

The problem: it's out of your budget. The solution: getting a roommate.

On the surface, this is a brilliant idea. It saves rent and bills. How often is that roommate *actually* going to hang out in the living room? You'll be able to cuddle up alone on the sofa while they're out working or living their single life. Well... Yes and no. A couple must be picky about their roommate because this situation has pros and cons. If you pick the wrong roommate, the roomshare will descend into anarchy and may ruin your relationship. In the unfortunate scenario where you picked the wrong roommate and are desperate to get rid of them but they've signed a contract, get ready to do the opposite of everything described in this chapter that fosters a healthy group dynamic. Hog the television, monopolize the kitchen, and create your starring role in the Gordon Ramsay–produced spin-off show *Hell's Couples*.[1] Eventually, the roommate will move out.

Navigating the Roomshare as a Couple

#137: A couple should live with someone sociable and older

The worst thing you can do, as a couple, is find a roommate who's only interested in staying at home, having glasses of wine on the sofa, while

---

1. I actually think this could be a great TV show. Gordon, if you're reading this, get in touch and let's chat.

watching reality television all night long. They will be at home often, and you'll have to forego any alone time as a couple.

In the interview, you'll want to know their roomsharing history, including whether they've lived with couples. Your ideal roommate is someone a bit older who has lived in a few roomshares and is sociable. That will immediately solve two issues:

1. They'll have an established circle of friends and be out regularly, giving you a higher chance of being alone.
2. Being older, they hopefully won't feel the need to get drunk and invite randoms back for afterparties.

Human beings are, by nature, unpredictable. Even if the roommate says all the right things, you never know what they'll do once they start living with you. So tread carefully, screen thoroughly, and hope against hope that your choice of roommate will give you the breathing room to be a happy couple.

#138: Expect there to be romance in the roomshare (hopefully not too much)

As an established couple, you might feel uncomfortable at the idea of another couple spending the night in your home. Whether your roommate has a partner or not, expect overnight guests. How many and how frequently is only possible to know once you start living together. It's not like you can ask them in the interview unless you want to deter them from moving in entirely. You can't stop your roommate from looking for love. Be prepared for randoms staying over and using your bathroom.[2] In parallel, you'll want to make your roommate feel comfortable, so avoid snuggling and overt displays of affection. No one likes being around a couple always holding hands, hugging, kissing, and whispering sweet nothings. You may be so in love that you can't help it, but it makes everyone around you feel awkward. Similarly, your roommate might have a date round, and they want to watch TV and snuggle up. Depending on the situation, it might be more appropriate for yourself and your partner to make yourselves scarce for the evening (either head out or stay in your room and put some earplugs in).

#139: Couples have one combined vote on matters

Everyone in a roomshare should agree on how to make decisions together. Democratically, it makes sense for everyone to have a vote,

---

2. Stock up on antiseptic wipes for the toilet seat...

including both halves of a couple. However, this isn't actually fair as the couple will always vote the same way (assuming a couple will always agree with each other). If everyone has an individual vote, a couple in a two-bedroom roomshare will always outvote the single roommate. Don't make the roommate feel like a third-wheel regarding roomshare-voting. This is the only time I can confidently write that one vote per person, as lauded by democracies around the world, is not the best solution for a roomshare. The better solution is one vote per bedroom.

The perfect roommate is hard to find, so when you have found a good one, it's essential to make them feel like equal partners and include them in all joint decisions. I like to call this version of democracy a "roomocracy"—particularly stupid, I know...

34

A Single Person Living with a Couple

You find the perfect two-bedroom apartment with a great living room and a wonderful terrace. There's even a regular cleaner. But you can only live there if all the costs are split three ways with a couple living in the other bedroom. According to Diggz, 77 percent of people looking to share are single, indicating that, although couples sharing is a minority, it's still something to be ready for in 23 percent of cases.[1] Living with a couple can be great.... Unless they're both idiots. Actually, it only takes one of them to be an idiot.

How to Live with a Couple

#140: Agree how to split rent and bills before moving in

Like any roomshare situation, ensure the rent and bills are divided fairly before signing on the dotted line. This is why you need to make sure that you agree on how much rent to pay per room.

Part of the reason a couple moves in is because rent is cheaper. The couple obviously wins when you split the rent by bedroom. On the surface, it might feel unfair, but it is the fairest way. The key difference, of course, are the bills. They must absolutely be split by the number of people living in that one roomshare. If there are two bedrooms (one couple is in one and the single person is in the other), the rent should be divided in two, and the amount each bedroom pays will depend on the size and amenities in that bedroom. With three people living in that roomshare, they should each be paying a third of every communal bill. Split any other way, someone is getting ripped off, and it's probably not the couple...

---

1. Diggz. 2023. "16 Questions to Ask Potential Roommates—Your Complete Roommate Questionnaire." Diggz Blog. March 30, 2023. https://blog.diggz.co/16-questions-to-ask-potential-roommates-your-complete-roommate-questionnaire-a858823ce75d.

#141: It might always feel like their place, and they'll likely want a quieter home

One thing to expect is that the house party days of yore will be far and few. Unless the couple you move in with are party animals (there are always exceptions to the rule), most usually settle and relax once they're home. All-night raves tend to be for singletons. Living with a couple is suitable for someone who's previously lived in a few roomshares and knows they prefer a quieter, nicer, and cleaner environment. On the flip side, it is perfect for a shy first-timer looking for a comfortable home.

Part of the reason to expect a quieter home is because moving in with a couple can feel like you're living in "their home" where you're renting the "spare room." It can also feel like the couple has more control in running the home. It's a topic the psychologist Bella DePaulo touches upon when she writes that a couple tends to "unconsciously believe that when they are dealing with a single person, their wishes and point of view should prevail."[2]

This power dynamic is a common thread in the research conducted by experts worldwide. Prof. Tuffin found that couples create a "power block," whereby "whatever they want, ends up ruling the day."[3] Dr. Maalsen goes as far as to recommend: "Never move in with a couple."[4] The dynamic of living with a couple is difficult to maneuver as, by default, you'll always be the third wheel. There's a possibility that the couple will go out of their way to make you feel included in decisions concerning the roomshare but, inevitably, they are the couple, and you're the "third tenant." This living situation is hard to change because the couple always looks out for each other. As long as you're prepared for this and the two roommates in the couple are kind enough to treat you as an equal, living with them has all the previously outlined financial and peripheral advantages.

#142: Living with a couple will end sooner than you expect

Living with a couple when it's going smoothly feels like a fairytale. Like all fairytales, they always come to an end. With a couple, this will come sooner than you think.

One of the following three things will occur 99 percent of the time:

1. They break up

    One of them moves out, and you're left with one half of the

---

2. Ross, Annabel. 2020. "'I'm so starved for human touch': A hell of its own for single people living with couples." *The Guardian*. April 21, 2020. https://www.theguardian.com/lifeandstyle/2020/apr/21/single-people-living-with-couples-coronavirus-lockdown.
3. Tuffin, Keith. 2021. Phone interview. January 19, 2021.
4. Maalsen, Sophia. 2020. Phone interview. December 22, 2020.

partnership. Sod's Law dictates you're left with the one you like the least. When this happens, there are four sub-scenarios:

    1A: You adapt—nothing changes, and you keep living with one roommate instead of a couple.
    1B: You move out—the bills are higher, and you can no longer afford to stay.
    1C: You find a replacement—the partner can't afford to pay their share of the rent and has to move.
    1D: You all move out—the lease depends on their names, so now you all need to find new places to live.

2. They get engaged

For the couple, this is the best news they could ask for. At first, they may tell you nothing will change and that they won't get married for years. The problem is, do you want to be living with a couple planning their nuptials? If you're single, they're throwing happiness in your face, and if you're in a relationship, they'll be pressurizing you with questions like, "When are you getting married, then?"

The options at your disposal here:

    2A: You replace them
    2B: You move out
    2C: Stay until you can no longer cope

    Either way, an engaged couple will eventually want their own space to grow in their relationship. They might be budget-conscious and keen to stay living with you while they save money for the wedding. When they finally hit their savings target, they will move out.

3. They start a family

Whether they're engaged or not, a couple will think about starting a family (assuming this is what they eventually want as almost half of U.S. households have children under 18).[5] And, once they do, either they find somewhere more suitable to live or you move out so they can take over the entire property to make space for their burgeoning family.

Whatever situation you end up facing, the one certainty about living with a couple is that your fairytale roomshare will end in the not-too-distant future.

---

5. Korhonen, Veera. 2024. "Share of family households with own children under 18 years in the United States from 1970 to 2022, by type of family." Statista. July 5, 2024. https://www.statista.com/statistics/242074/percentages-of-us-family-households-with-children-by-type.

Part G—Romance Kills the Roomshare

#143: *If the couple moves out, you can take over the tenancy*

Unless this is something you definitely don't want, one advantage of a couple moving out is that it allows you to become the "lead" tenant in the property. You can pick your next roommate, decide how much they'll pay, and dictate the rules of the roomshare. Not everyone is interested in doing this or wants the responsibility, but deciding who lives with you puts you in an advantageous position of picking someone compatible for a healthy group dynamic.

Living with a couple is like card-counting at Blackjack in Vegas if you know how to play the game. Get the math right with a side dish of luck, and you'll be winning. I've lived with great couples in the past. When the group dynamic works, it's a brilliant solution. You'll always get a bigger and nicer home than if you lived with just one other person, and you'll be able to save more money. Besides, if the couple is sociable, you'll get to meet their friends and grow your own network. And who knows... They might even introduce you to the love of *your* life.

35

Living with a Partner

This chapter is for a couple living in their own home without roommates. I'm fully aware I'm breaking my own rule here, as exclusively living with a partner doesn't qualify as a "roomshare." It's important to include this because individuals regularly change from living in a roomshare to living as a couple, then break up and return to roomsharing. No official government organization keeps track of this, but it happens regularly. Do you think I would leave anyone behind after an entire book on roomsharing grace and decorum? To all couples out there, I got you. Besides, living with a partner is like a tiny roomshare. The difference is you have one roommate and are in love (in theory).

The Art of Living with a Partner

#144: If you have the luxury of time before moving in together, take it

Suppose you're in a position where you can take your time moving in together, you'll want to maximize that to your advantage. The last thing you want to do is rush because your leases are running out and, financially, it makes sense to be speedy. Moving in together is a big step. It should happen organically. It's like getting married. Just because you said yes doesn't mean you have to drop into the registry office on the way back from the engagement. You want to plan. You want to prepare. You want to set a date. You want to look forward to your wedding.

As you excitedly move in, there will be niggles and disagreements. You can't expect everything to go smoothly. You'll discover things you didn't know (and might not want to know). Living together is like going from care-free college to responsible adulthood. Things really get real. Rent, utilities, and storage space—all the boring, practical, but real details of living together should be discussed before committing. It's like two companies merging and needing to make redundancies. Assuming you each have your own television, do you get rid of your 50-inch television because your partner has a 65-inch? Or is there room to keep both? What about the bed? Do you buy afresh or use one you already own? And then what if it all falls apart and you realize you're not meant to be?

When I was 28, my father gave me a good piece of advice: "When signing a contract, agree on the exit strategy so that you've already agreed on what will happen if it all goes wrong." In this case, he was concerned about a joint mortgage I signed with my partner. We were in love. We planned on being together forever. My dad's advice almost broke us up as my partner couldn't believe I would even contemplate a scenario where we'd break up. We stayed strong, signed the mortgage and moved in together. We broke up four months later. Luckily, I had listened to my father and had the exit strategy in place.

You don't want to envisage it, but most couples break up. According to relationship expert Hellen Chen, the ratio is as high as 85 percent.[1] You don't want to end up financially worse off because you didn't plan. I have seen friends stuck in long-term leases they couldn't afford when their partners moved out and stopped paying rent. When you don't plan, you'll pay the price when things fall apart. And that's true for anything in life, not just a roomshare with a partner.

#145: *Living together will make or break your relationship*

In the olden days, getting married was a precursor to living together. In the 1950s, only 0.7 percent of couples lived together before getting married. Nowadays, living together is the precursor to marriage, with over 70 percent of couples doing so before tying the knot.[2] Financially, it's the smart thing to do. Ending a lease is a hell of a lot cheaper than hiring divorce lawyers and arguing for months (if not years) over who gets to keep the 65-inch television. That's because living together is the quickest way to find out if you're really life partners at all. You get a real-time glimpse into life together, warts and all. Gone are the arranged dates dancing around each other's social schedules, gym workouts, and professional

---

1. Media Relations. 2013. "Over 85% of Dating Ends Up in Breakups—Upcoming New Book on Relationships Sheds Light." PR Web. October 29, 2013. https://www.prweb.com/releases/over_85_of_dating_ends_up_in_breakups_upcoming_new_book_on_relationships_sheds_light/prweb11278931.htm.

2. Kuperberg, Arielle. 2018. "Premarital Cohabitation and Direct Marriage in the United States: 1956–2015." Taylor & Francis Online. October 8, 2018. https://www.tandfonline.com/doi/10.1080/01494929.2018.1518820.

commitments. "I'll see you at home!" is what you can now tell each other as you walk out the door every morning.

If living together makes you happier than before, you've struck gold and should hold onto this person for as long as possible. When you're part of the 15 percent of couples who stay the course and live happily ever after, that's the dream relationship everyone is looking for.

36

Living with Your Ex

This happens more often than people realize. You're broken up, but neither can afford to leave the home you're both paying for. A typical scenario is that you are both co-signers and can't afford to pay rent elsewhere, or your ex doesn't want to let go of the property. Ouch.

So, you can't break the lease for another six months unless you pay out the contract, and you're faced with the prospect of paying for two homes simultaneously. Even if you could afford it, the drain on your personal finances is a complete waste of money.[1] You're likely living in a one-bedroom apartment, so you can't move into a different bedroom. Subletting the entire place isn't an option, as your lease won't let you. If you risked it anyway and were found out, it would be an automatic breach of contract, and you could be out on the street while still being liable to pay the remainder of the lease. You're in a doomsday scenario. Stay with friends and family as much as you can or go away a lot. If you travel for work, count your lucky stars. If, every time you see your ex, you'd rather stick pins in your eyes, best to get away as much as you can.

Wait it out, and eventually, your lease will end, and you'll be free again. Until then those remaining months sharing that home will be torture. There's no hiding from that. Just know that there is an end in sight. In this case, hope is very real. Hold onto it.

#146: Don't rush a sale for emotional reasons

Co-owning a home with your ex is like having nits. You hate them. They're hard to get rid of. And you're prepared to pay any price to do so. Being desperate to sell means you could end up selling at a loss. The key here is patience. If you rush a sale for emotional reasons, it will be like you're punching yourself in the face and cutting off your nose. With extra

---

1. Unless you're in the top 1 percent of the world's richest, of course. In that case, this would all just be a minor inconvenience.

36. Living with Your Ex

spite sprinkled on top. The last thing you want is to have a broken bank account on top of a broken heart. Stay smart. Think of the end goal. Get a good lawyer. You'll want to, at least, salvage some financial recompense with profit from the property sale.

All good things come to an end, and conversely, all bad things come to an end, too. The best plan you can work on is figuring out your next move so you have the end in sight. Make a plan for when you can finally stop living together. Whether in three, six, or 12 months, decide on a date to work towards so that you know, physically and mentally, when you'll be able to get yourself out of the situation. Perhaps you're secretly hoping that with time you'll reconcile, get back together, and live happily ever after on the second try? There's always hope. However, after his latest break-up, an old monogamist playboy friend once said, "Exes are like tax returns. Once they're filed, you never want to look at them again."

Part H

The End of the Roomshare

"I like my roommates. I just like my next roommates even more."

—Anonymous

When One Roomshare Ends, Another (Better) Roomshare Will Start

All roomshares, no matter how great they are, will come to a natural finish. It's just a matter of time. Either someone moves out, or you all have to leave, and before you know it, you're living with completely different people than you were 12 months prior. How you deal with the change determines how you find and move into your (hopefully better) next roomshare.

This section of the book is about dealing with scenarios where you're no longer in a roomshare, which was out of your control. My hope is that you'll come away with the knowledge and skills to handle the inevitable. Remember, it's not you. It's them.

37

Accidentally Living Alone

Living alone is like Marmite. You either love it or hate it. Many end up living alone for a while, whatever the reason. It can happen when your partner or roommate moves out, and you're picking up the pieces. And when living alone is something you hate as much as Marmite, remember to keep your eyes on the prize and find a roommate.

Whether it's to fill the spare bedroom or to move into a proper roomshare, at least prepare yourself for the future. However, you should never rush into anything that feels uncomfortable. When it comes to shared living, it's better to be slow and steady to make the right move, than fast and nimble just to get it done, which sounds like a terrible innuendo.

When It Comes to Living by Yourself

#147: It's normal to not want to live alone, and normal to want to live alone

As Sam Gosling explains, "Some people can't stand to be alone, and the difference is extroversion."[1] Extroverted people love being around others because they thrive on social connections. When extroverts find themselves alone, they flounder. On the other hand, as Peter van der Bel explains, introverts usually love being alone because "introverted people are already fulfilled being among themselves."[2] He goes on to elaborate: "There is a difference between being alone and being lonely. When you're lonely, you're in the wrong company. But you're in a situation that fits if you are enjoying it."[3]

I wish I could be happy living alone, but it has always been and always will be a nightmare for me. I'm not the only one to think this. A study in

---
1. Gosling, Sam. 2021. Phone interview. February 23, 2021.
2. van der Bel, Peter. 2021. Phone interview. February 25, 2021.
3. van der Bel, Peter. 2021. Phone interview. February 25, 2021.

Psychology Today found that those who lived alone had a 42 percent higher risk of depression and premature death, as well as increased pain sensitivity.[4] Although the study doesn't mention a difference between introverts and extroverts, it found that people living alone are prone to overspending, materialism, and increased activity on social media out of a "fear of missing out."[5]

So, you see? Living with people is scientifically proven to be healthier. Living alone is like eating junk food. The first bite of a burger, fries, and ice cream is delicious. The feeling lasts about 20 minutes, and then you're crashing, feeling fat and bloated.

If you've lived in roomshares and hated them, this is perfectly normal too. In fact, the trend of living alone is on the up, with the number of single-person households in the U.S. rising from 7.7 percent in 1940 to 27.6 percent in 2020.[6] The stats don't prove that more and more people *want* to live alone. Only that more people *are* living alone. One of the biggest factors for single-adult households is the increasingly high divorce rate.

Even when you're in love and living happily ever after, the risk of a spouse dying and leaving you alone increases as you get older. An 80-year-old is ten times likelier to die than a 60-year-old.[7] Some people love being home alone because they can do whatever they want and watch whatever they please. I'm like a needy dog who gets excited seeing a familiar face and thrives on having company. If you're like a cat and are happy being alone for days, all the more power to you.

#148: Being nice to neighbors can minimize loneliness (or borrow a dog)

Almost 28 percent of Americans don't even know their neighbors' names.[8] This is positively neighborly compared to the UK, where 73

---

4. Emamzadeh, Arash. 2022. "How Living Alone Increases the Risk of Depression." *Psychology Today*. November 27, 2022. https://www.psychologytoday.com/gb/blog/finding-new-home/202211/how-living-alone-increases-the-risk-depression.
5. Emamzadeh, Arash. 2022. "How Living Alone Increases the Risk of Depression." *Psychology Today*. November 27, 2022. https://www.psychologytoday.com/gb/blog/finding-new-home/202211/how-living-alone-increases-the-risk-depression.
6. Anderson, Lydia, Washington, Chanell, Kreider, Rose M., and Gryn, Thomas. 2023. "Home Alone: More Than a Quarter of All Households Have One Person." United States Census Bureau. June 8, 2023. https://www.census.gov/library/stories/2023/06/more-than-a-quarter-all-households-have-one-person.html.
7. Dattani, Saloni. 2023. "How does the risk of death change as we age—and how has this changed over time?" Our World in Data. November 7, 2023. https://ourworldindata.org/how-do-the-risks-of-death-change-as-people-age.
8. Fitzgerald, Ryan. 2022. "Benefits of Being Friends with Your Neighbors." uphomes. July 25, 2022. https://uphomes.com/blog/benefits-of-being-friends-with-your-neighbors.

percent of British people have no idea what their neighbors are called.[9] Where you live affects how you interact with your neighbors. In rural areas, 40 percent of residents claim to know all or most of their neighbors, but this falls to 28 percent for those in the suburbs and even lower for urban residents at 24 percent.[10] Whether you're living alone or not, you'll still need a support system, including your neighbors. From the heating malfunctioning to borrowing a bottle opener, your neighbors are the first port of call when something goes wrong (that doesn't warrant the police), particularly if you're alone.

This is why being nice to your neighbors pays dividends, especially in city apartment buildings, which can be unfriendly, from smiling in the corridors to holding doors open for others to making small talk when you collect your post. You'll develop these neighborly connections if you're genuinely kind and friendly. You'll start seeing faces you recognize. You don't want to be the overenthusiastic, pushy neighbor, but over time, you'll get to know other tenants and exchange tips or advice regarding the building. Introducing yourself to neighbors will provide useful information, especially when living somewhere new. Most importantly, you might even start to make some new friends. According to a study by LendingTree, 74 percent of Americans say they're friends with at least one of their neighbors.[11] I just hope your neighbors aren't a pastiche of the actual movie *Neighbors* starring Seth Rogen and Dave Franco (although they did seem to have a lot of fun…).[12]

Alternatively, walking a dog is a shortcut to meeting fellow dog lovers in your neighborhood. Buying one because you hadn't planned on living alone and want some company will feel like a knee-jerk reaction to what is (usually) a short-term situation, which is why it's not always necessary. You can just borrow a dog. A website like TrustedHouseSitters.com (a dedicated pet-sitting search function) connects you to dog owners needing sitters. This is a great way to connect with others. Some say it's even better than Tinder…

---

9. Elsworthy, Emma. 2018. "More than half of Britons describe their neighbours as 'strangers.'" *The Independent*. May 29, 2018. https://www.independent.co.uk/news/uk/home-news/britons-neighbours-strangers-uk-community-a8373761.html.

10. Davis, L., and Parker, K. 2019. "A half-century after 'Mister Rogers' debut, 5 facts about neighbors in the U.S." Pew Research Center. August 15, 2019. https://www.pewresearch.org/fact-tank/2019/08/15/facts-about-neighbors-in-u-s.

11. Ceizyk, Denny. 2022. "Nearly 75% of Americans Dislike a Neighbor—Most Common Among Gen Zers, Apartment Dwellers and Northeasterners." LendingTree. April 26, 2022. https://www.lendingtree.com/home/mortgage/neighbors-survey.

12. Stoller, Nicholas, dir. 2014. *Neighbors*. Universal Pictures.

38

When the Landlord Asks You All to Leave

You've been living in the perfect home. It is clean, is spacious, and has great roommates. You even have a 70-inch (70 inches!!!) smart television in the living room packed with apps and streaming services (including Apple TV!!!). It's great. Life is sweet, and nothing can ruin it. Until you get an email from the agent, which usually goes like this…

"*Dear Tenant,*
The owner of [insert address] is putting the property on the market and is giving you two months to vacate the premises."

Or…

"*Dear Tenant,*
The owner of [insert address] is increasing the rent by $750 a month per person and giving you one month to agree, or you'll be issued an eviction notice."

I've also had…

"*Dear Tenant,*
The owner of [insert address] will refurbish the property and is giving you two months to vacate the premises."

Goodbye, favorite roommates. Goodbye, beautiful television. Goodbye, comfy sofa watching Apple TV. The curtains are closing, and it's time to find somewhere new. And this is okay! Regularly moving is inevitable when renting. This is true whether you're renting a whole house or a room in a six-bedroom, one-bathroom apartment in the city. According to BMG, a quarter of private tenants are evicted through no fault of their own.[1] This means that, out of four of your friends living in roomshares, at least one will be forced to move, and it won't be their choice.

---

1. Harris, Lauren. 2016. "Generation Rent/BMG poll: One in four tenants have, at some point, been evicted from their home by their landlord." BMG Research. January 28, 2016. https://www.bmgresearch.co.uk/generation-rent.

Part H—The End of the Roomshare

When it happens to you, remember that a perfect roomshare is down to the group dynamic. Assuming you're happy as a group, talk to your roommates about moving together. You should live with and cherish that group for as long as you can. It's cheesy but living with the right people is more important than a 70-inch television with Apple TV. Although, if I had to suffer a few idiots to live in a five-star resort that had all that and more, I definitely would.

39

You're Technically Homeless

I once bought a property with a partner, which didn't work out. While we negotiated the details of the sale, I couldn't afford to live elsewhere, so I stayed in the apartment throughout the process. Only once we got into escrow could I finally find somewhere else, and I had only a week to do so. This meant that I had nowhere to live by the time the keys were handed over. This was my first (and last) experience being "homeless." A couple of friends with spare rooms kindly took me in. I was mortified I had to rely on their generosity. I felt like I was imposing and didn't know what the best way forward was. I was so distressed I hurried into a roomshare within three weeks. Unluckily for me, I rushed into living with idiots. I made mistake after mistake; the next six months of my life were the worst in my roomsharing journey.

Perfect material for the book, though.

When You've Got Nowhere to Go

#149: When you're stuck for somewhere to live, reach out to all your friends and friends of friends

Some of you might think this entire chapter is pointless because you can stay in an Airbnb while looking for something permanent. If you're rich, absolutely. If you're part of the majority not earning in the top 1 percent of salaries, Airbnbs are expensive. As soon as you realize you're going to need temporary accommodation, post about it on social media. Get in touch with friends. The best message to send is one which doesn't bully them into inviting you to stay. Something along the lines of:

"Hey, I'm in a bit of a jam. I have only *[insert timeframe] to find somewhere to live and all the hotels I've looked at are so expensive. Even Airbnb is pricey! Know of somewhere I could crash while I find something permanent?"*

Obviously, it needs tweaking to ensure the message is in "your voice," but something along these lines usually works. This kind of situation is also a true test of friendship. When this happened to me, I received offers from the most unexpected people, which warmed my heart. The sooner you can do this, the higher your chances of success. It won't solve all your problems and may not work out at all, but it's worth trying to see where you land.

Worst case: Airbnb.
Worst worst case: move in with the family (and you know all about that now).
Worst worst worst case: Ask your ex for help (I'd rather down a vat of acid).

#150: Manage your exit date when crashing with a friend and don't rush into a roomshare because you're desperate

Once a friend has offered you a place to stay, their first question will be, "How long do you need…?" Emphasis on the ellipsis. The reality is that you have no idea (probably). Could be a day, week, month, or a year? Ask your friend what's acceptable, but also remember to be reasonable. It's entirely possible your friend can only let you stay the weekend. Once you know and agree, stick to this timetable. And be grateful! When relying on people's generosity, you can't overstay your welcome, or you'll ruin a friendship in the process.

The reality is that you'll likely have to move between friends for a while. The short-term pain is better than signing up for the first roomshare that comes your way. That's one big lesson to take away: don't sign up for the first roomshare that's available because you feel you need to. You'll end up in a far worse situation than what you started with…

The best policy here is honesty. Your friends (assuming they're real friends) will want to know about your viewings and check your progress. If you're seeing horrible roomshares, they won't want you to move into them either. It's also a balance, right? They'll have their own drama they're dealing with, too. Everyone has a starring role in their own movie called *My Life*, and you don't want to be the secondary character ruining this for them. You're already starring in your own version of that movie!

#151: Use the proper guest etiquette (that includes buying dinner and a gift!)

A guest who sleeps past midday, never cleans, and acts like they're in a five-star hotel is an idiot on the crash course to learn how to ruin friendships. Take it upon yourself to clean and tidy. Make yourself useful. They're doing you a huge favor, so the least you can do is wash the dishes and make your bed. They may not be saying it, but as the guest, you are being judged even on how neatly you keep your clothes in your suitcase. Every detail matters, so make every action count. Channel your inner Monica from *Friends,* and you'll be on a good path. Whatever you do, avoid being a Joey.

One of the quickest ways to get kicked out is stumbling back home hammered with an overnight guest. Not only is it disrespectful, but it also mocks your friend's generosity. Bringing a random back to their home is a slap in the face and potentially dangerous. That random you met in a bar could steal a laptop or kidney and sneak out before anyone wakes up—unless your friend is lonely and looking to party with whomever… In this case, all bets are off.

One thing you can count on is that on arrival, you'll need to come with a gift to say thank you, and, throughout your stay, make sure you buy them dinner or lunch and top up their staples like toilet paper and trash bags. They're letting you stay and would probably refuse your offers if you asked, so just go ahead and buy them these little things. No matter how often or loudly they claim it's unnecessary, they'll be grateful and always remember these acts of kindness. Everyone loves a gift and a free meal. It's just being human.

Talking of being human… It goes without saying that if a friend of yours finds themselves in a similar situation, make sure you return the favor. After all, you never know when you'll need that hospitality again. Or not. Depending on how much you like them…

Of course, ending up homeless is a rare scenario, especially when most have the nuclear option available: moving back in with the family.

40

Moving In with Family

Everyone is born into a family. It could be a family of two parents and ten siblings or an only-child situation. Or you could have grown up in an orphanage, and your friends became your family. Whatever childhood you had, the people around you are your "family" in whatever form this may take. The thing about family is that they'll always have their door open for you if they're nice. But if that isn't the case, they're not the kind of family you want anyway.

If you suddenly need to save money or require emergency shelter, and living with your family helps you, you're in good company. It happens to a lot of people. For the first time since the Great Depression of the 1930s, most young people (52%) aged between 18 and 29 live with their families.[1] And it's not just a U.S. thing. In the last 20 years, the UK has seen the number of adults aged between 20 and 34 returning to live with family increase by 46 percent.[2] It's the highest proportion of young adults living at home since records began.

Despite what the headlines lead you to think, it's not a frightening prospect. It should be celebrated. How beautiful is it that people have families they can rely on for help?

If you are part of the boomerang generation of people going back to live with family, that process has its own recommendations to ensure you don't end up at each other's throats like *The Simpsons*.[3]

---

1. Fry, Richard, Passel, Jeffrey S., and Cohn, D'Vera. 2020. "A majority of young adults in the U.S. live with their parents for the first time since the Great Depression." Pew Research Center. September 4, 2020. https://www.pewresearch.org/fact-tank/2020/09/04/a-majority-of-young-adults-in-the-u-s-live-with-their-parents-for-the-first-time-since-the-great-depression.

2. Sanders, Sophie. 2019. "Families and households in the UK: 2019." Office for National Statistics. November 15, 2019. https://www.ons.gov.uk/peoplepopulationandcommunity/birthsdeathsandmarriages/families/bulletins/familiesandhouseholds/2019.

3. Groening, Matt, creat. 1989. *The Simpsons*. Disney+.

How to Handle Living with Family

#152: Establish how long you'll be living with family

If the move is temporary, manage your family's expectations. It's similar to how you must manage your boss and colleagues with project deadlines. You need to align proactively. Perhaps you have a savings goal or deadline by which you need to find a roomshare. Without an end date in sight, planning for the future is impossible. Even if your family insists you can stay as long as you need to, they want to firm up their own plans for the future. Vacations, family commitments, work trips, life keeps going, and they need to work around your schedule. If they know when you'll be moving out, they can adjust.

Remember that even when you lived in the family home as a child, they prepared for your departure the closer you grew to adulthood. The reality for a family is that kids are like cold sores. Once you get one, they'll be with you forever, waiting to make a comeback.

#153: Be flexible and helpful when staying with family

Make a conscious effort to determine how the family home is run, as things might have changed since you first left. What are the expectations around bathroom usage, bedtime, and cooking? As a rule of thumb, depending on how long you're set to live with them, make sure you're aware of their routines. Every household is different, and it's your job, as the guest, to be flexible and minimize disruption, even when it comes to family. They're doing you a favor, so don't make it harder than it needs to be. The number one rule is to be judgment-free. Your family might have developed some habits that didn't exist when you were living there before. Perhaps they keep their bread in a tin, and you put it in the freezer. Whatever works for them needs to be respected. How you usually live at home is now superseded by the people welcoming you into theirs.

Of course, this doesn't mean you can't do anything and have to agree with everything your family does. What I mean is make sure your choices don't negatively impact the lives of those welcoming you into their home. You're on someone else's property, and everyone has different rules and routines. If taking shoes off and wearing slippers is something they do, do the same. It's a small and symbolic step that you're acknowledging and respecting their values and choices. If you usually get up at five in the morning for a run and they don't wake up until seven, make sure you don't wake anyone up when you leave and come back. You need to literally be as quiet as a mouse.

Adapting or giving up your own routine is the price to pay when you temporarily move into someone else's home. The one thing to remember is that this is temporary, so you don't need to feel like you're giving up your life. It's a transitional sacrifice while your family gives you the freedom to work on your next steps (whatever they are).

Just like you would when crashing with friends, be as helpful as you can around the home. Easy wins include taking the trash out (and recycling if they do so), clearing plates after a meal, and doing the dishes. Don't ask to do it. Just do it.[4] Find out your family's favorite meals and cook them. Do small maintenance repairs like changing a lightbulb. Purchase replaceable grocery items like soap and toilet paper. And always buy the same brand as it shows you pay attention to their preferences. All these little things demonstrate your gratitude.

Put another way: not conducting these small acts of kindness guarantees your family are trash-talking you on a separate family WhatsApp group. Not being helpful is a surefire way of never being welcomed back. You'll be seen as a real-life Veruca Salt from *Charlie and the Chocolate Factory*.[5] Entitled, spoiled, and the brat everyone is glad to see the back of.

#154: *Moving back in with the family to take care of a family member*

In the unfortunate scenario of moving into the family home to care for a relative due to health concerns, every piece of advice you've read about moving back in with the family should be adapted or ignored to suit your situation.

Only you will know what this is like, so there's no point in giving meaningful advice for this scenario. The only thing I would say is to do what feels right for the family. The second piece of advice I would also add is to make sure you don't lose sight of your own life. This starts with you. Just because you're caring for a family member doesn't mean you need to lose your identity. For your own health and well-being, remember to take care of yourself physically and mentally. Every situation like this is unique, and the best thing this book can do is wish this family member a speedy recovery. This is the one situation where I really do hope moving back in with the family means everyone lives happily ever after à la Disney.

---

4. Nike's famous slogan is pretty universal, am I right?
5. Dahl, Roald. 1964. *Charlie and the Chocolate Factory*. New York: Alfred A. Knopf.

41

What Next?—Buying Your Own Home?

This is not a financial advice book. There are millions of those to help you with finances. *Living with Others: A Survival Guide* is not the place to learn how to make a boatload of cash. It'd be like buying a dictionary, thinking you can use it as a guide to make a time machine. And yet, as a shared-living advocate writing a book about how to best live communally with others, there are three elephants in the room to be addressed:

Elephant #1: How does shared living work when you buy a home?
Elephant #2: Can you or should you buy a home when you're roomsharing?
Elephant #3: What if buying property is financially out of reach?

At the time of writing, Googling "Why is owning your own home important?" brings up over 7.4B results. People across the world are clearly thinking, discussing, and searching for an answer. There is a cultural obsession with home ownership in countries like the UK, Ireland, USA, Australia, and New Zealand. As Dr. Maalsen explains, it's "what everyone aspires to."[1] In this context, roomsharing is seen as a young person's game, and it's assumed that older people should live in their own property.

Why are people obsessed with home ownership in the first place? It's not a fad like owning a Tamagotchi in the 1990s. Homeownership has always been a milestone to hit, and with spiraling rent prices, it's only more important. Matt Phillips, a reporter for Quartz, theorizes that after World War II, different governments' responses to rebuilding people's homes had a part to play in the quality of the properties being built.[2] In the U.S., the federal government doubled down on property investments

---

1. Maalsen, Sophia. 2020. Phone interview. 22 December 2020.
2. Phillips, Matt. 2014. "Most Germans don't buy their homes, they rent. Here's why." Quartz. January 23, 2014. https://qz.com/167887/germany-has-one-of-the-worlds-lowest-homeownership-rates.

by enacting laws allowing investors to generate wealth from real investment trusts, spearheading the U.S. culture of buying and selling homes for profit.[3]

In the UK, the rich bought their homes while the poor rented. In Germany, renting was considered perfectly acceptable, with high-quality homes made affordable by law. As a result, the UK and the U.S. came to see homeownership as the beacon of success, whereas Germany sees renting as a normal part of life, no matter your income. People can have whatever life goals they want. I, for one, would never advocate against saving money to buy your own place. Wherever you stand in the buying vs renting debate, the younger and poorer you are, the likelier you are to rent. Across the U.S., 39 percent of those under 35 own their own home[4] compared to 79 percent of those aged 65 and over,[5] leaving 61 percent of those under 35 in the rental market. These numbers are actually high compared to a country like the UK, where 10.1 percent of those under 35 own their own homes.[6]

For most people, saving for a mortgage deposit while paying rent and enjoying life (eating out, vacations, shopping) is impossible. A mortgage is seen as a pipe dream reserved for people who have either been lucky in finance, received an inheritance, or had parents help them (and often it's all three). Or it's for people who live somewhere with cheap real estate and can buy a property for peanuts compared to hotspots like New York and LA. This leaves most people with no other option but to roomshare as renting a place alone is too expensive, lonely, or both.

Dr. Maalsen explains: "Housing prices are so unaffordable in areas where people need to work that sharing becomes the only option. Unless there's a considerable shake-up of the housing market, then [roomsharing is] just going to continue to grow."[7] So, even if people want to buy their own property, they may not have a choice but to roomshare until they can buy.

---

3. Beattie, Andrew. 2023. "No Longer Nomads: The History of Real Estate." Investopedia. September 28, 2023. https://www.investopedia.com/articles/07/history-real-estate.asp.

4. USAFacts Team. 2024. "Homeownership is rebounding, particularly among younger adults." 2024. USAFacts. January 29, 2024. https://usafacts.org/articles/homeownership-is-rebounding-particularly-among-younger-adults/.

5. Joint Center for Housing Studies of Harvard University. 2023. "Housing America's Older Adults." Joint Center for Housing Studies of Harvard University. 2023. https://www.jchs.harvard.edu/sites/default/files/reports/files/Harvard_JCHS_Housing_Americas_Older_Adults_2023.pdf.

6. Statista Research Department. 2024. "Distribution of homeowners in England in 2023, by age." Statista. https://www.statista.com/statistics/321065/uk-england-home-owners-age-groups.

7. Maalsen, Sophia. 2020. Phone interview. 22 December 2020.

41. What Next?—Buying Your Own Home?

And for those on this path, Professor Heath found that "The group that were in their twenties saw it as a transitional phase and of this act of constraint. And many of them were actively saving to buy a house but what was really interesting was that many were saying, 'Well I know that the only way I will be able to afford to have that house is to take in a lodger.'"[8]

"And so they were anticipating that they were going to be creating another form of shared household at that point. So they'd be moving out of the shared tenancy and into their own home, but they would have a lodger. So they were going to continue to share."[9]

Part of the motivation for owning your own home is that you'll have paid off the mortgage by the time you retire, and your pension will cover your living expenses. "But this is no longer a reality for most Americans. Dr. Molinsky's research highlights that between 1989 and 2022, the number of homeowners aged 80 and over with mortgages jumped from 3% to 31%."[10] Put another way, over a third of people who would traditionally no longer worry about housing costs still need to worry about that even when they're supposed to be enjoying their twilight years. And that trend is on the up.

In parallel, there is a whole generation of people from their 20s to their 50s who have rented their entire lives and are perfectly content to continue doing so. But what happens when you retire and your pension doesn't cover your expenses? Kath Scanlon believes future generations are at high risk of retirement poverty, explaining, "If you rented your whole life, [when you retire] your income goes down, but your rent doesn't go down."[11] Rents will go up, which means that, within a few decades, there will be a "wave of people in that situation [retirement poverty]... And that's going to be a big social issue."[12]

The Downside of Long-Term Renting

#155: Beware of renting your entire life

Even though this book is all about shared living in rented homes, assuming renting is cheaper in the long run is delusional. Depending on

---

8. Heath, Sue. 2021. Phone interview. 6 January 2021.
9. Heath, Sue. 2021. Phone interview. 6 January 2021.
10. Joint Center for Housing Studies of Harvard University. 2023. "Housing America's Older Adults." Joint Center for Housing Studies of Harvard University. 2023. https://www.jchs.harvard.edu/sites/default/files/reports/files/Harvard_JCHS_Housing_Americas_Older_Adults_2023_Revised_040424.pdf.
11. Scanlon, Kath. 2020. Phone interview. 11 December 2020.
12. Scanlon, Kath. 2020. Phone interview. 11 December 2020.

your country and the legislation (which could change at any point), renting costs will always increase in the long term. No matter where you are in the world. And there's nothing you can do about it for as long as the world economy functions as it currently does. The founder of SeniorHomeshares.com Stephanie Heacox explains that the "challenge of renting is that someone else has the control. And so suddenly if rents skyrocket, you're kind of screwed. There's just that inability to control your finances to the degree to which you might want to be able."[13] Once you own a home, you have control. Your mortgage payments are steady (unless interest rates get hiked). No one but yourself (and the bank if you don't keep up with your mortgage payments) can get you kicked out of your own property.

Another aspect of having a mortgage is that inflation makes debt cheaper in the long term. When you borrow $250,000 in 2024, and all goes well for you salary-wise, you'll earn a lot more in 2034, making that $250,000 much easier to pay off. This is the gift and the curse associated with inflation. It is every homeowner's best friend and a renter's worst enemy.[14]

When I first started living in London in 2007, I was paying $400 a month (all bills included) for a single room in a four-bedroom apartment living with four other randoms (a lovely Scottish couple, a singleton trainee lawyer, and a sometimes single, and sometimes not, trainee physiotherapist). It was small, overcrowded, and didn't have a living room. I wouldn't have moved in if I knew what I know now. Still, it was cheap and worked for me at the time. Fast-forward 17 years, and I'm paying close to $2,900 monthly for a two-bedroom apartment in London. This apartment is bigger and nicer, but my salary hasn't gone up by a multiple of 7.25. Although I earn more than in 2007, my general living costs have also increased. My commute to work on public transport is three times more expensive. Groceries cost more. Restaurants are pricier. Vacations are harder to pay for.

What costs a dollar today will cost two dollars in the future. This applies to every item you'll buy for the rest of your life, including rent. Between 2000 and 2020, nationwide inflation hovered around 2 percent yearly, shooting up to 10 percent following the pandemic. This means that, if something costs $10,000 one year, 12 months later it'll be worth between $10,200 (2 percent inflation) and $11,000 (10 percent inflation). Great if you're selling, terrible if you're buying.

An easier way to think about inflation is that your $10,000 of cash savings can be worth, at best, $9,800 and at worst, $9,000 within a year.

---

13. Heacox, Stephanie. 2023. Phone interview. 30 April 2023.
14. Mortgages are great until interest rates get hiked. Then you're in a whole different area of trouble financially. Out of scope for this book, though.

Governments love inflation because it makes housing debt cheaper and encourages spending.[15] This means the country's overall economic value increases, creating a virtuous circle of employment opportunities, higher salaries, and wealth. But, for the average person making ends meet, inflation is a killer that makes everything more expensive as years go by. This is just the reality of modern economics. The only way you can achieve any control regarding how much you pay to keep a roof over your head is if you have an affordable mortgage on a property you own.[16] This means that unless you're part of the lucky few who live in rent-controlled apartments or have inherited a mortgage-free home, your rent will be more expensive next year, no matter where you are.

Except for the 1 percent of people earning millions of dollars yearly, your salary will not increase to keep up with the same rate as inflation. Imagine your salary being your best friend and inflation their irritating partner you can't stand. You try and ignore them, but they're always there when you see your BFF. So, you can try to be polite and hope they go away, but the next thing you know, your best friend is engaged, getting married, and then (worst of all) having kids. Their spouse will be there forever and they're only ever going to get more annoying as the years fly by.

That's why, no matter how impossible it seems, save when you can. As soon as you get paid, put 10 percent to 30 percent of your income into savings. You'll get used to living on less. This is the one time in life when being a penny-pinching Scrooge is actually healthy for you.

#156: *The first property you buy doesn't have to be one you live in*

The focus on getting on the property ladder can get in the way of the bigger picture. Your first owned property doesn't have to be one you live in. Best-selling author and financial guru Robert Kyosaki advises against your first property being the one you live in.[17] Instead, he recommends buying a property you can rent out to generate income. If you follow this advice, it doesn't matter where you buy it as long as you can rent it out. Which means you can afford to buy something cheaper.

As soon as you buy this first property and it starts generating money, save that cash to buy a second one. Then rinse and repeat, and before you

---

15. This comes back to the fact that borrowing $250,000 today will be cheaper to pay back in 10 years' time, assuming you're earning more by then.
16. The dream is obviously to own your home outright. No mortgage.
17. Kiyosaki, Robert T. 2000. *Rich Dad, Poor Dad*. New York: Warner Books, p. 105.

know it, you own three, then four homes with more on the way. It sounds like a Ponzi scheme. It's not. You're buying an income-generating asset (a buy-to-let property) to generate wealth that you can accumulate to buy more money-generating assets (more buy-to-lets). It makes financial sense. Just check with your accountant first on the best way to proceed from an accounting perspective.

In fact, speaking to your accountant is a golden rule whenever you're making a large investment. They'll be able to advise on tax liabilities and know things you wouldn't even think of asking about. Not speaking to an accountant before buying a property would be like trying to eat a bowl of soup with your hands tied behind your back because you "love to challenge yourself." You're bound to spill it all over your front and make a complete mess.

#157: You can rent and own simultaneously

Being in a roomshare doesn't exclude you from owning property. Whether it's a property you move into or rent out is up to you. If you decide to rent a property while renting out one you own, it can be a more affordable lifestyle. Sounds quite comfortable, doesn't it? Earning money from your property and building a nest egg on your salary.

I'll repeat myself: speak to an accountant to ensure you're tax-efficient before making an informed decision. No one likes paying taxes because any amount of tax is too much tax. Smart people like accountants know how to legally advise to maximize tax efficiency.[18]

You could also rent out the rooms in a home you own, and you become an agent and tenant simultaneously. This popular concept known as "house hacking" is promoted by self-professed millionaire gurus such as Chad Carson.[19] The strategy involves purchasing a two-bedroom (or bigger) home. You live in one bedroom and take in a lodger to cover your living and property costs. Using this method, you can live effectively for "free" while saving your spare cash to invest in other things (such as more properties).

The benefits are that your mortgage costs will decrease while the rent you charge will increase. It sounds like a rip-off, which it is, unless you're the owner. Congratulations! This is a tiny taste of what being part of the 1 percent is like.

---

18. "Tax efficiency" is, of course, a euphemism for "paying the least amount of tax you can legally get away with."
19. Carson, Chad. 2019. "The House Hacking Guide—How to 'Hack' Your Housing, Live for Free, & Start Investing in Real Estate" Coach Carson. September 25, 2019. https://www.coachcarson.com/house-hacking-guide.

41. What Next?—Buying Your Own Home?

#158: Do not rely only on a pension to live out your days

If you're trying to build wealth, splurging on Chanel handbags and Jimmy Choo shoes is a surefire way to stay trapped in poverty. Unless you're rich already. Real estate is an investment which can get you out of the poverty trap. When I say "real estate," I don't mean buying a bunch of properties you can't afford and having them sit empty while you hope they'll increase in value over time so you can sell them at a profit. I mean buying properties to rent them out and generate an annual income you can live off in your twilight years (if not sooner).

As you get older, you realize you can't rely on your salary forever. The company you work for may change, you might not like it there anymore, or you've been asked to leave. If any of these scenarios happen to you and you're not yet financially independent, you'll be on the search for a new job. You may have a pension, but what if it disappears? In 2005, United Airlines wiped out its $7.4 billion pension fund, leaving 123,957 participants without retirement savings. This has happened to many others in the last 20 years.[20]

Assuming all your pensions are intact, with inflation eroding the value of cash every year, it's unlikely your pension will be enough to cover your living costs when you retire. Employers seldom hire pensioners, and of those who do, you might be too unwell to work in the first place. Your family and friends may help, but they'll have money worries of their own and might be unable to.

Government subsidies won't be enough. You might secure the basic benefits, but I have never heard of a government paying their citizens enough for them to be truly happy (whatever being truly happy means to you). And, even if they did, this could change at any moment. Relying on a pension would be like watering a lemon tree for forty years. One day you stop watering it as you've given it everything and now it's time to reap the benefits and live off the lemons. Eventually, the tree will die out for lack of water, and you're wondering what happened because you've been looking after it and not touching it for 40 years. The same will happen to your pension. At some point it will also shrivel and die. Your finances must always be watered to keep growing.

Renting and roomsharing come with a lot of freedom, and if you want to continue doing this for years to come, you need to prepare for when you're either out of a job or retired. If you have been relying on a monthly

---

20. Brandon, Emily. 2010. "The 10 Biggest Failed Pension Plans." *U.S. News*. August 23, 2010. https://money.usnews.com/money/blogs/planning-to-retire/2010/08/23/the-10-biggest-failed-pension-plans.

salary without consideration for when it ends, you are on a path to destitution. Eventually, your rent will become unaffordable, and you'll spiral into debt trying to cover your expenses and keep a roof over your head. So, my final piece of advice? Save and invest like you'll live forever so that you can live every day like it's your last.

PART I

Actually Living with Idiots

> "Dear Roommate, I have been really dirty lately. Please do me.
> Love,
> Dishes x"
>
> —Anonymous

Idiots Are Real and the Signs Can't Be Ignored…

Everyone has pet peeves. This is universal. Whether it's being woken up before their alarm or feeling disgusted by hair in the bathroom sink, we become irritated at some point by something someone else does. Particularly with roommates. It's inevitable. It's human nature. It's called roomsharing.

The difference is the extent of annoyance you can put up with. Like a romantic relationship, your partner annoys you occasionally, but you can't imagine life without them. You're willing to deal with the irritations to make your relationship work.

A roomshare is the same. Your roommates will do things you find exasperating. They might leave the toilet seat up or forget to clean the hobs and other surfaces after cooking. Hopefully, you like them enough to let those things slide as you'd prefer to keep living together than with someone else. Yet, when it comes to living with idiots, these pet peeves aren't little things you could live with. These "OMG WHAT IS THIS" outbursts are reasonable reactions to unreasonable situations.

Everyone who has ever roomshared has a roommate horror story. Plenty of great books have been written about terrible roommates such as *He Died with a Felafel in His Hand* by John Birmingham.[1] Even *I Lick My Cheese and Other Notes: From the Frontline of Flat-Sharing* by Oonagh

---

1. Birmingham, John. 1994. *He Died with a Felafel in His Hand*. Australia: Duffy & Snellgrove.

O'Hagan.[2] In fact, these books will probably put you off roomshares forever. So, I am trying to say that you must recognize infuriating traits in roommates early. Or, even better, avoid them in the first place. If this book helps you avoid living with just one idiot or escape living with one, *Living with Others: A Survival Guide* will have done its job.

---

2. Oonagh, O'Hagan. 2009. *I Lick My Cheese and Other Notes: From the Frontline of Flat-Sharing.* New York: Harry N. Abrams.

42

This Is Literally Idiot Central

It's Monday. You've signed the contract. You've moved in. Not everyone's home, but the roommates who are, welcome you warmly. After sharing your plans and interests, discussing movie nights with homemade popcorn, and planning some evenings out, you head to bed smiling. Your new living situation seems perfect.

Suddenly, it's four in the morning, and a roommate comes crashing through the front door, drunk, with two randoms looking to party. You hope they won't barge into your room since you can't lock your door. A moment later, one of the strangers staggers into your bedroom, asking for help finding the bathroom. You yell at them to leave. They drunkenly apologize, fumble around, and slam the door on the way. By the sounds of it, they've found the toilet. The next morning, as you head into the shower, you step in vomit.

At breakfast, no one mentions this, and you decide to avoid it altogether. You don't want to "throw the cat amongst the pigeons." Throughout the week, you watch the dishes piling high, and the ashtray spewing cigarette butts across the table. On the WhatsApp group you ask when the cleaner is due. They say the cleaner has been cancelled. You suggest hiring a replacement, and no one replies.

By the time the weekend comes around your roommates have been:

- Playing music in the middle of the night
- Showering for an hour which makes you late for work
- Using the kitchen hosting a dinner party you're not invited to
- Ignoring your suggestion for a roommates dinner

You're living with idiots.

I wish the above were fictional. This sequence of events happened to me in a roomshare in East London. I eventually put a lock on my door. I wore earplugs to sleep. The bathroom would get so dirty that I went to the gym to shower and brush my teeth. I'd walk into the kitchen, and the roommates pretended I didn't exist.

It was horrific. Yet, I only had myself to blame because I made rookie mistakes before moving in. I hadn't:

- Met all the roommates
- Compared our schedules
- Asked if there was a cleaner
- Discussed lifestyles
- Checked if anyone smoked weed (the stench really does stick to everything)

I walked straight into living with idiots like the young, naïve roommate I was, and I couldn't wait to walk straight out.

#159: Get ready to be unlucky and move from living with idiots to living with even bigger idiots

In an ideal world, you'll gladly run away from any car crash of a roomshare and move into one that ticks all of your boxes. If this is the case, huge congratulations. But... If you're like 99 percent of people living in roomshares, and if it hasn't happened to you, it will do soon, you will go from living with idiots to moving in with bigger idiots.[1] This is the risk of modern living.

You might have incorporated all the advice in this book and asked the right questions, made sure the location was convenient, sized up your room, and checked the rent is affordable. All it takes is one—one idiot—who can make you want to move. Living alone sucks for a lot of people but living with idiots is worse.

You can do what I did to mitigate living with idiots (earplugs, door lock, paying for a cleaner yourself), but if you get to a point where you have to hide dishes in your room because someone will always use them and never wash up, then move out. Everyone has a breaking point. You need to move out before you reach yours.

Life is too short to continue living with idiots, and the quicker you can move out, the happier you'll be.

---

1. Anecdotally.

43

How to Get Out of Living with Idiots

You think you found an exemplary place with quintessential roommates but, within two days, you realize it's a nightmare because your roommate:

- Wakes up at five a.m. to pump iron
- Smokes weed for dinner
- Names the rats infesting the cupboard under the stairs

What's nuts about the above examples is they happened to me or someone I know. Agents don't care, though. They can and will hold you to your contract. They will force you to pay the outstanding rent if you want to move out early. And let's face reality: who can actually afford to pay that much rent upfront and move somewhere else?

What to Do When Living with Idiots

#160: When living with idiots, activate a break clause to move out quickly

I wish there were a magic bullet to solve your problems. It'd be great if one email to the agent fixed everything. For example, a quick chat with the agent, and the idiot gets kicked out.

Unless the roommate has stopped paying rent (in which case you'll have bigger problems), getting someone kicked out is hard. As long as the property isn't being trashed and the rent is getting paid, the agent will not be interested in your roomshare woes. Living with idiots is such a regular occurrence I've lost track of the number of times it's happened to me. If it hasn't happened to you yet, it's not a question of *if* but *when*. The best thing to do is to move out and move on. The idiots aren't going to change.

Your home is your safe space. You want to come home from work and feel relaxed, which is impossible when living with idiots. This is why if you are living with idiots, you need to move out. And move out fast.

As you have no idea what it's like to live there until you do, ask for a month's trial to settle in. Within those first four weeks, you should have the right to move out without penalty and get your deposit back. This is a big ask, and an agent may just offer the contract to someone else. But you'd be surprised how many will happily agree. The reason? It's difficult to find good tenants. If the agent is smart and there has been no other offer, they'll bend over backwards to secure the law-abiding tenants who pay their rent on time. The agent may be "traditional" and insist on a six-month break clause instead. And to be fair, when you first move in, a 12-month lease gives you peace of mind that the agent can't raise the rent for a year. But maybe you've found the living situation isn't ideal. This could be anything; the floors creak too much, your neighbors are noisy, the street is sketchy. Now, it's not entirely unlivable, but you want to move out as soon as possible.

Which is when a six-month break clause is ideal. You have the right to give the agent one month's notice to get out of there and get your deposit back, no questions asked. One-third of renters break their leases early, so having at least a six-month break clause in a year-long contract is critical and usually standard practice.[1]

#161: *If you want to leave outside of a break clause, find someone to replace you*

No agent wants an empty room (less money and less profit), so they'll be likely open to finding a replacement tenant. Most agents don't care who's actually living in their property; they just want rent. So, if you can offer to find a replacement tenant who will take over your tenancy, they're usually receptive and will let you out of your contract. The replacement tenant might have different sensibilities and not mind the roommates you consider idiots.

An alternative would be to sublet your room. You'll be out of the roomshare; you won't be paying double rent, and you'll be free. If the agent won't let you out of the lease, subletting your room to someone else with the blessing of your roommates can be a short-term solution. It's tricky as it depends on your roommates, but you could explain that you need to

---

1. B, Michelle. 2017. "What is the percentage of people want to move out before their rental lease agreement ends in the U.S.?" Ask Wonder. March 21, 2017. https://askwonder.com/research/percentage-people-want-move-rental-lease-agreement-ends-us-x3pb5tjc1.

43. How to Get Out of Living with Idiots

leave but can't afford to due to unreasonable financial demands on the part of the agent.

If you don't know your roommates at all (and if they're idiots, you won't want to), tell them you have a family emergency. Tell them you need to move out, and subletting is the only way you can afford to. In an ideal world, the person you sublet to is brilliant and happy to take over the lease. The risk is it'll get messy if they start causing trouble or stop paying rent. You won't know until it happens.

#162: Pack and run out of the roomshare

The last-choice scenario. Skipping out on a lease can affect your credit score (a metric you should care about if you want to purchase property), but if nothing you've tried has worked, you'll be left with two choices: stay living with idiots until the end of your contract or pack and run. It works if you're leaving the country. You can say you're going on vacation and never come back. Doing so means losing your deposit, but at least you'll come out of the lease. And what's losing a security deposit if it means you get your mental health back on track? This is a bold choice, of course. You'll need to be sure you don't mind not coming back to live in the country as that debt will be tied to your name until the day you die. Sounds dramatic? Oh yes. That's because it is (debt collectors don't mess around).

PART J

Actually Living in Paradise (As Close as You Can, Anyway)

"Home is the place where you feel happy."
—Salman Rushdie

44

What It Takes to Live in Paradise (Metaphorically)

I wrote this book because the reality of moving somewhere new, big or small, at any age, can be scary, lonely, and intimidating. I would know. I've done it in Dublin, LA, New York, and London. Countless friends and acquaintances of mine have also moved states and countries and had to make new friends and start new lives. It's almost the same process as a witness protection program. Minus the whole "I'll be killed if someone finds out who I really am" thing of course.

Moving is one of the hardest things anyone can do, especially when you're by yourself. It can be tough on your mental health and finances, and when moving countries, your friends, your family and your home comforts will top the list of things you miss the most.[1] This is why roomsharing can be so brilliant. Roommates provide a safety net. A roomshare is a ready-made social network you can tap into. It's the beginning of your new life.

There's no secret formula for a successful roomshare. What I have done throughout the book is lay out everything you need to know to set you up for success.[2] In other words, *Living with Others: A Survival Guide* should be able to set you up to live in paradise (as close as you can anyway).

Hold on. Paradise? Yeah. Paradise.

What do you mean paradise?

The Cambridge Dictionary defines paradise as "a place or condition of great happiness where everything is exactly as you would like it to be."[3] Which in a roomshare is when everything runs perfectly. It's a home you love where you like all your roommates and you enjoy living there. It's close to where you work and like to hang out, and it feels like you belong

---

1. On the flipside you may be relieved to start fresh and make new friends and build a new life. In which case, yay! You'll still need to start building a network somehow, hence roomsharing can be a great way to kick that off.
2. That sounds so corporate, doesn't it?
3. Cambridge Advanced Learner's Dictionary & Thesaurus. n.d. "Paradise." Cambridge Dictionary. n.d. https://dictionary.cambridge.org/dictionary/english/paradise.

44. What It Takes to Live in Paradise (Metaphorically)

(and it's affordable). Nothing goes wrong and your agent abides by all the laws and is supportive and friendly.

And that actually exists? On paper absolutely. In reality I've never seen it.

Call me unlucky, or picky or difficult, but in my 40 years on the planet I have yet to witness or hear of a flawless and perfect roomshare that would qualify as paradise.[4] With paradise defined as the perfect roomshare, paradise is impossible. No human is perfect. No home is perfect. Nothing is perfect. And if it's not perfect, then it's not paradise. Right?

The perfect roomshare is like a flying unicorn—it doesn't exist. You dream and hope to find it one day, but you never will. After all, what makes a perfect roomshare is different for everyone. What works for one person might be anathema to another. Every roommate will have their quirks and foibles. What you *can* do is like a roomshare and your roommates enough to forgive those annoying niggles. And this is the key. A perfect roomshare is somewhere you like and get on with the roommates enough, that no matter what happens (within reason and the law), you would rather live there than anywhere else.

The nuance is how you perceive paradise. Your home may have imperfections like the front door squeaking when you walk in, your sofa being too small to snuggle on, or your roommate crunching chips loudly while watching your favorite show. In the literal sense of perfection, living with those annoyances isn't so, but if you can love your home and roommates and live happily, that *is* paradise.

To think the perfect roomshare exists sets you up for failure. And you can't simply throw money at the problem. Billionaires living in their mega-mansions have issues too. Maybe it's a leaky roof, a faulty swimming pool, or a lawsuit from an angry neighbor regarding their renovations. I'd still rather swap my roomshare issues for a billionaire's problems though…

For the rest of the planet, the 99 percent of us, the problem isn't finding paradise but finding what feels like the right home. Technically, a home has four walls, a roof over your head, and running hot water (ideally limitlessly hot), but it's much more than that. A home is made by the people who live in it. You could share a one-bedroom shack in the rural countryside with two people and feel this is paradise, or move into a mega-mansion where your housemates are horrible slobs and you want to activate the break clause as soon as you can. You might even rent a single room in a rundown apartment and find the people you're living with are kind, caring, and clean, making this the most beautiful roomshare you've ever experienced.

---

4. Please do get in touch if you have some stories to share! Would love to hear them.

This is the key: living with the right people.

Nobody is perfect, and things will go wrong. It's inevitable that, when it comes to your roommates, you'll sometimes disagree with them, disapprove of their actions, or be let down. If this weren't the case, I'd argue life would be boring. We must learn to live with that imperfection. *That* is what makes life interesting.

So, instead of looking for paradise, look for roommates you like and get on with. Paradise is created by people living together and doing it well with a healthy and supportive group dynamic, regardless of their flaws. Once you have that, it won't feel like you're paying rent just to stay off the street and have a hot shower in the morning. It will feel like you're waking up and falling asleep on your own paradisiac island.

At the end of the day... Paradise *is* other people.

Final Thoughts

"Happiness is roommates becoming a family."
—David Ruby

The concept of living with other people has been around since the dawn of civilization. Many people say their "real" family are the friends they make and choose to keep (alongside the family they decide to start with a partner). It's similar when deciding who you live with. Your choice of roommates and what they become to you are within your control.

To an extent, we're the product of our experiences and choices. Where you end up living is more often through circumstance than choice. Given the option, we'd all be living in Kardashian-style homes with acres of land, swimming pools, and tennis courts with staff on hand 24/7 to take care of us.[1]

The reality is we're born unequal. We live unequally. We aspire for different things and settle into disparate lives, families, and friendships. Despite this, one common factor is universal across generations, incomes and time zones: companionship. Humans universally seek friendship wherever they are in the world from the homeless person living in a shelter to the billionaire relaxing in one of their compounds. You've just read an entire book which can be summarized into a few words: live with people who you want and can be friends with.

When you take in all the different types of living situations (families, couples, and roommates), we all live with others for the majority of our lives. As human beings, we can only sustain living with others if we like them enough to do so. That companionship from sharing experiences with people you like is key to unlocking a better life. Not only will you have a better life, it's been scientifically proven to provide a healthier life.

The Harvard Study of Adult Development, currently led by Professor Robert Waldinger, is a groundbreaking human developmental study

---

1. I really doubt Kim Kardashian scrubs her own toilet after going for a number two, or does she? I think the most fun part of this footnote is you now have an image of Kim Kardashian with a toilet brush in her hand. She would still make it look good.

that started tracking 268 Harvard students in 1938.² The research has now expanded across three generations, with over 1,300 participants, making it officially the world's longest continuous study of humans and their descendants, tracking their health, jobs, and social mobility.

Armed with close to nine decades of data, Waldinger delivered a TED talk in 2022 which at the time of writing had garnered over three million views, where he explains that he believes that "relationships matter in our lives" as they "affect our health."³ And in the study who were the happiest and healthiest? They were the people with "warm connections to others."⁴ What does Waldinger mean when talking about "warm connections"? Companionship, of course, also known as the joy of spending time with others.

When the study identified participants as having warm connections, it found that those very same people were happier and less ill than others.⁵ Waldinger also discovered that as time passed and age took its toll on everyone, those with warm connections stayed fitter and neurologically stronger.⁶

One of the biggest factors in this trend came down to the simple discovery that "Good relationships turn out to be stress regulators. People feel better when they freely share their worries, stresses, and day-to-day lives. Their stress levels decrease, and their overall happiness improves."⁷

This is in contrast to people in the study who lacked that companionship. As Waldinger explains, those who were lonely and removed from regular social contact lacked the "stress regulators that we get from good relationships."⁸ Those people stay in "chronic fight or flight mode" and their "bodies have this chronic stress, chronic levels of inflammation and

---

2. Waldinger, Robert, and Schulz, Marc. 2023. *The Good Life and How to Live It*. London: Rider.

3. Waldinger, Robert. 2022. "The Secret to a Happy Life—Lessons from 8 Decades of Research." TED. November 2022. https://www.ted.com/talks/robert_waldinger_the_secret_to_a_happy_life_lessons_from_8_decades_of_research.

4. Waldinger, Robert. 2022. "The Secret to a Happy Life—Lessons from 8 Decades of Research." TED. November 2022. https://www.ted.com/talks/robert_waldinger_the_secret_to_a_happy_life_lessons_from_8_decades_of_research.

5. Waldinger, Robert. 2022. "The Secret to a Happy Life—Lessons from 8 Decades of Research." TED. November 2022. https://www.ted.com/talks/robert_waldinger_the_secret_to_a_happy_life_lessons_from_8_decades_of_research.

6. Waldinger, Robert. 2022. "The Secret to a Happy Life—Lessons from 8 Decades of Research." TED. November 2022. https://www.ted.com/talks/robert_waldinger_the_secret_to_a_happy_life_lessons_from_8_decades_of_research.

7. Waldinger, Robert. 2022. "The Secret to a Happy Life—Lessons from 8 Decades of Research." TED. November 2022. https://www.ted.com/talks/robert_waldinger_the_secret_to_a_happy_life_lessons_from_8_decades_of_research.

8. Waldinger, Robert. 2022. "The Secret to a Happy Life—Lessons from 8 Decades of Research." TED. November 2022. https://www.ted.com/talks/robert_waldinger_the_secret_to_a_happy_life_lessons_from_8_decades_of_research.

circulating stress hormones that wear away our happiness and break down different body systems. Having at least one person in your life who you really feel has your back, who you could go to if you were in trouble, that's essential for maintaining our happiness and our health."[9]

This doesn't imply you need to double down on finding "the one" if you haven't already. Especially when as discussed earlier, relationship expert Hellen Chen believes that 85 percent of relationships break down. Reassuringly, Waldinger explains that "All types of relationships support our well-being. Friendships, relatives, colleagues, casual contacts. The person who gets you coffee every morning at Starbucks…. Even talking to strangers has that benefit."[10]

Which is why Waldinger advocates the concept of "social fitness," similar in principle to physical fitness. In addition to working on your muscles and cardio, it's critical to practice developing your ability to create warm connections with others. This is because all relationships take work. Connections and contacts don't remain connections and contacts in your life without effort on your part. Even strong friendships you've developed over decades need nurturing.

We're social beings. Humans always prefer to be with other humans. An experience shared with someone else is infinitely more enjoyable than experiencing it alone.[11] And that's the case even with a stranger.[12] Whether it's a movie, a meal or a sunset, sharing that moment with another human being makes it more enjoyable. You can both express how you feel about it to each other and you're creating a shared memory you can treasure forever.

Waldinger specifically calls out the relationships with the people we live with as relationships we risk taking for granted.[13] Shared living is the bedrock on which people build their happiness. You can't have a happy life without a happy home. Which is why having a great relationship with the people you live with is so important.

---

9. Waldinger, Robert. 2022. "The Secret to a Happy Life—Lessons from 8 Decades of Research." TED. November 2022. https://www.ted.com/talks/robert_waldinger_the_secret_to_a_happy_life_lessons_from_8_decades_of_research.
10. Waldinger, Robert. 2022. "The Secret to a Happy Life—Lessons from 8 Decades of Research." TED. November 2022. https://www.ted.com/talks/robert_waldinger_the_secret_to_a_happy_life_lessons_from_8_decades_of_research.
11. There are always exceptions to the rule, of course. I hate sharing my cheesecake. I definitely prefer experiencing that alone.
12. Optimist Performance. 2022. "The Power of Shared Experiences—By Optimist Performance." Optimist Performance. August 8, 2022. https://www.optimistperformance.com/captains-blog/news/the-power-of-shared-experiences-by-optimist-performance.
13. Waldinger, Robert. 2022. "The Secret to a Happy Life—Lessons from 8 Decades of Research." TED. November 2022. https://www.ted.com/talks/robert_waldinger_the_secret_to_a_happy_life_lessons_from_8_decades_of_research.

So here's a toast to shared living: the key to a financially better, healthier, and happier life. Whether it's sharing with a friend, a relative, or a romantic partner, as long as you're living with at least one person with whom you have a warm connection, you're already ahead in the bigger game of life. I just hope that after reading this book, you're able to up your game just that little bit more.

And remember: it's people, not money, which determine how happy you are.

Appendix

Checklists

"You don't know what you don't know."
—Donald Rumsfeld

To help in your roomsharing journey I've created three different checklists for you to take with you to print out before signing up for a roomshare. Each item is there as a reminder of what's key in ensuring you'll be able to happily live in that property. The more ticks there are, the higher the chance that this is a great roomshare.

Checklist #1: Visiting a roomshare

- ☐ Met all roommates and none of them seem to be an idiot
- ☐ Living room is suitable to eat and relax in
- ☐ Fridge is large enough for all
- ☐ Dishwasher works
- ☐ Between rent and bills, the place is affordable
- ☐ There's a system to split bills
- ☐ A cleaner comes regularly
- ☐ The agent has a physical office
- ☐ There is a phone number for after-hours emergencies

Checklist #2: Signing a contract

- ☐ Rent liability:
  - Option A: Responsible for just the room (bills included)
  - Option B: Shared responsibility between all roommates for the whole place
- ☐ There's an acceptable break clause
- ☐ Pets are allowed
- ☐ Doing small decorative improvements (ex: putting up frames) is allowed
- ☐ The agent is explicitly responsible for all white goods
- ☐ Emergency repairs are the responsibility of the agent

- ☐ The security deposit is secure via a third party
- ☐ Subleasing is allowed (tough ask but worth trying)

Checklist #3: After you've moved into the roomshare

- ☐ All roommates are likable
- ☐ Everyone is friendly and sociable
- ☐ The cleaner comes around regularly
- ☐ All bills get paid on time
- ☐ The agent responds promptly
- ☐ Although there is one idiot, it's easily managed

Index

Adamo, Matt 22, 85
Adams, Rebecca G. 100
adulthood 7, 26, 99, 175, 191
Airbnb 73, 137–138, 187–188
Alabama 31, 52
alcohol 15, 28, 107, 133
Amazon 41, 96, 160
Aspen 136
Australia 36, 78, 193
Avail 31

Bahamas 137
Bank of Mom and Dad 82
Beverly Hills 85
Big Apple 39
bills 7, 17, 44, 47–48, 61, 63–66, 88, 93, 167–168, 171, 173, 196, 217
Birkman Colors 96
birthday 131–132
Boston 55
Burstein, Rany *see* Diggz
buy-to-let 30, 198

California 6, 31, 52, 60
Camden 34, 53
Cancun 136
capitalism 32
career 20–22, 26, 135, 153
Carson, Chad 198
Chambers, Lee 24, 26, 83, 85, 88, 110, 116
Chen, Hellen 176, 215
childhood 7–8, 149, 190
Christmas 19, 132–134
Cialdini, Robert 138
Clark, Margaret 45, 99, 144
compatibility 73, 91, 95–97, 152
contract 14, 31–32, 36–37, 50–52, 54, 58, 61, 67, 74, 110, 119–120, 124, 137, 139, 154, 168, 176, 178, 203, 205–207, 217
cost of living 11, 20, 22
Crocs 13

Dawson, Donna 25, 45, 94, 98, 104, 106, 109, 140
Day, Elizabeth, *How to Fail* 144
debt 23, 84, 87, 196–197, 200, 207
DePaulo, Bella 27, 172
deposit: mortgage 21, 23, 27–28, 31, 33–34, 36–37, 50, 83, 87, 194; security 16–17, 206–207, 218
Diggz 25, 80, 85, 92, 104–105, 148, 171
discrimination 77–80
divorce 53, 83, 176, 183
dorm 10–12, 14–16
drugs 75, 107
Dublin 12, 146, 149, 210
Duckworth, Angela, *Grit: The Power of Passion and Perseverance* 8
Dwellsy 33
dynamic pricing 55

education 19–20
Equality Act 2010 78
etiquette 3, 44, 46, 93–94, 99, 115, 151, 167, 188
European Union 22

Fair Housing Act 79
fee 4, 14, 31–33, 64, 87
first-timer 46–47, 172
Florida 52
Ford, Henry 59
France 22, 34
Franco, Marisa G.: *Platonic* 100; *The Secret to Making New Friends as an Adult* 99
Franklin, Benjamin 12, 158
fraud 33
Friends (TV show) 52, 66, 117, 189
friendship: big occasions 133; college 13, 16; cooking 111; having friends over 120; homeless 188; mental health 144, 146; money 63; relationships 213, 215;

219

romance 48; roomshares 26–27, 45, 98–100, 102–103; taboos 140

Germany 194
Gladwell, Malcolm 3; *Talking to Strangers* 91
Google 31, 38, 51–53, 82
Gosling, Sam: cleanliness 39; extroversion 182; *Snoop: What Your Stuff Says About You* 29, 95
Gould, Dana 19
Green, Richard K. 87; see also Wachter, Susan M.
Grinch 132
grit 8, 12; see also Duckworth, Angela
group dynamic: communication 94; discrimination 80; friendship 100; romance 168, 174; roomshares 90–92, 130–131, 142, 186; taboos 95, 97, 139, 146, 212; see also compatibility; Personal User Guide

Hagura, Dr. Nobuhiro 14
hangover 44, 90
Harvard 84, 86; Harvard Study of Adult Development 213–214
Heacox, Stephanie 196
Heath, Sue 27, 82, 195
high school 10, 82
Human Rights Act 78

inflation 11, 20, 59–60, 68, 87, 196–197, 199
intimacy 27
inventory 35, 37
iPhone 17, 93
Ireland: college 11–12; family 22; home ownership 193; Trinity College Dublin 146
Italy 8, 22

Kozinski, Alex 79–80; see also Fair Housing Act
Kyosaki, Robert 197

landlord 5, 51–53
Landlord and Tenant Act 153
Las Vegas 174
loan 10, 60
London 19; bills 196; contract 32; discrimination 79; fee 31; living alone 24; money 22; roomshares 21, 34, 42, 72, 149, 203, 210; Sam Gosling 29
London School of Economics 21; see also Scanlon, Kath
Long Island 89
Los Angeles 21–22, 55, 72, 149, 194, 210

Maalsen, Sophia 27, 98, 172, 193–194
management company 5–6
Manhattan 89
marriage 48, 53, 104, 165, 176
Martin, Chris 26, 50, 78, 86–87
mature student 11–12
mental health 43, 84–85, 117–118, 142–145, 155, 207, 210
MET council 51
Meta 92
Michigan 60
millennials 24, 54, 149
Molinsky, Jennifer 86, 195
mortgage 7, 23–24, 56, 60, 82–84, 87, 176, 194–198

National Occupancy Standards 38
neighborhood 92; Amy Winehouse 34; commute 40; personality 28–29; rent 61; roomshare 46, 163, 184; strangers 25, 88
Netflix 74, 93, 96, 115, 149
Never Split the Difference 141; see also Voss, Chris
New Jersey 34, 60
New Year's Eve 134
New York: homeownership 194; law 53; money 22; moving 210; parents 21; roomshares 29, 39, 42, 51, 72, 161; see also Shapiro, Andrea
New York University 142; see also Shrout, Patrick
New Zealand 22; homeownership 193; law 78; see also Human Rights Act; Tuffin, Keith
NFL 71
North Carolina 60
Nudge (Cass R. Sunstein and Richard H. Thaler) 52

pandemic 41, 43, 72, 85, 88, 116–118, 143, 196
Paris 34, 72
Personal User Guide 97–98; see also Van Der Bel, Peter
pets 122, 217
Platonic (Marisa G. Franco) 100
politicians 32, 140
privacy 25, 27, 51, 80, 128, 165–166
property owner 5–6, 30, 34, 56; law 153; see also management company
psychology 57, 95–96, 138
Psychology Today 183

randoms 7, 103, 112, 115, 196, 203; adulthood 26, 46–47; college 12; definition 6; finance 67; group dynamic 90; romance 163, 169; taboos 139, 146

Index

red flag 5, 28; agency 36–37; interview 73, 106; mental health 145; rent 59
regulations 6, 30–31, 34
rental 56, 72, 86–87; cost 68; fraud 33; law 50, 53; market 7, 61, 125, 194
renters 32, 44, 56, 61, 86; costs 163; fraud 33; interview 72; law 31, 52, 54, 206
retirement 86, 195, 199
romance 48, 164–165, 169
roomsmart 49

San Francisco 41
San Jose 83
scam 32, 34, 37
Scanlon, Kath 21, 26, 76, 195; *see also* London School of Economics
Schedule 5 78; *see also* Equality Act 2010
school 7–10, 26, 30, 34, 49, 82
Scotland 72
Secret Santa 133
The Secret to Making New Friends as an Adult 99; *see also* Franco, Marisa G.
Seinfeld, Jerry 147
SettleUp 64; *see also* bills
Shapiro, Andrea 51, 80
Shrout, Patrick 142–143
Snoop: What Your Stuff Says About You 29, 95; *see also* Gosling, Sam
Sod's Law 173
Spain 34
Splid 64; *see also* bills
Splitwise 17, 64; *see also* bills
stage 4, 24, 76, 155
staples 15–16, 65, 114–115, 189
stigma 21, 24, 83, 88
student 3, 16–17, 88; cleanliness 14–15; dorms 10–12; food 115; Harvard 214; *see also* deposit
subleasing 136–139, 218
subletting 136, 178, 206–207
Superbowl 71; *see also* NFL
Sustein, Cass R. 52; *see also Nudge*; Thaler, Richard H.
Sydney 26; *see also* University of Sydney

taboo 135
Talking to Strangers 91; *see also* Gladwell, Malcolm
television 132, 138, 141, 158, 168–169, 185–186; friendship 120; interview 74; romance 176; roomshares 47; weekend 129
tenancy 54, 139, 174, 195, 206; contract 31, 50–51; law 34, 52–53; *see also* subleasing
Tenant Protection Act of 2019 52
Thaler, Richard H.: *Nudge* 52; *see also* Sunstein, Cass R.
toxicity 123
Trinity College Dublin 12, 146
Tuffin, Keith 22, 27, 88, 91, 128, 144, 172

United States 5, 19–20, 24, 40, 82–83, 86, 122, 132, 135, 163, 173, 183, 193–194; cleanliness 149; dorms 12; family 21–22, 190; law 16, 34, 38, 52, 79, 153; rent 60; student 10–11; *see also* college; deposit; mortgage; pets
United Kingdom 31, 132, 183; cleanliness 149; college 11; deposit 16; family 22, 190; home ownership 193–194; law 51, 78–79, 153
universities 11
University of London 14; *see also* Hagura, Dr. Nobuhiro
University of Manchester 27; *see also* Heath, Sue
University of Massey 22; *see also* Tuffin, Keith
University of Sydney 27; *see also* Maalsen, Sophia

Van Der Bel, Peter 95, 97–98, 182; *see also* Personal User Guide
veteran 46, 47
Voss, Chris 141–142, 152; *see also Never Split the Difference*

Wachter, Susan M. 87; *see also* Green, Richard K.
Waldinger, Robert 213–215; *see also* Harvard
Washington D.C. 31
WhatsApp 92–95, 111, 126, 128, 130, 192, 203; *see also* group dynamic
Wi-Fi 60, 65, 74, 88, 116–118
World War II 21, 24, 193
Wyoming 52

Yale University 45; *see also* Clark, Margaret

www.ingramcontent.com/pod-product-compliance
Ingram Content Group UK Ltd.
Pitfield, Milton Keynes, MK11 3LW, UK
UKHW021527050825
461577UK00020B/231